BUT *WE* LOVE YOU, CHARLIE BROWN

Titan Facsimile Editions by Charles M. Schulz

On sale now:
Peanuts
More Peanuts
Good Ol' Charlie Brown
Good Grief, more Charlie Brown
Snoopy
You're Out of your Mind, Charlie Brown
Peanuts Revisited

Coming soon:
Go Fly a Kite, Charlie Brown
Peanuts Every Sunday

BUT *WE* LOVE YOU, CHARLIE BROWN

A NEW PEANUTS BOOK

By CHARLES M. SCHULZ

TITAN COMICS

BUT WE LOVE YOU, CHARLIE BROWN
ISBN: 9781782761617
PUBLISHED BY TITAN COMICS, A DIVISION OF TITAN PUBLISHING GROUP LTD,
144 SOUTHWARK ST, LONDON SE1 0UP. TCN 306.
© 2015 BY PEANUTS WORLDWIDE LLC.
PRINTED IN INDIA.

10 9 8 7 6 5 4 3 2 1

WWW.TITAN-COMICS.COM
WWW.PEANUTS.COM

ORIGINALLY PUBLISHED IN 1959 BY RHINEHART & CO. INCORPORATED
NEW YORK & TORONTO

A CIP CATALOGUE RECORD FOR THIS TITLE
IS AVAILABLE FROM THE BRITISH LIBRARY.
THIS EDITION FIRST PUBLISHED: NOVEMBER 2015

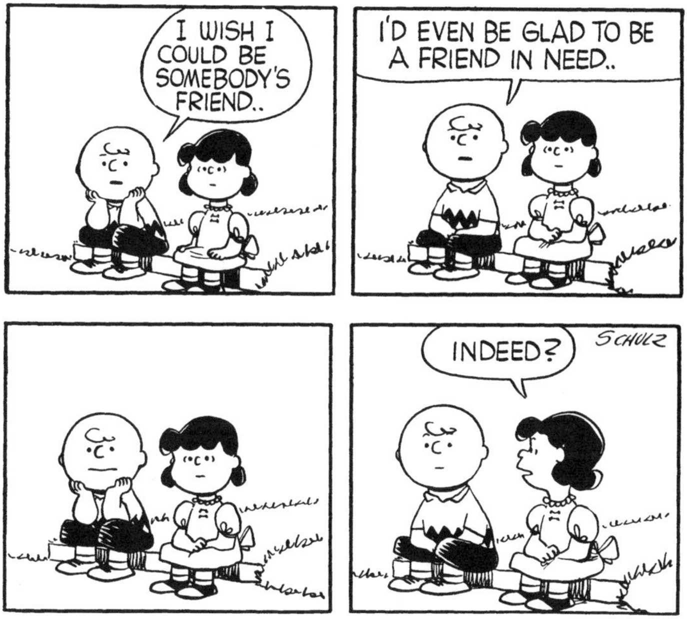
I WISH I COULD BE SOMEBODY'S FRIEND..
I'D EVEN BE GLAD TO BE A FRIEND IN NEED..
INDEED?
SCHULZ

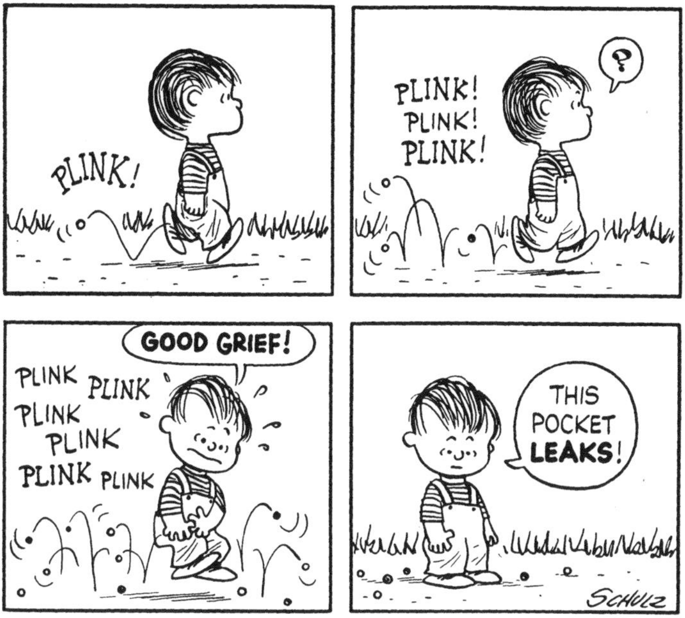
PLINK!
PLINK! PLINK! PLINK!
?
GOOD GRIEF!
PLINK PLINK PLINK PLINK PLINK PLINK
THIS POCKET **LEAKS**!
SCHULZ

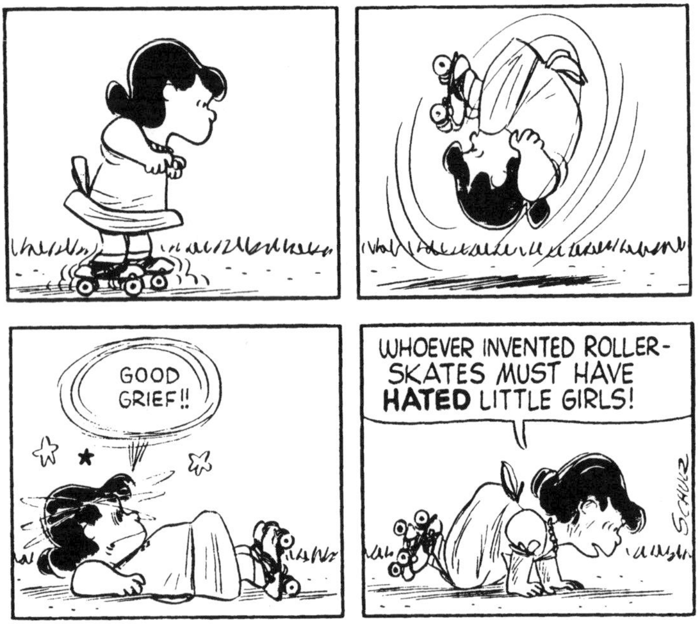
GOOD GRIEF!!
WHOEVER INVENTED ROLLER-SKATES MUST HAVE **HATED** LITTLE GIRLS!
SCHULZ

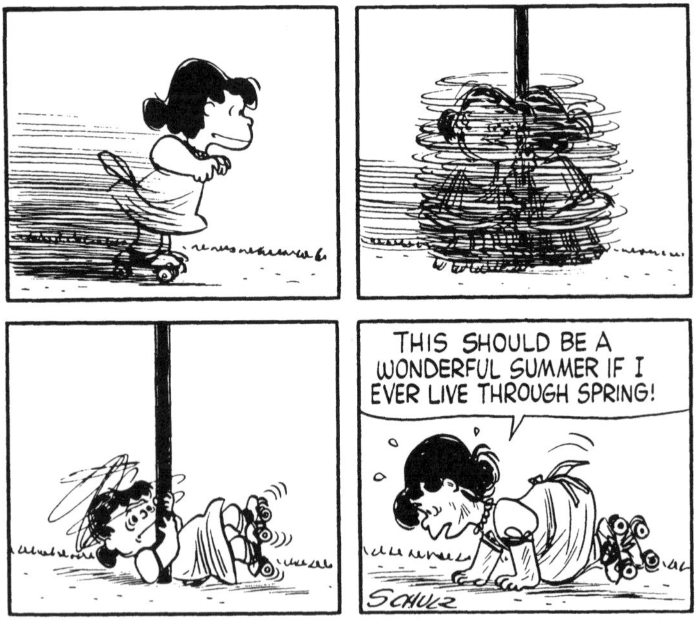
THIS SHOULD BE A WONDERFUL SUMMER IF I EVER LIVE THROUGH SPRING!
SCHULZ

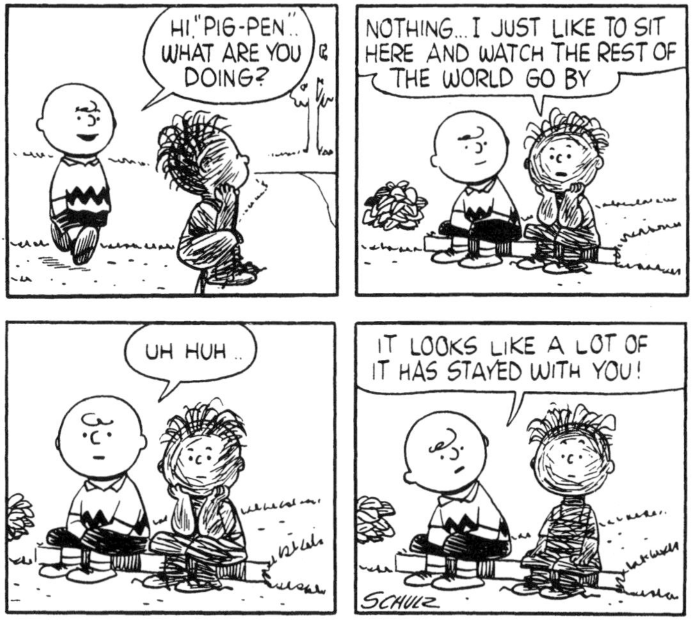
HI, "PIG-PEN".. WHAT ARE YOU DOING?
NOTHING... I JUST LIKE TO SIT HERE AND WATCH THE REST OF THE WORLD GO BY
UH HUH ..
IT LOOKS LIKE A LOT OF IT HAS STAYED WITH YOU!
SCHULZ

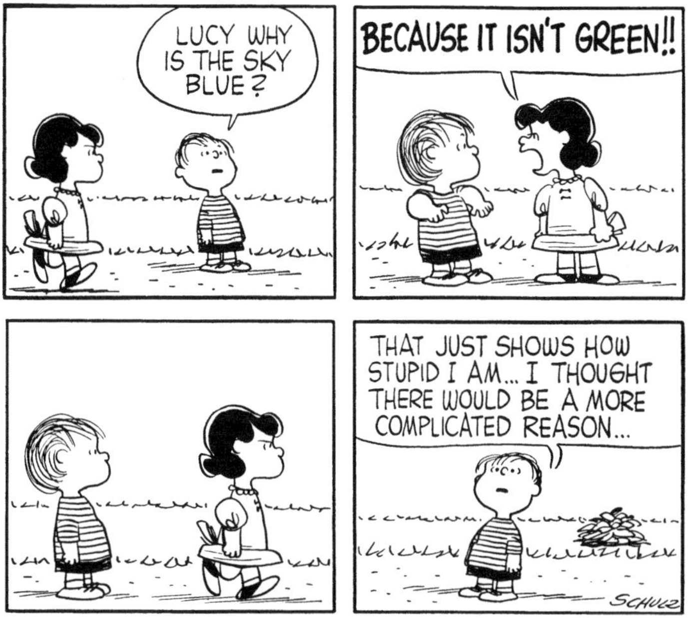
LUCY WHY IS THE SKY BLUE?
BECAUSE IT ISN'T GREEN!!
THAT JUST SHOWS HOW STUPID I AM... I THOUGHT THERE WOULD BE A MORE COMPLICATED REASON...
SCHULZ

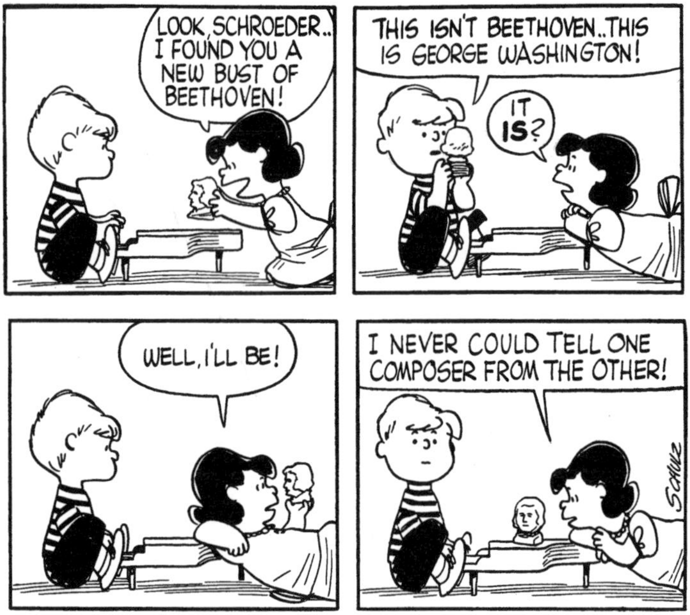
LOOK, SCHROEDER.. I FOUND YOU A NEW BUST OF BEETHOVEN!
THIS ISN'T BEETHOVEN..THIS IS GEORGE WASHINGTON!
IT IS?
WELL, I'LL BE!
I NEVER COULD TELL ONE COMPOSER FROM THE OTHER!
SCHULZ

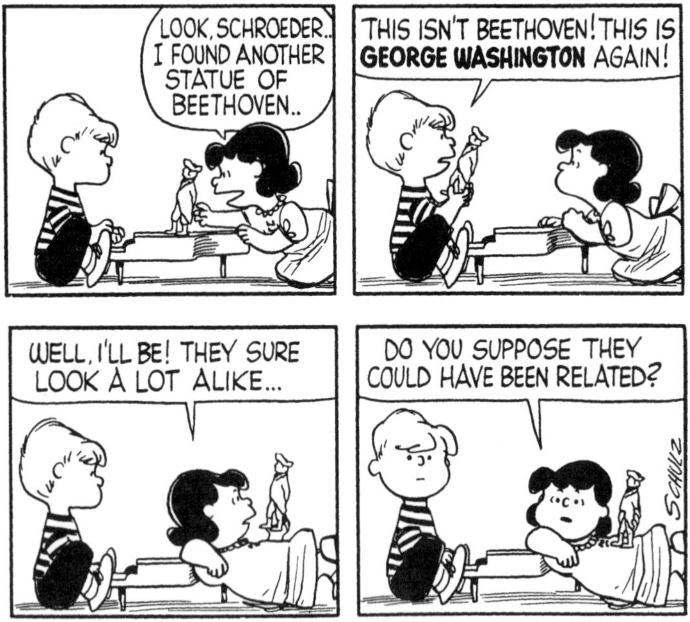
LOOK, SCHROEDER.. I FOUND ANOTHER STATUE OF BEETHOVEN..
THIS ISN'T BEETHOVEN! THIS IS GEORGE WASHINGTON AGAIN!
WELL, I'LL BE! THEY SURE LOOK A LOT ALIKE...
DO YOU SUPPOSE THEY COULD HAVE BEEN RELATED?
SCHULZ

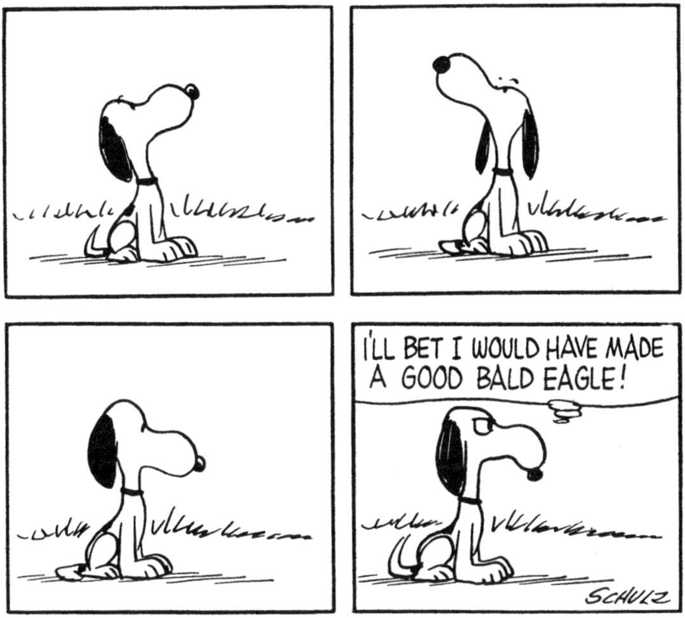
I'LL BET I WOULD HAVE MADE A GOOD BALD EAGLE!
SCHULZ

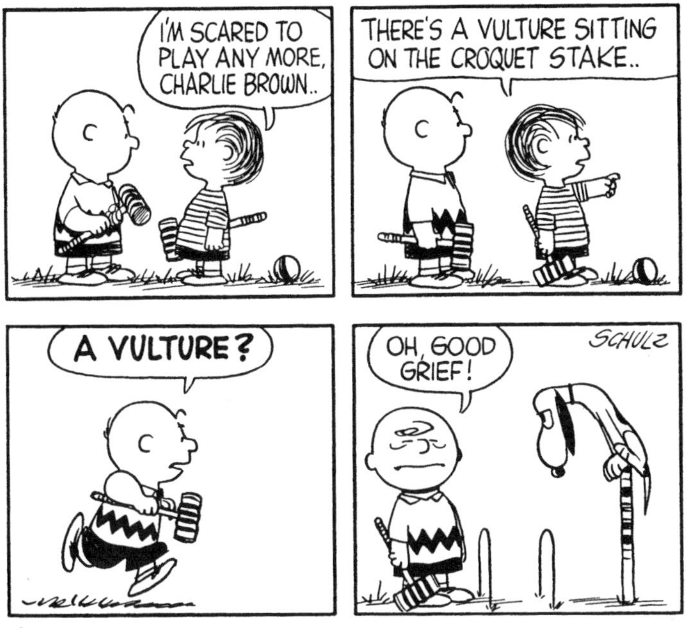
I'M SCARED TO PLAY ANY MORE, CHARLIE BROWN..
THERE'S A VULTURE SITTING ON THE CROQUET STAKE..
A VULTURE?
OH, GOOD GRIEF!
SCHULZ

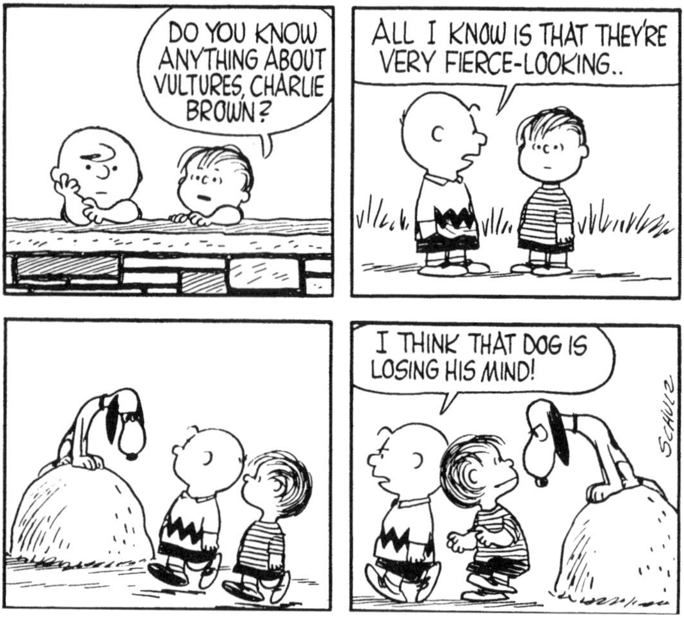
DO YOU KNOW ANYTHING ABOUT VULTURES, CHARLIE BROWN?
ALL I KNOW IS THAT THEY'RE VERY FIERCE-LOOKING..
I THINK THAT DOG IS LOSING HIS MIND!
SCHULZ

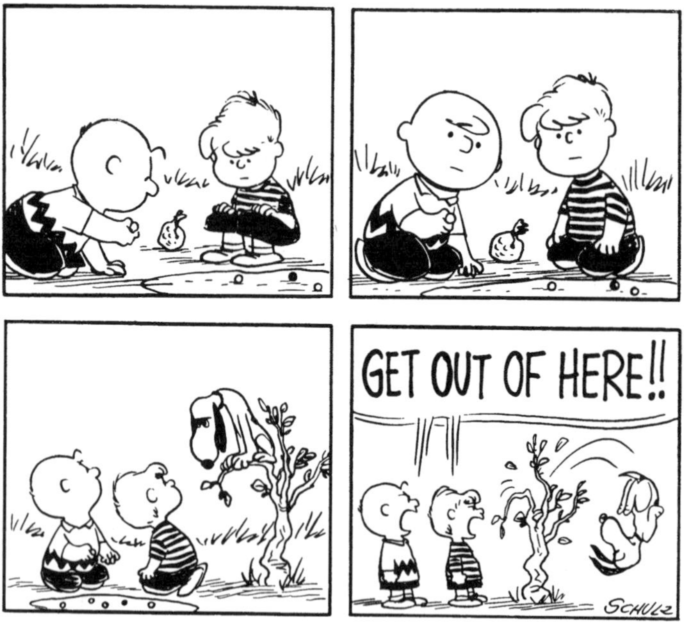
GET OUT OF HERE!!
SCHULZ

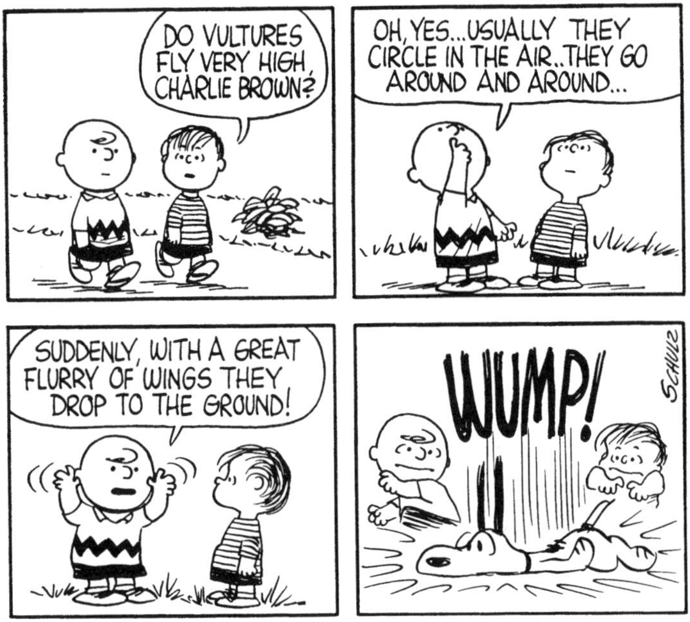
DO VULTURES FLY VERY HIGH, CHARLIE BROWN?
OH, YES...USUALLY THEY CIRCLE IN THE AIR..THEY GO AROUND AND AROUND...
SUDDENLY, WITH A GREAT FLURRY OF WINGS THEY DROP TO THE GROUND!
WUMP!
SCHULZ

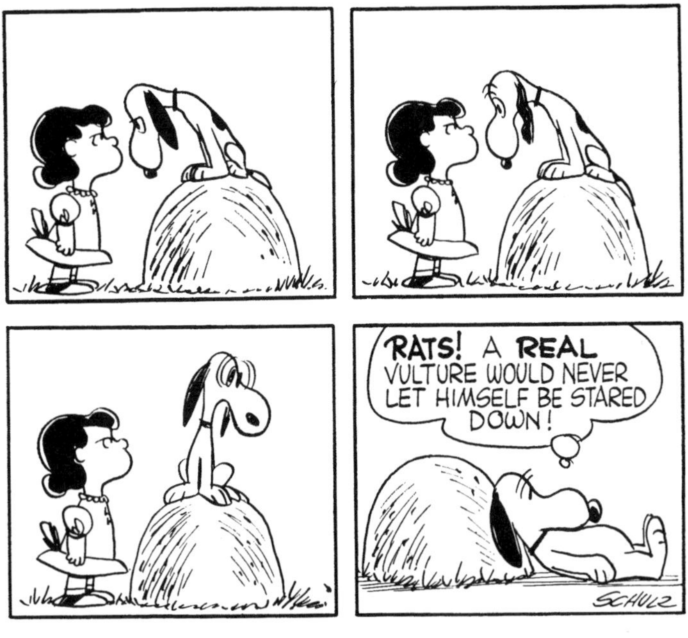
RATS! A REAL VULTURE WOULD NEVER LET HIMSELF BE STARED DOWN!
SCHULZ

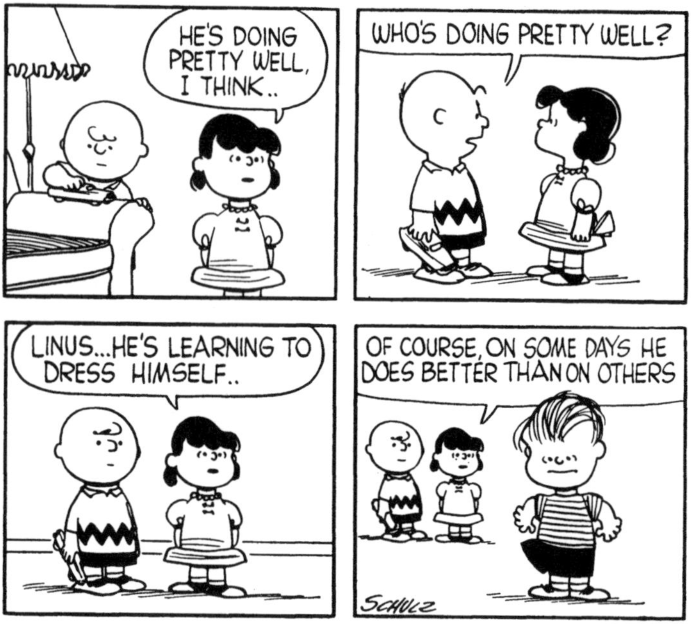
HE'S DOING PRETTY WELL, I THINK..
WHO'S DOING PRETTY WELL?
LINUS...HE'S LEARNING TO DRESS HIMSELF..
OF COURSE, ON SOME DAYS HE DOES BETTER THAN ON OTHERS
SCHULZ

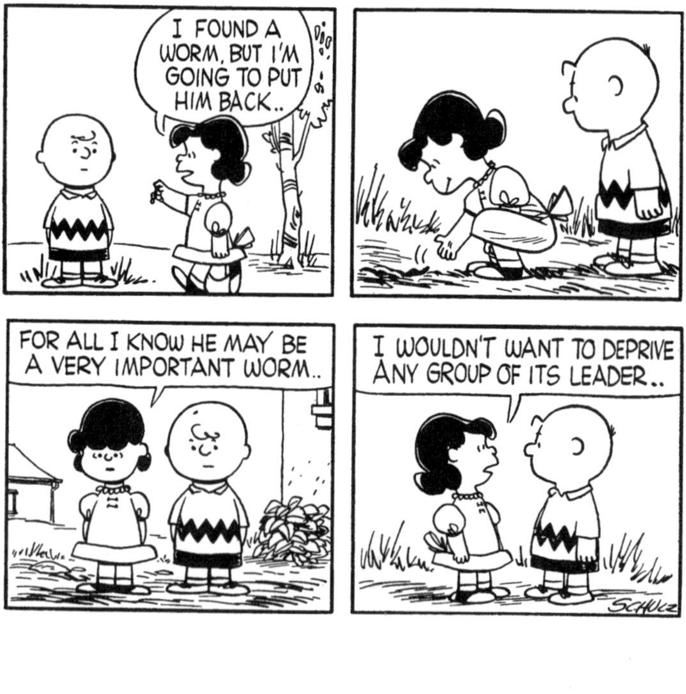
I FOUND A WORM, BUT I'M GOING TO PUT HIM BACK..
FOR ALL I KNOW HE MAY BE A VERY IMPORTANT WORM..
I WOULDN'T WANT TO DEPRIVE ANY GROUP OF ITS LEADER..
SCHULZ

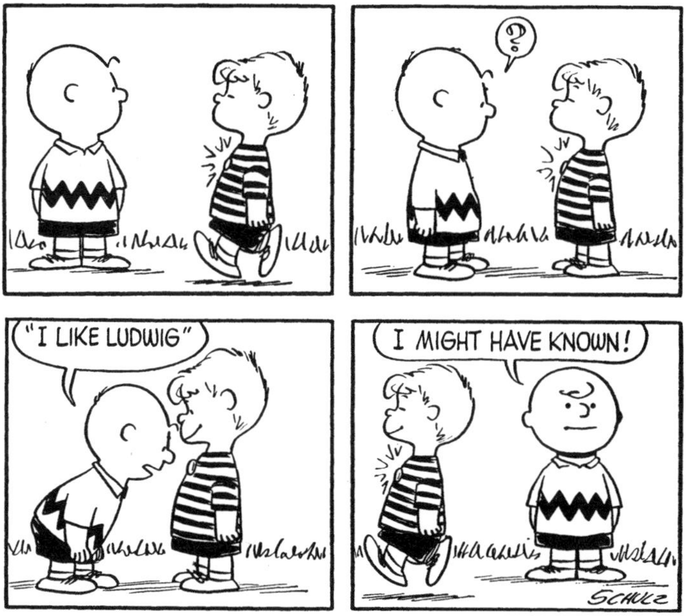
?
"I LIKE LUDWIG"
I MIGHT HAVE KNOWN!
SCHULZ

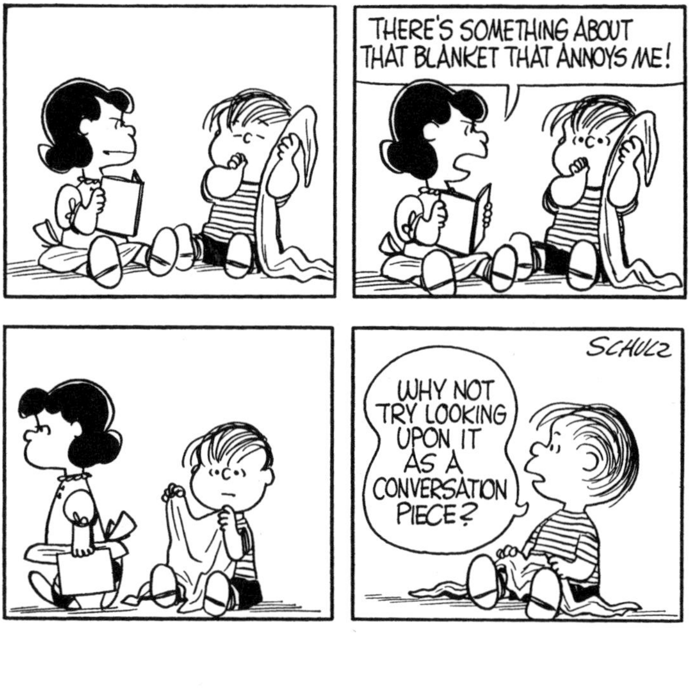
THERE'S SOMETHING ABOUT THAT BLANKET THAT ANNOYS ME!
SCHULZ
WHY NOT TRY LOOKING UPON IT AS A CONVERSATION PIECE?

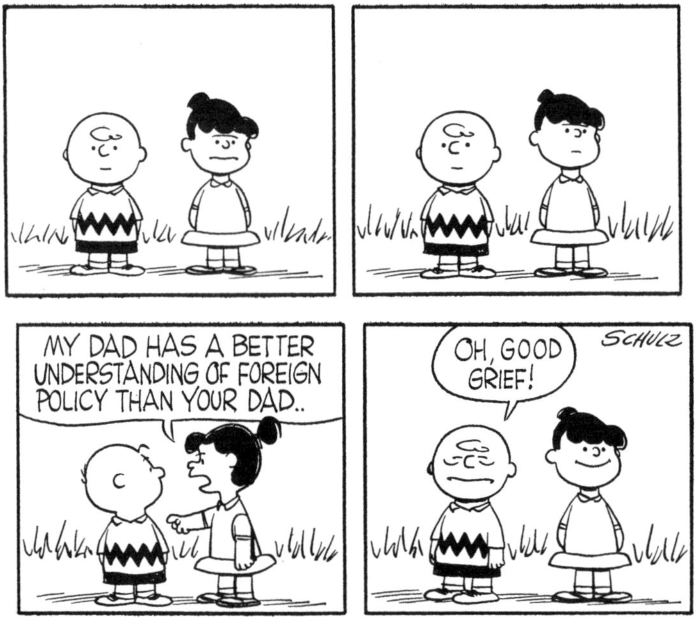
MY DAD HAS A BETTER UNDERSTANDING OF FOREIGN POLICY THAN YOUR DAD..
OH, GOOD GRIEF!
SCHULZ

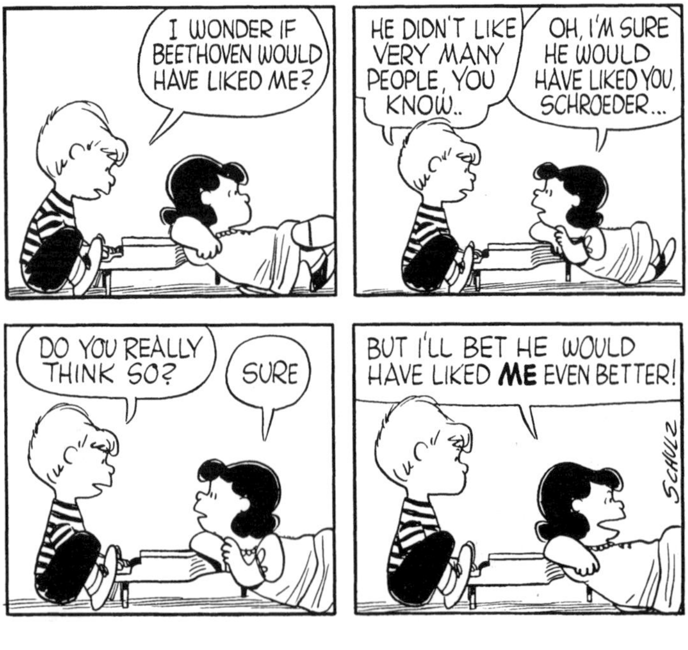
I WONDER IF BEETHOVEN WOULD HAVE LIKED ME?
HE DIDN'T LIKE VERY MANY PEOPLE, YOU KNOW..
OH, I'M SURE HE WOULD HAVE LIKED YOU, SCHROEDER...
DO YOU REALLY THINK SO?
SURE
BUT I'LL BET HE WOULD HAVE LIKED **ME** EVEN BETTER!
SCHULZ

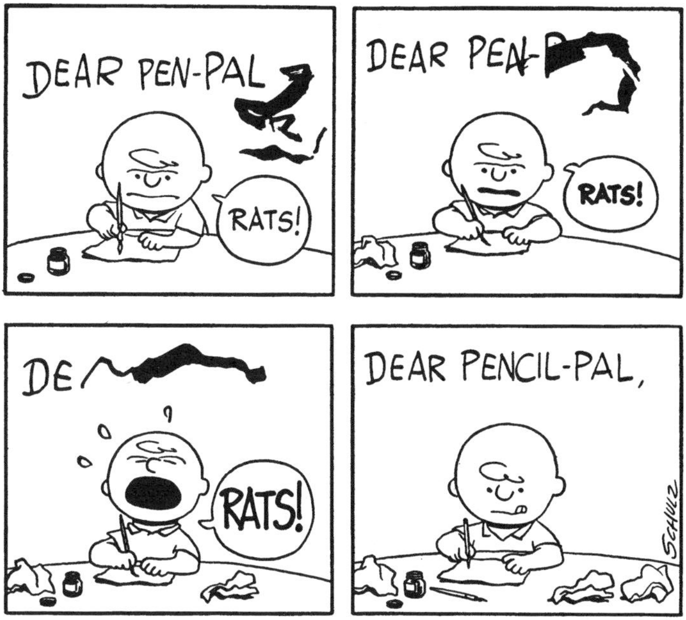
DEAR PEN-PAL
RATS!
DEAR PEN-
RATS!
DE
RATS!
DEAR PENCIL-PAL,
SCHULZ

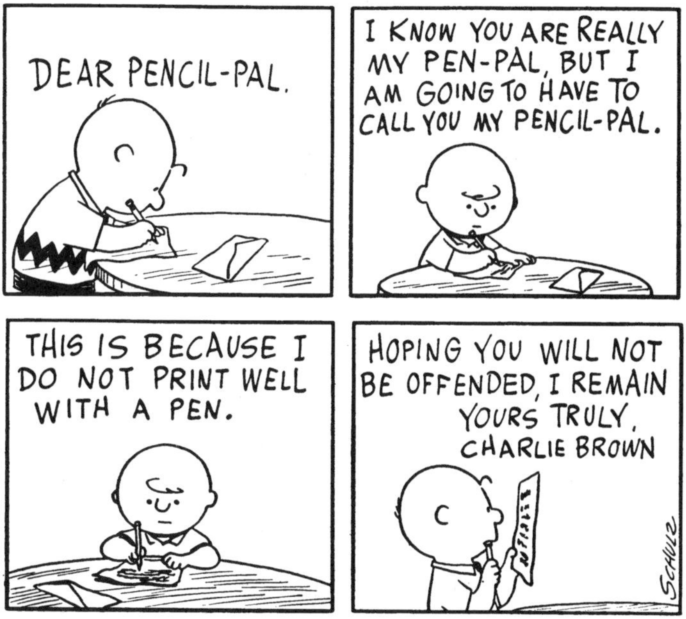
DEAR PENCIL-PAL.
I KNOW YOU ARE REALLY MY PEN-PAL, BUT I AM GOING TO HAVE TO CALL YOU MY PENCIL-PAL.
THIS IS BECAUSE I DO NOT PRINT WELL WITH A PEN.
HOPING YOU WILL NOT BE OFFENDED, I REMAIN YOURS TRULY, CHARLIE BROWN
SCHULZ

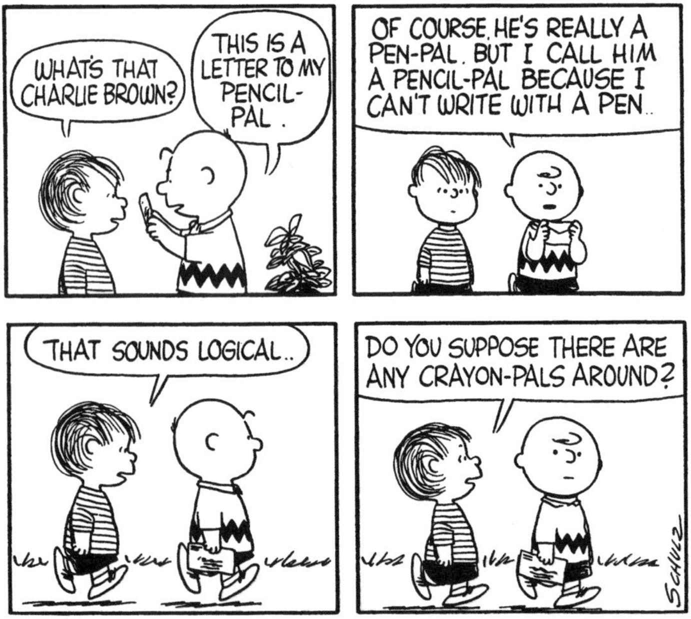
WHAT'S THAT CHARLIE BROWN?
THIS IS A LETTER TO MY PENCIL-PAL .
OF COURSE, HE'S REALLY A PEN-PAL. BUT I CALL HIM A PENCIL-PAL BECAUSE I CAN'T WRITE WITH A PEN..
THAT SOUNDS LOGICAL..
DO YOU SUPPOSE THERE ARE ANY CRAYON-PALS AROUND?
SCHULZ

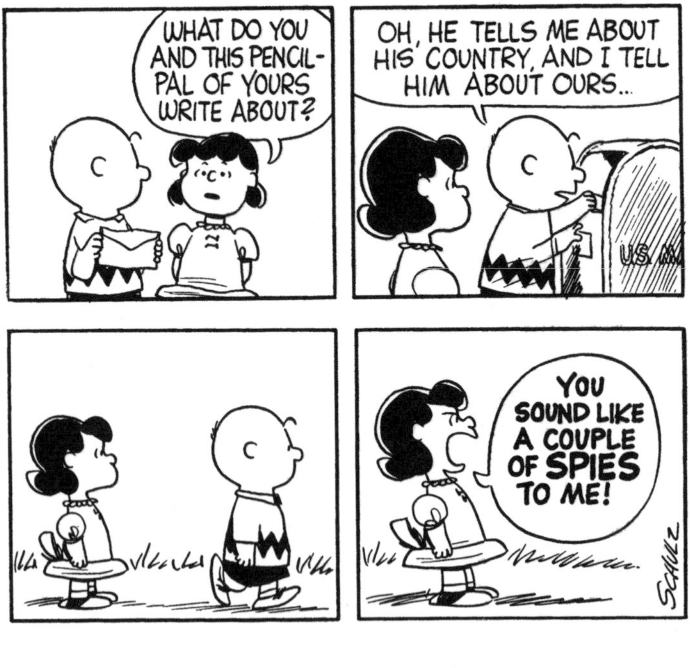
WHAT DO YOU AND THIS PENCIL-PAL OF YOURS WRITE ABOUT?
OH, HE TELLS ME ABOUT HIS COUNTRY, AND I TELL HIM ABOUT OURS...
U.S. M
YOU SOUND LIKE A COUPLE OF SPIES TO ME!
SCHULZ

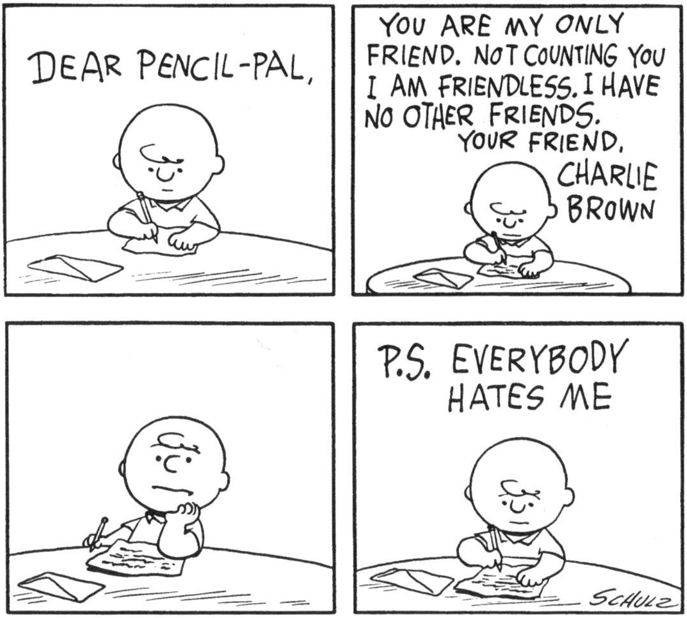
DEAR PENCIL-PAL,
YOU ARE MY ONLY FRIEND. NOT COUNTING YOU I AM FRIENDLESS. I HAVE NO OTHER FRIENDS.
YOUR FRIEND, CHARLIE BROWN
P.S. EVERYBODY HATES ME
SCHULZ

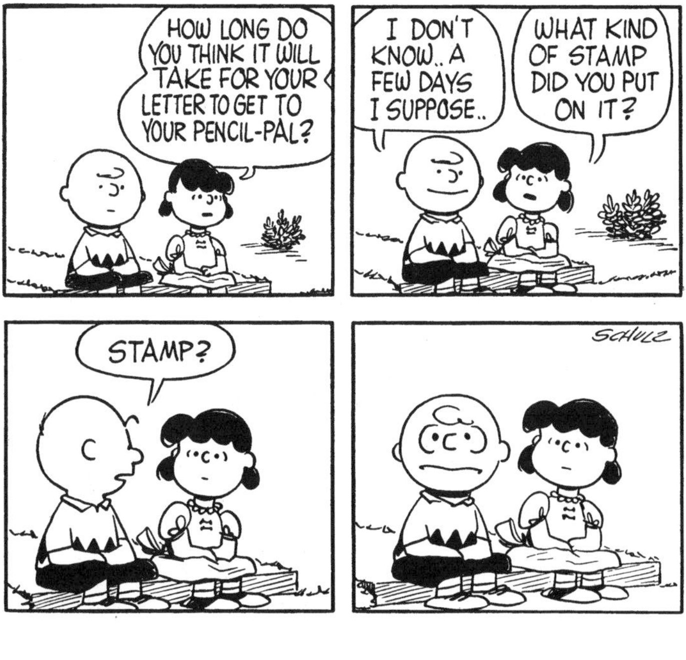
HOW LONG DO YOU THINK IT WILL TAKE FOR YOUR LETTER TO GET TO YOUR PENCIL-PAL?
I DON'T KNOW.. A FEW DAYS I SUPPOSE..
WHAT KIND OF STAMP DID YOU PUT ON IT?
STAMP?
SCHULZ

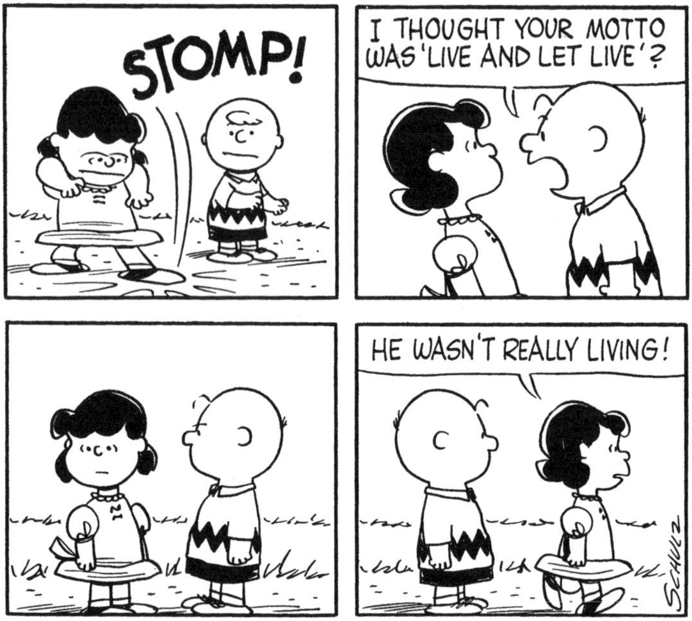
STOMP!
I THOUGHT YOUR MOTTO WAS 'LIVE AND LET LIVE'?
HE WASN'T REALLY LIVING!
SCHULZ

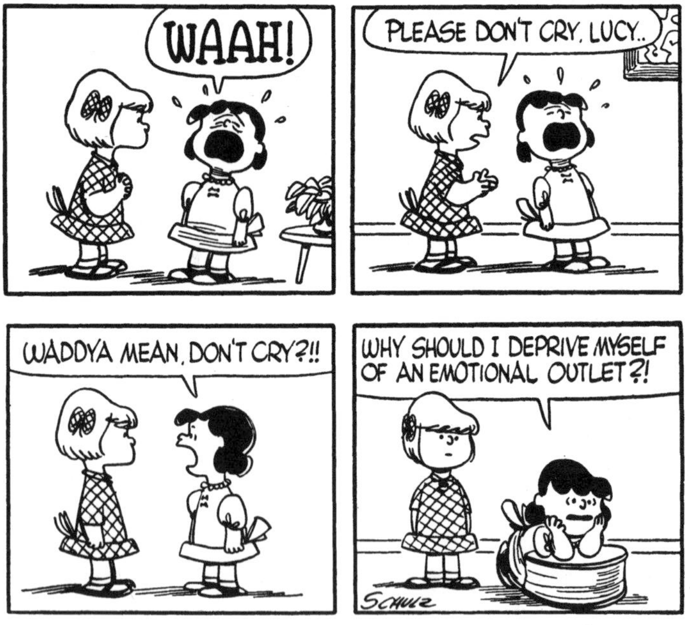
WAAH!
PLEASE DON'T CRY, LUCY..
WADDYA MEAN, DON'T CRY?!!
WHY SHOULD I DEPRIVE MYSELF OF AN EMOTIONAL OUTLET?!
SCHULZ

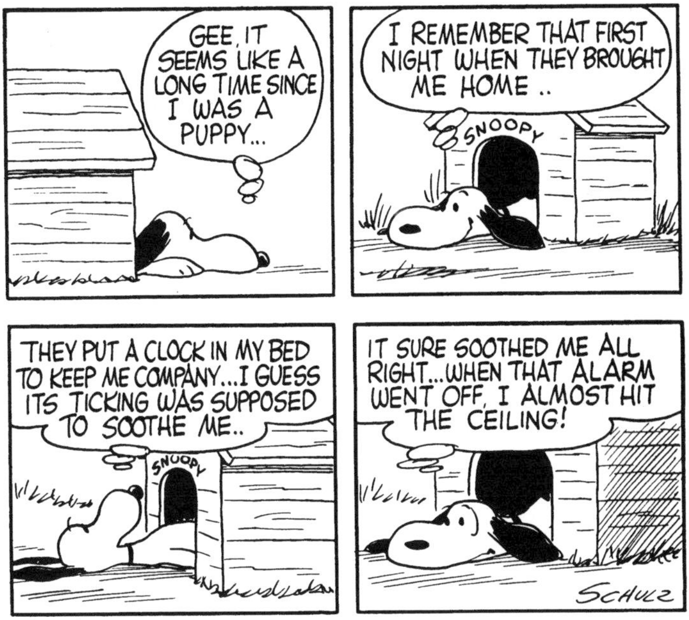
GEE, IT SEEMS LIKE A LONG TIME SINCE I WAS A PUPPY...
I REMEMBER THAT FIRST NIGHT WHEN THEY BROUGHT ME HOME ..
SNOOPY
THEY PUT A CLOCK IN MY BED TO KEEP ME COMPANY...I GUESS ITS TICKING WAS SUPPOSED TO SOOTHE ME..
SNOOPY
IT SURE SOOTHED ME ALL RIGHT...WHEN THAT ALARM WENT OFF, I ALMOST HIT THE CEILING!
SCHULZ

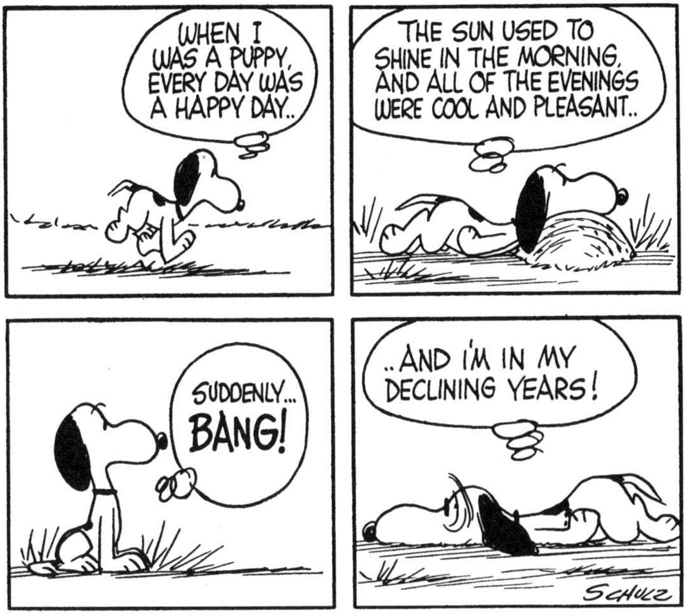
WHEN I WAS A PUPPY, EVERY DAY WAS A HAPPY DAY..
THE SUN USED TO SHINE IN THE MORNING, AND ALL OF THE EVENINGS WERE COOL AND PLEASANT..
SUDDENLY... BANG!
..AND I'M IN MY DECLINING YEARS!
SCHULZ

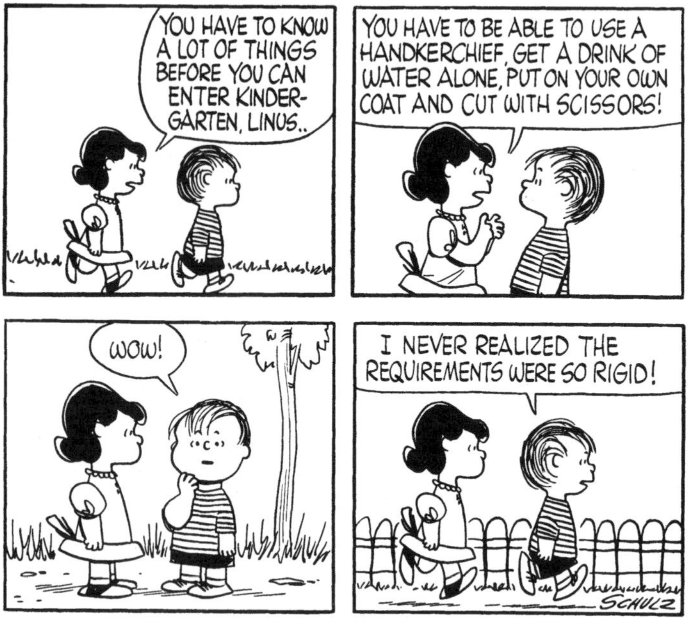
YOU HAVE TO KNOW A LOT OF THINGS BEFORE YOU CAN ENTER KINDER-GARTEN, LINUS..
YOU HAVE TO BE ABLE TO USE A HANDKERCHIEF, GET A DRINK OF WATER ALONE, PUT ON YOUR OWN COAT AND CUT WITH SCISSORS!
WOW!
I NEVER REALIZED THE REQUIREMENTS WERE SO RIGID!
SCHULZ

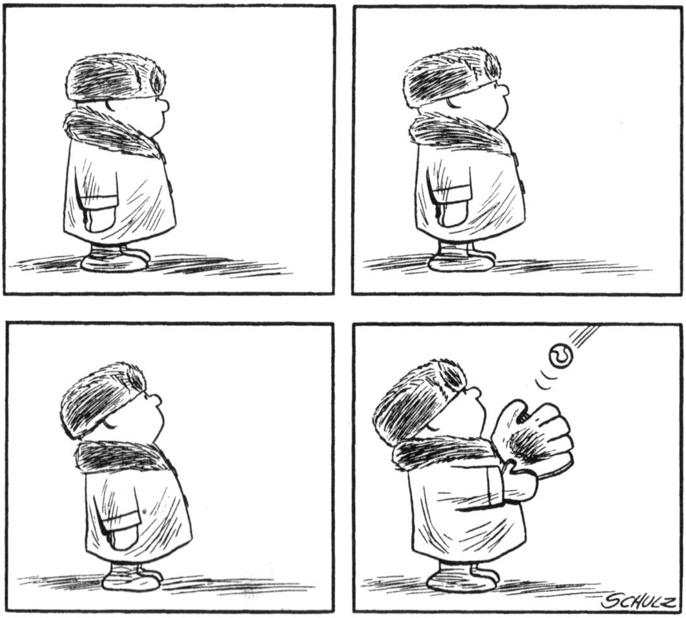
SCHULZ

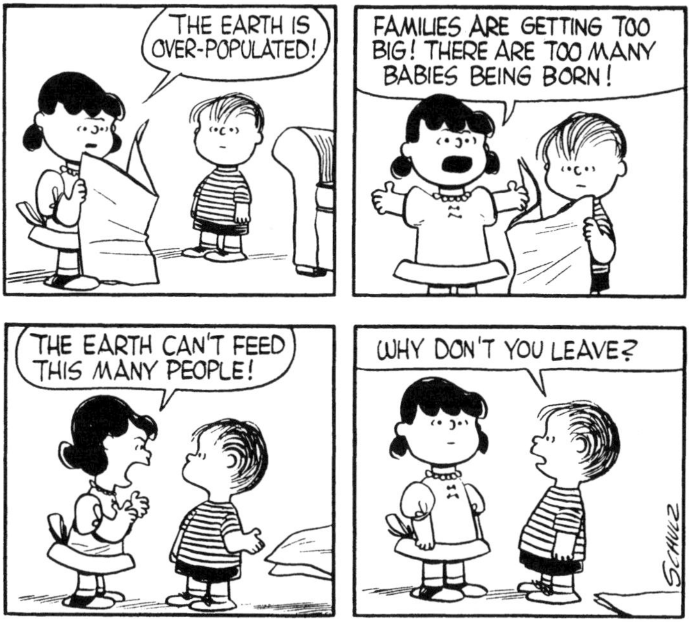
THE EARTH IS OVER-POPULATED!
FAMILIES ARE GETTING TOO BIG! THERE ARE TOO MANY BABIES BEING BORN!
THE EARTH CAN'T FEED THIS MANY PEOPLE!
WHY DON'T YOU LEAVE?
SCHULZ

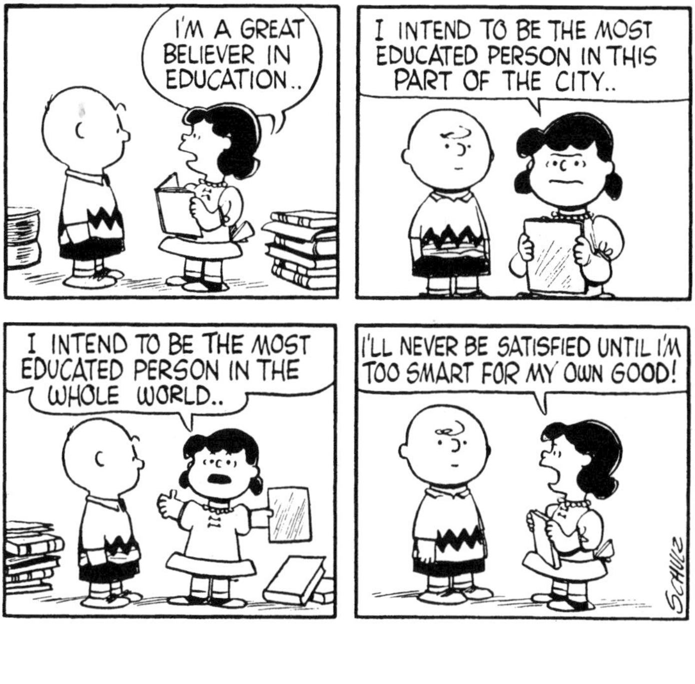
I'M A GREAT BELIEVER IN EDUCATION..
I INTEND TO BE THE MOST EDUCATED PERSON IN THIS PART OF THE CITY..
I INTEND TO BE THE MOST EDUCATED PERSON IN THE WHOLE WORLD..
I'LL NEVER BE SATISFIED UNTIL I'M TOO SMART FOR MY OWN GOOD!
SCHULZ

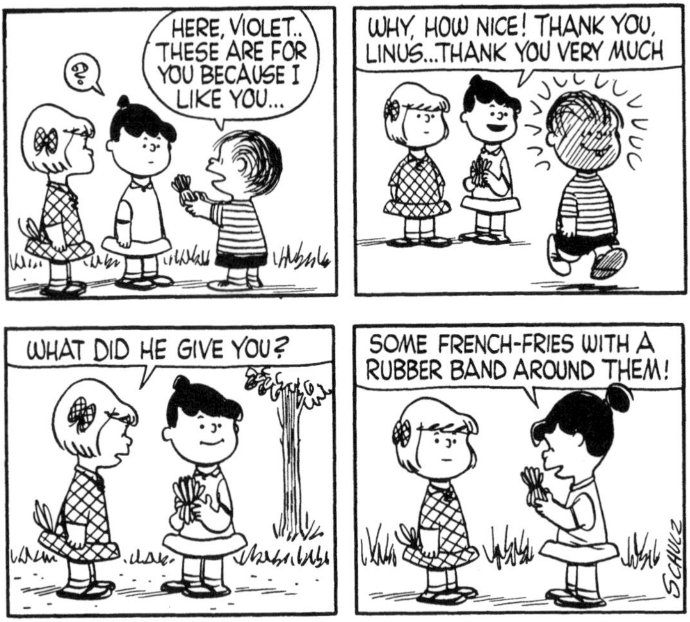
?
HERE, VIOLET.. THESE ARE FOR YOU BECAUSE I LIKE YOU...
WHY, HOW NICE! THANK YOU, LINUS...THANK YOU VERY MUCH
WHAT DID HE GIVE YOU?
SOME FRENCH-FRIES WITH A RUBBER BAND AROUND THEM!
SCHULZ

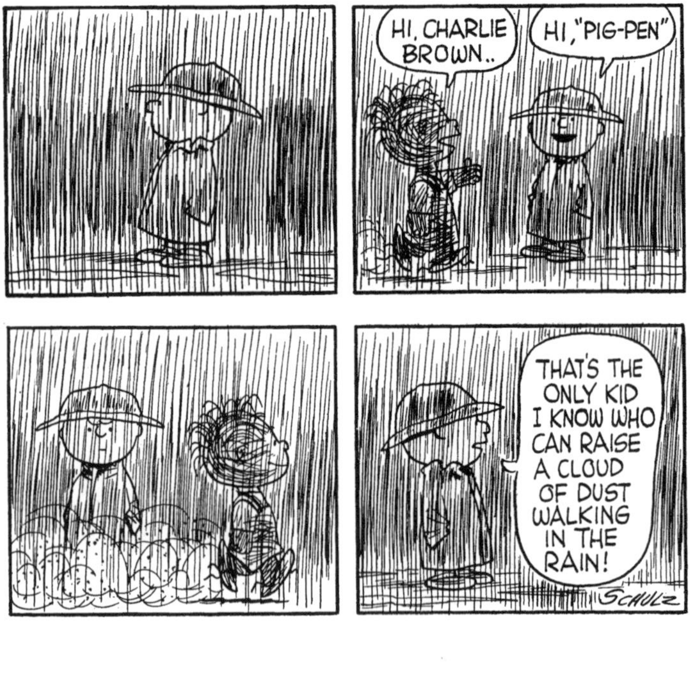
HI, CHARLIE BROWN..
HI, "PIG-PEN"
THAT'S THE ONLY KID I KNOW WHO CAN RAISE A CLOUD OF DUST WALKING IN THE RAIN!
SCHULZ

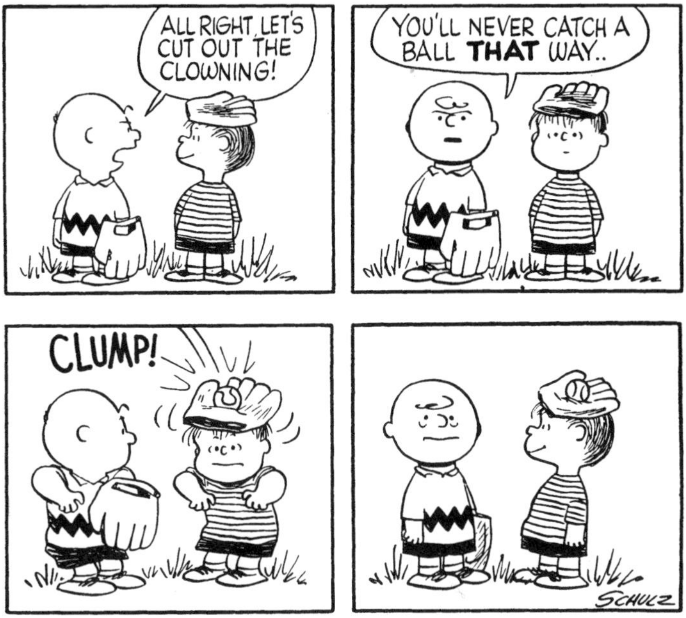
ALL RIGHT, LET'S CUT OUT THE CLOWNING!
YOU'LL NEVER CATCH A BALL **THAT** WAY..
CLUMP!
SCHULZ

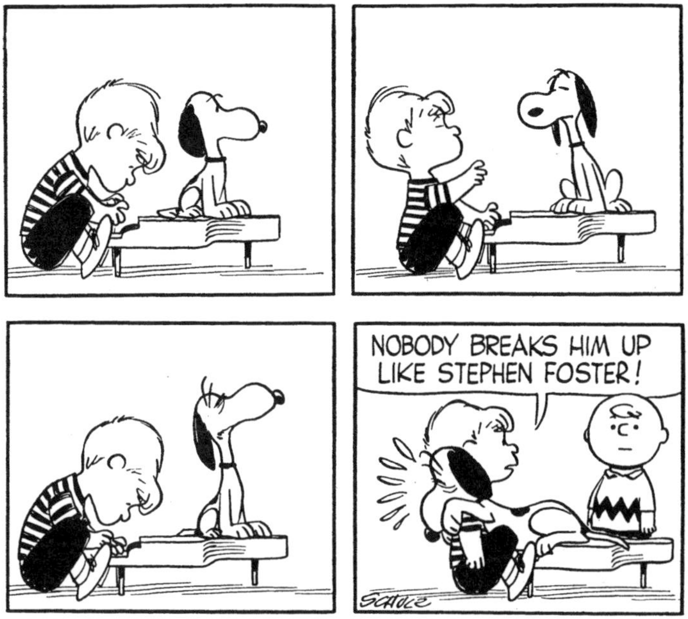
NOBODY BREAKS HIM UP LIKE STEPHEN FOSTER!
SCHULZ

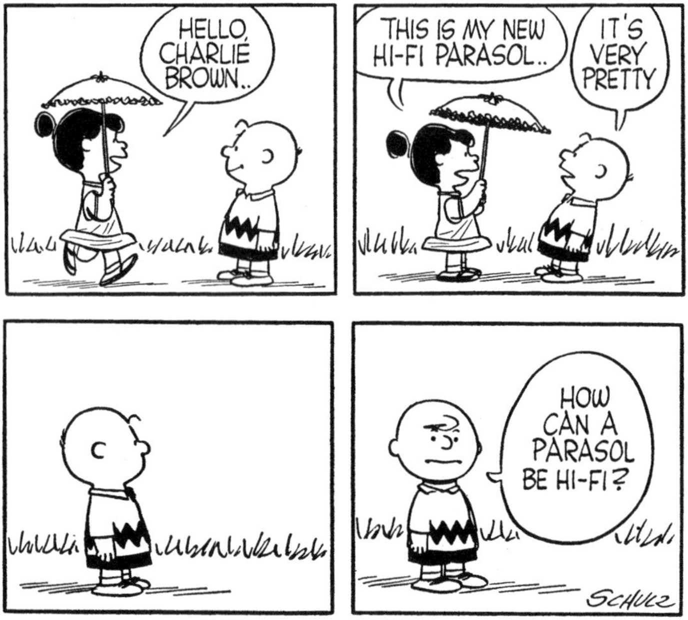
HELLO, CHARLIE BROWN..
THIS IS MY NEW HI-FI PARASOL..
IT'S VERY PRETTY
HOW CAN A PARASOL BE HI-FI?
SCHULZ

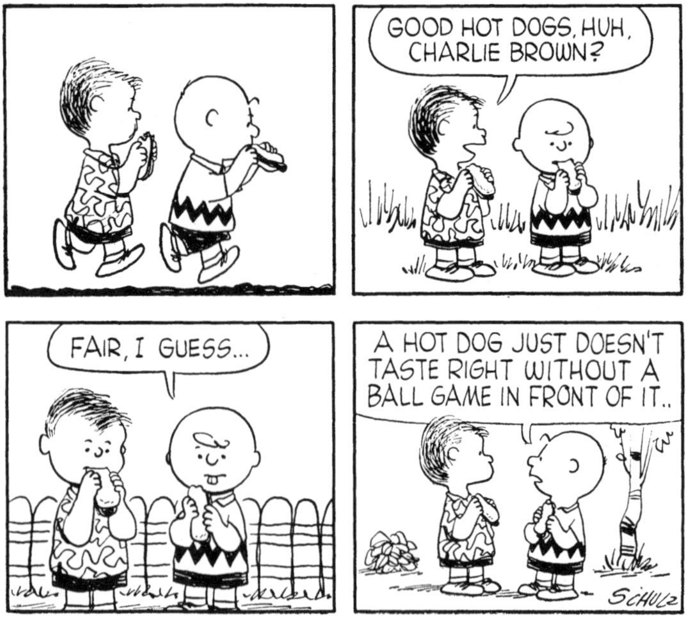
GOOD HOT DOGS, HUH, CHARLIE BROWN?
FAIR, I GUESS...
A HOT DOG JUST DOESN'T TASTE RIGHT WITHOUT A BALL GAME IN FRONT OF IT..
SCHULZ

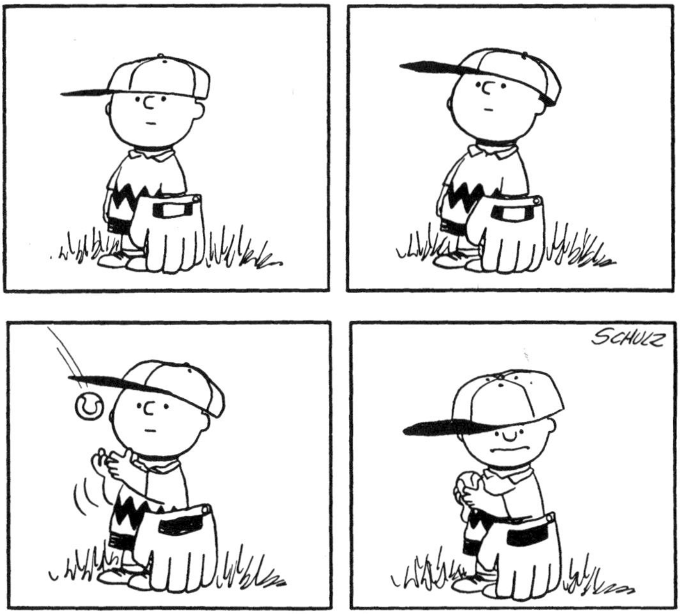
SCHULZ

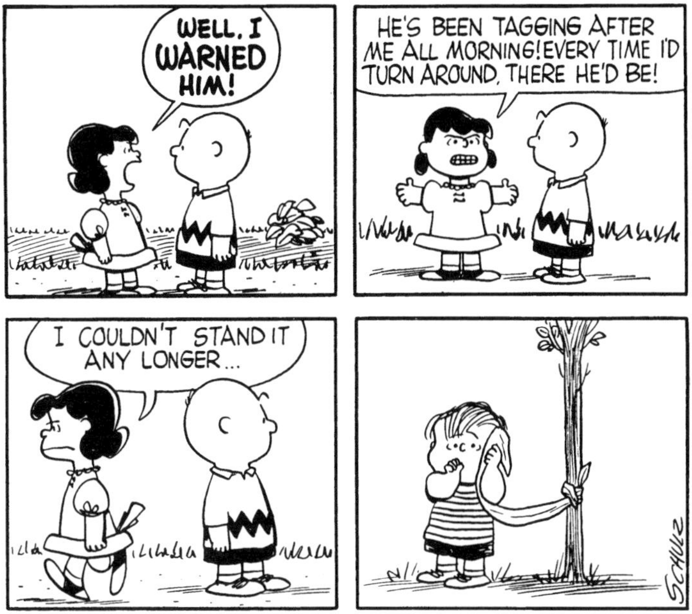
WELL, I WARNED HIM!
HE'S BEEN TAGGING AFTER ME ALL MORNING! EVERY TIME I'D TURN AROUND, THERE HE'D BE!
I COULDN'T STAND IT ANY LONGER...
SCHULZ

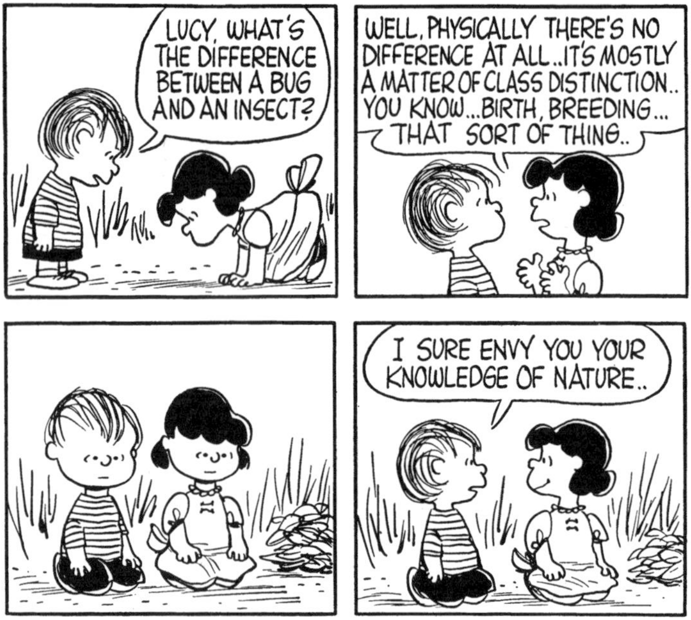
LUCY, WHAT'S THE DIFFERENCE BETWEEN A BUG AND AN INSECT?
WELL, PHYSICALLY THERE'S NO DIFFERENCE AT ALL..IT'S MOSTLY A MATTER OF CLASS DISTINCTION.. YOU KNOW...BIRTH, BREEDING... THAT SORT OF THING..
I SURE ENVY YOU YOUR KNOWLEDGE OF NATURE..

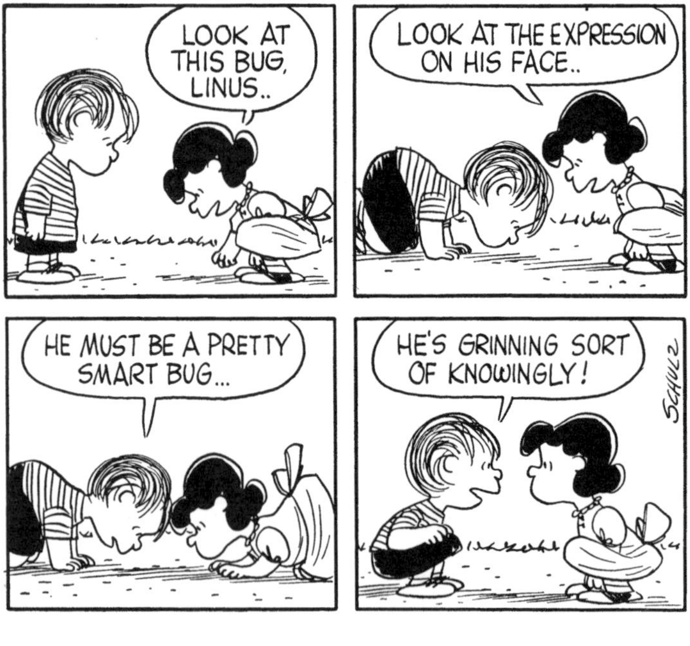
LOOK AT THIS BUG, LINUS..
LOOK AT THE EXPRESSION ON HIS FACE..
HE MUST BE A PRETTY SMART BUG...
HE'S GRINNING SORT OF KNOWINGLY!
SCHULZ

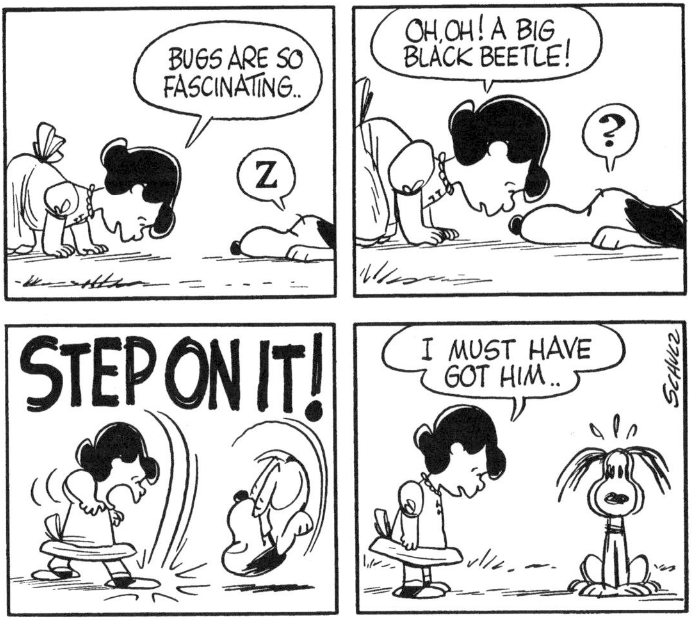
BUGS ARE SO FASCINATING..
Z
OH, OH! A BIG BLACK BEETLE!
?
STEP ON IT!
I MUST HAVE GOT HIM..
SCHULZ

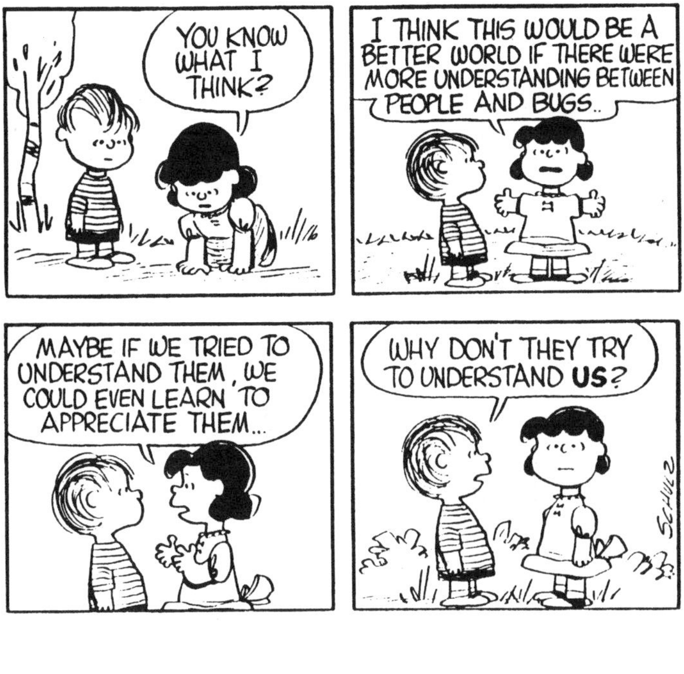
YOU KNOW WHAT I THINK?
I THINK THIS WOULD BE A BETTER WORLD IF THERE WERE MORE UNDERSTANDING BETWEEN PEOPLE AND BUGS..
MAYBE IF WE TRIED TO UNDERSTAND THEM, WE COULD EVEN LEARN TO APPRECIATE THEM...
WHY DON'T THEY TRY TO UNDERSTAND **US**?
SCHULZ

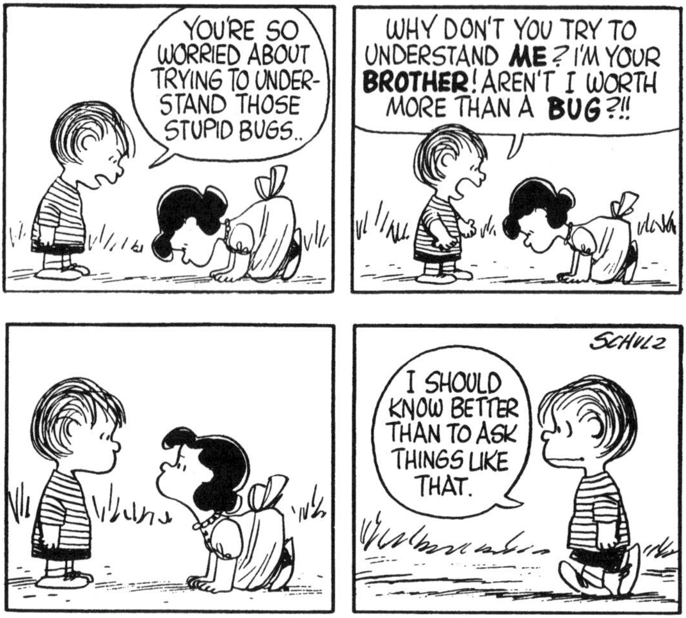
YOU'RE SO WORRIED ABOUT TRYING TO UNDER-STAND THOSE STUPID BUGS..
WHY DON'T YOU TRY TO UNDERSTAND **ME**? I'M YOUR **BROTHER**! AREN'T I WORTH MORE THAN A **BUG**?!!
SCHULZ
I SHOULD KNOW BETTER THAN TO ASK THINGS LIKE THAT.

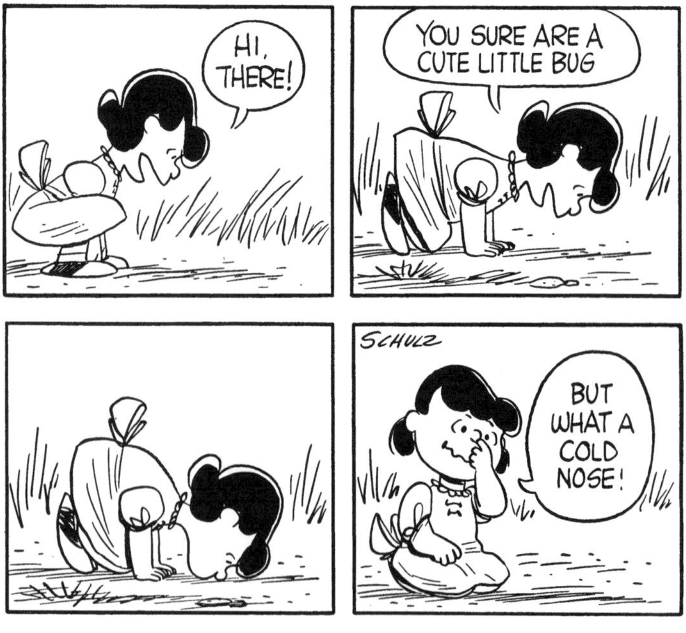
HI, THERE!
YOU SURE ARE A CUTE LITTLE BUG
SCHULZ
BUT WHAT A COLD NOSE!

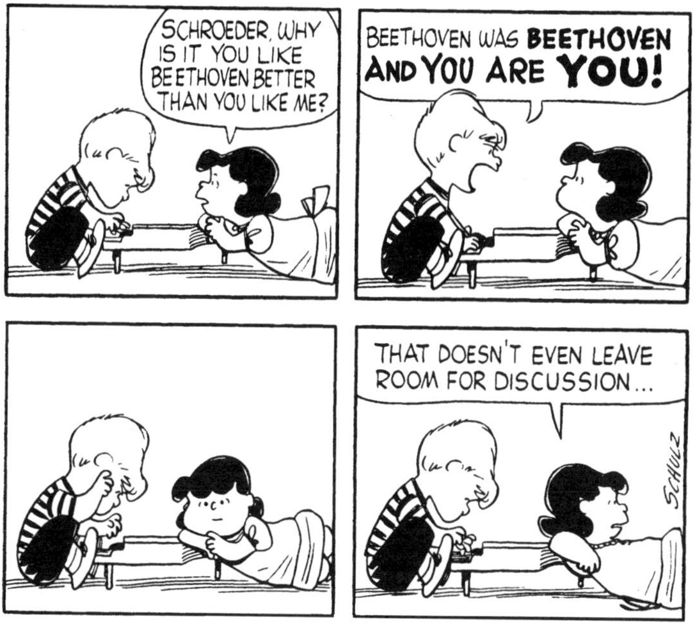
SCHROEDER, WHY IS IT YOU LIKE BEETHOVEN BETTER THAN YOU LIKE ME?
BEETHOVEN WAS **BEETHOVEN** AND YOU ARE **YOU!**
THAT DOESN'T EVEN LEAVE ROOM FOR DISCUSSION...
SCHULZ

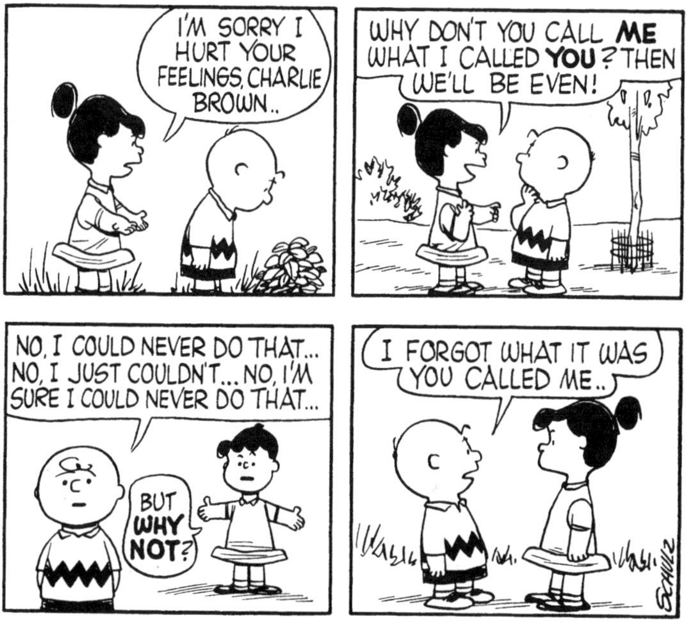
I'M SORRY I HURT YOUR FEELINGS, CHARLIE BROWN..
WHY DON'T YOU CALL **ME** WHAT I CALLED **YOU**? THEN WE'LL BE EVEN!
NO, I COULD NEVER DO THAT... NO, I JUST COULDN'T... NO, I'M SURE I COULD NEVER DO THAT...
BUT **WHY NOT**?
I FORGOT WHAT IT WAS YOU CALLED ME..
SCHULZ

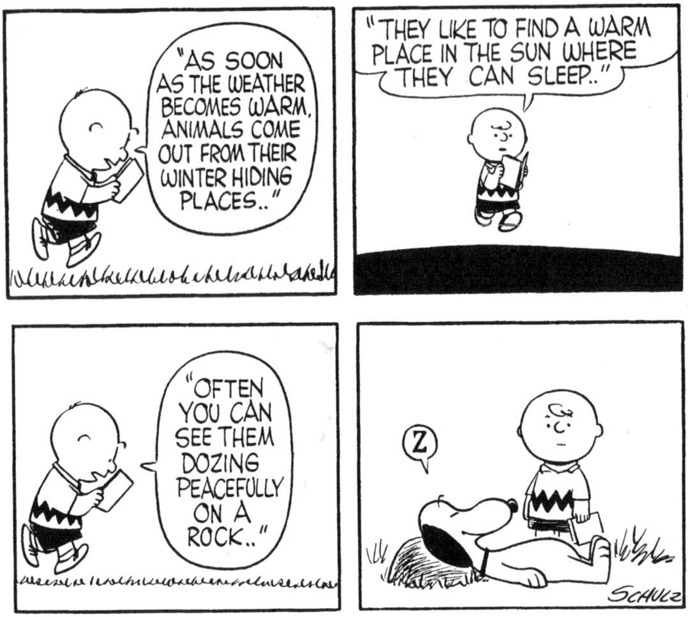
"AS SOON AS THE WEATHER BECOMES WARM, ANIMALS COME OUT FROM THEIR WINTER HIDING PLACES.."
"THEY LIKE TO FIND A WARM PLACE IN THE SUN WHERE THEY CAN SLEEP.."
"OFTEN YOU CAN SEE THEM DOZING PEACEFULLY ON A ROCK.."
Z
SCHULZ

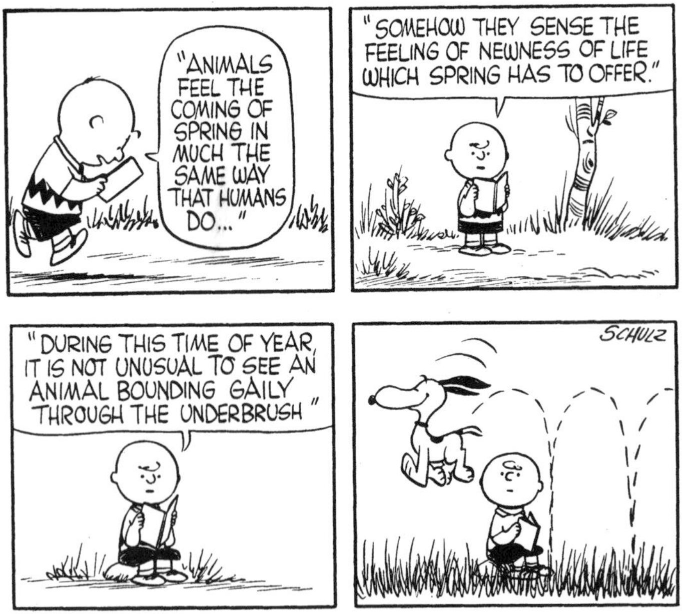
"ANIMALS FEEL THE COMING OF SPRING IN MUCH THE SAME WAY THAT HUMANS DO..."
"SOMEHOW THEY SENSE THE FEELING OF NEWNESS OF LIFE WHICH SPRING HAS TO OFFER."
"DURING THIS TIME OF YEAR, IT IS NOT UNUSUAL TO SEE AN ANIMAL BOUNDING GAILY THROUGH THE UNDERBRUSH"
SCHULZ

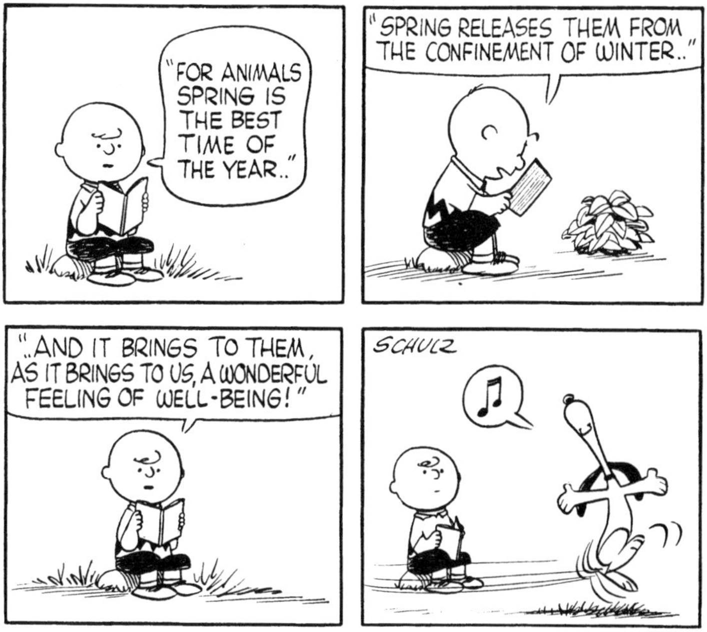
"FOR ANIMALS SPRING IS THE BEST TIME OF THE YEAR.."
"SPRING RELEASES THEM FROM THE CONFINEMENT OF WINTER.."
"..AND IT BRINGS TO THEM, AS IT BRINGS TO US, A WONDERFUL FEELING OF WELL-BEING!"

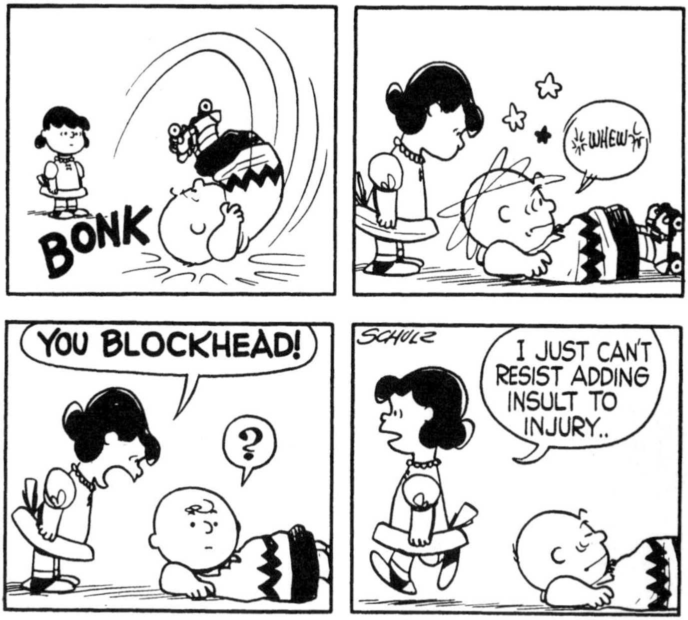
BONK
WHEW
YOU BLOCKHEAD!
?
I JUST CAN'T RESIST ADDING INSULT TO INJURY..

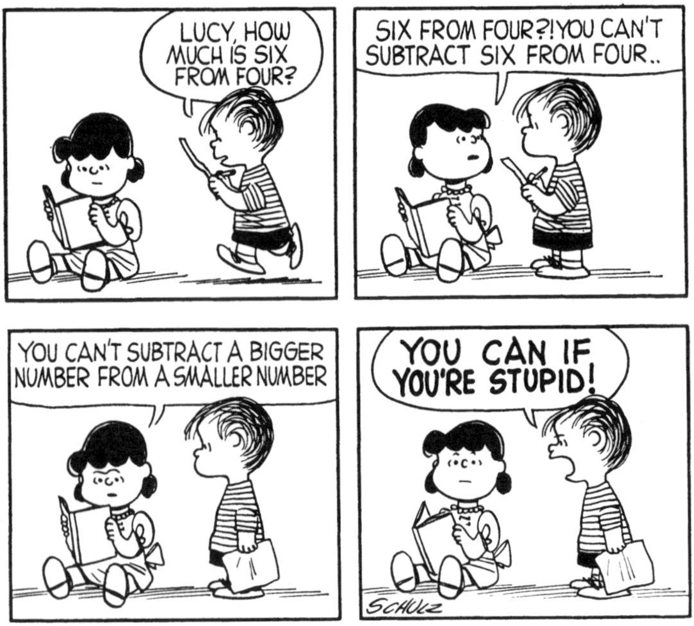
LUCY, HOW MUCH IS SIX FROM FOUR?
SIX FROM FOUR?! YOU CAN'T SUBTRACT SIX FROM FOUR..
YOU CAN'T SUBTRACT A BIGGER NUMBER FROM A SMALLER NUMBER
YOU CAN IF YOU'RE STUPID!
SCHULZ

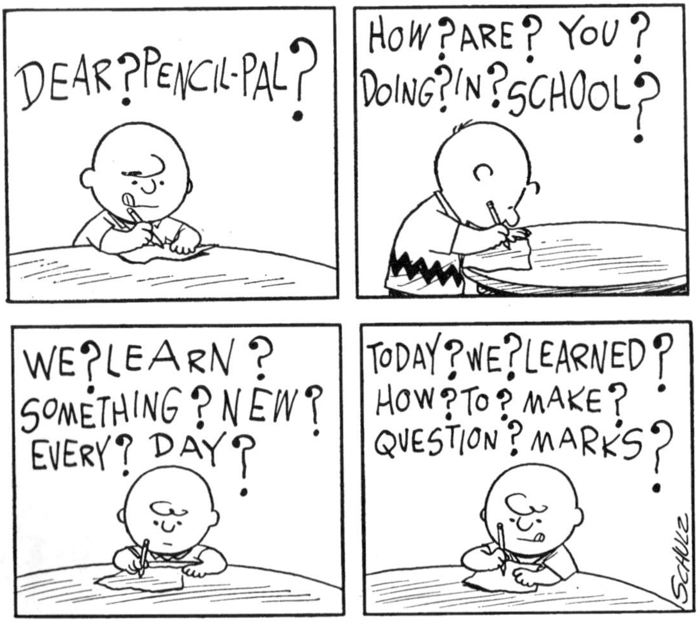
DEAR?PENCIL-PAL?
HOW?ARE?YOU?DOING?IN?SCHOOL?
WE?LEARN?SOMETHING?NEW?EVERY?DAY?
TODAY?WE?LEARNED?HOW?TO?MAKE?QUESTION?MARKS?
SCHULZ

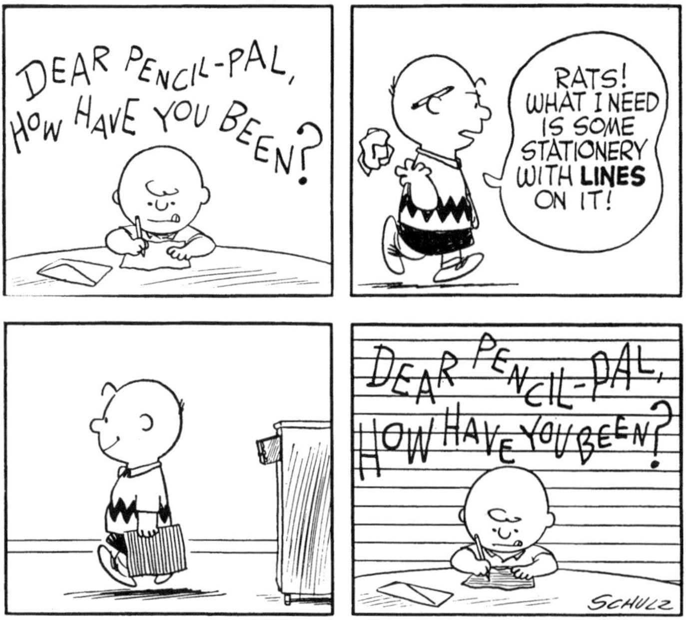
DEAR PENCIL-PAL,
HOW HAVE YOU BEEN?
RATS! WHAT I NEED IS SOME STATIONERY WITH **LINES** ON IT!
DEAR PENCIL-PAL,
HOW HAVE YOU BEEN?
SCHULZ

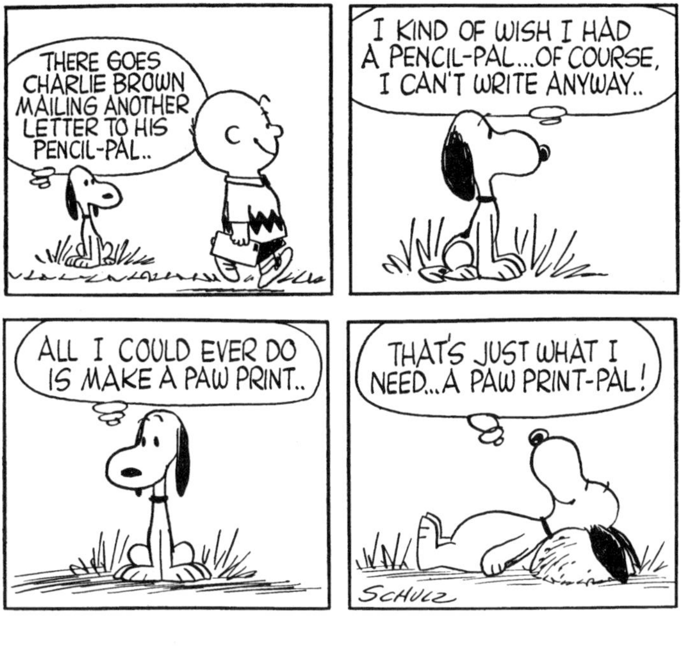
THERE GOES CHARLIE BROWN MAILING ANOTHER LETTER TO HIS PENCIL-PAL..
I KIND OF WISH I HAD A PENCIL-PAL...OF COURSE, I CAN'T WRITE ANYWAY..
ALL I COULD EVER DO IS MAKE A PAW PRINT..
THAT'S JUST WHAT I NEED...A PAW PRINT-PAL!
SCHULZ

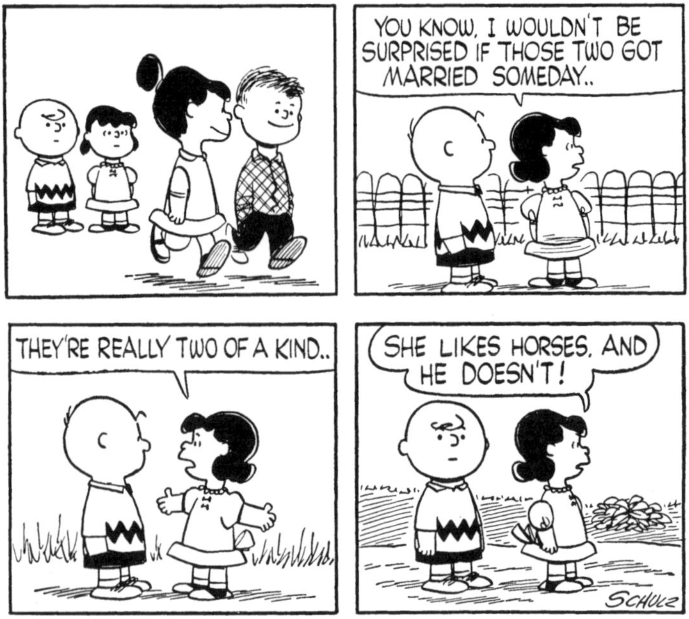
YOU KNOW, I WOULDN'T BE SURPRISED IF THOSE TWO GOT MARRIED SOMEDAY..
THEY'RE REALLY TWO OF A KIND..
SHE LIKES HORSES, AND HE DOESN'T!
SCHULZ

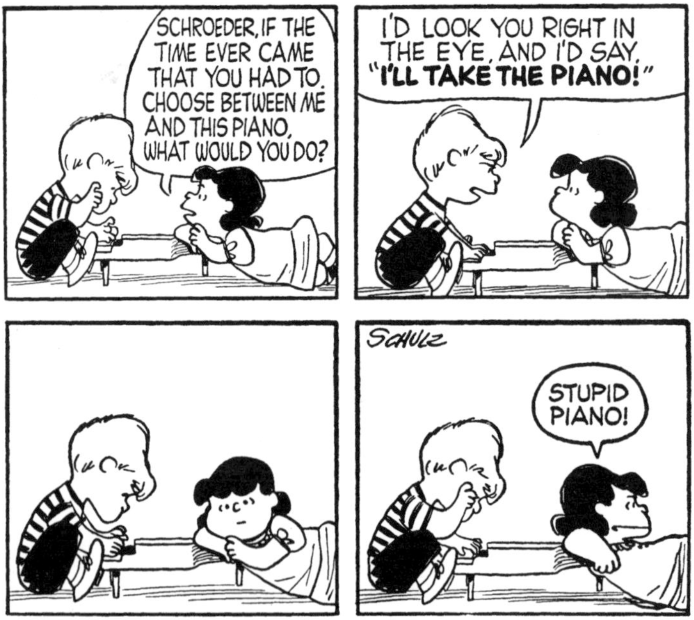
SCHROEDER, IF THE TIME EVER CAME THAT YOU HAD TO CHOOSE BETWEEN ME AND THIS PIANO, WHAT WOULD YOU DO?
I'D LOOK YOU RIGHT IN THE EYE, AND I'D SAY, "I'LL TAKE THE PIANO!"
SCHULZ
STUPID PIANO!

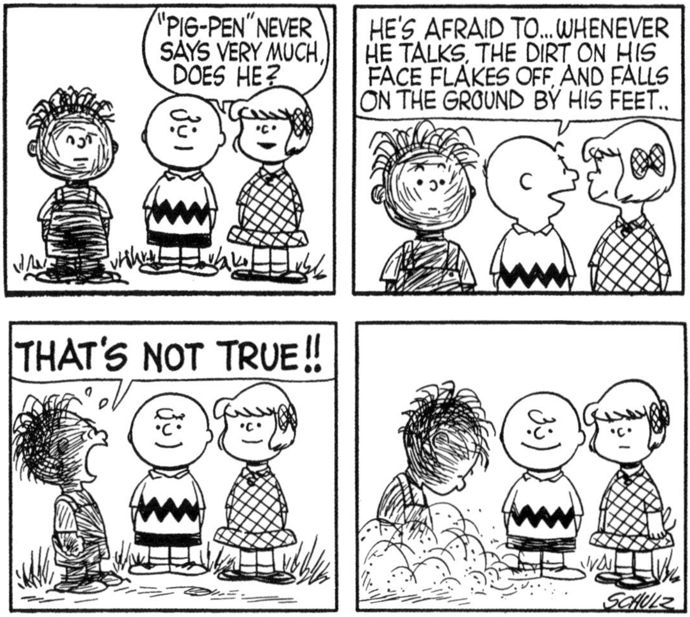
"PIG-PEN" NEVER SAYS VERY MUCH, DOES HE?
HE'S AFRAID TO...WHENEVER HE TALKS, THE DIRT ON HIS FACE FLAKES OFF, AND FALLS ON THE GROUND BY HIS FEET..
THAT'S NOT TRUE!!
SCHULZ

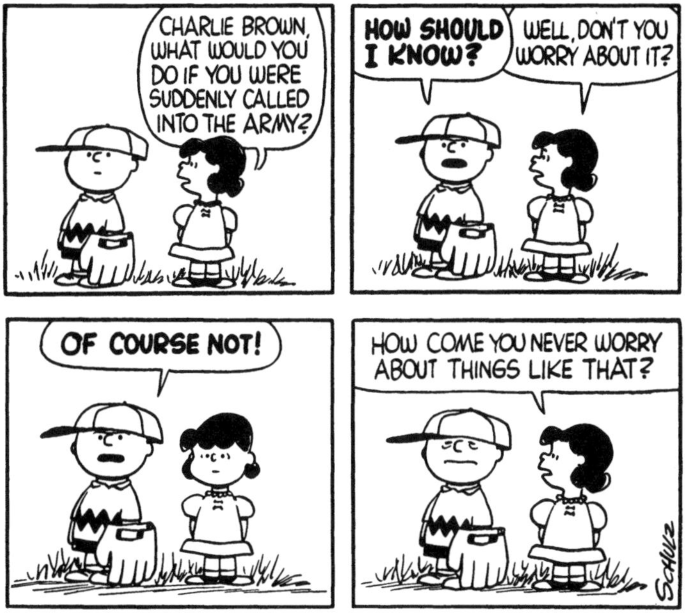
CHARLIE BROWN, WHAT WOULD YOU DO IF YOU WERE SUDDENLY CALLED INTO THE ARMY?
HOW SHOULD I KNOW?
WELL, DON'T YOU WORRY ABOUT IT?
OF COURSE NOT!
HOW COME YOU NEVER WORRY ABOUT THINGS LIKE THAT?
SCHULZ

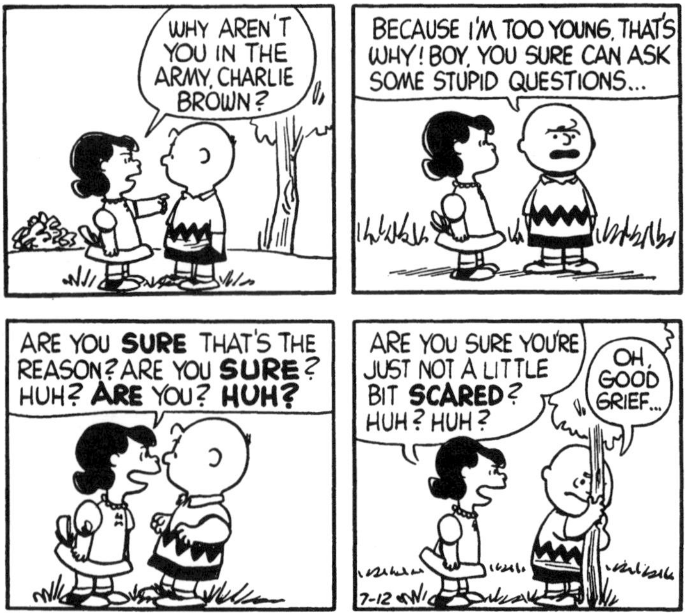
WHY AREN'T YOU IN THE ARMY, CHARLIE BROWN?
BECAUSE I'M TOO YOUNG, THAT'S WHY! BOY, YOU SURE CAN ASK SOME STUPID QUESTIONS...
ARE YOU **SURE** THAT'S THE REASON? ARE YOU **SURE**? HUH? **ARE** YOU? **HUH?**
ARE YOU SURE YOU'RE JUST NOT A LITTLE BIT **SCARED**? HUH? HUH?
OH, GOOD GRIEF...
7-12

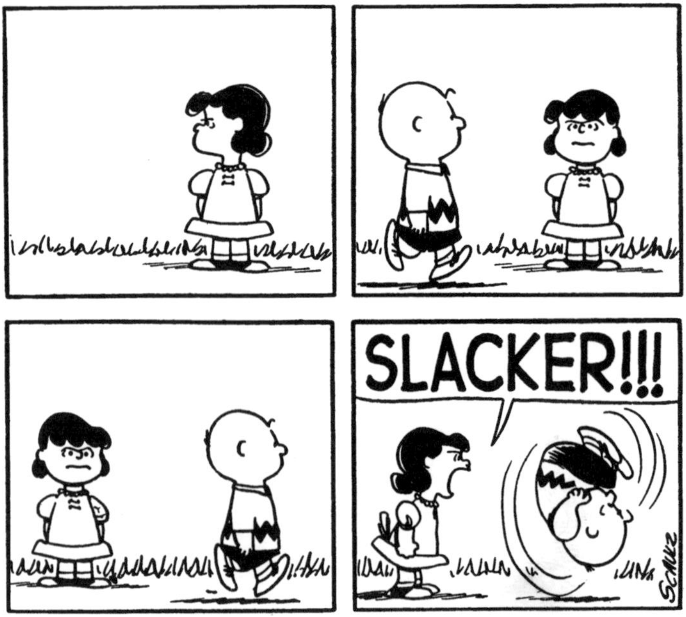
SLACKER!!!
SCHULZ

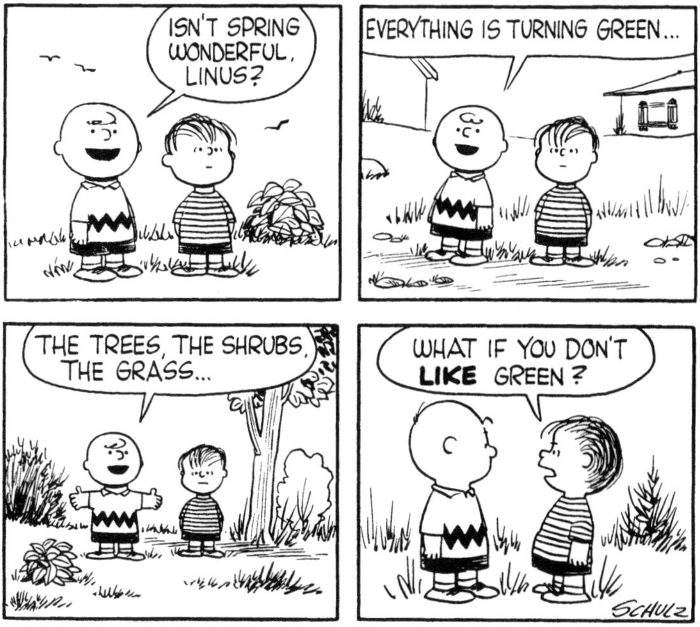
ISN'T SPRING WONDERFUL, LINUS?
EVERYTHING IS TURNING GREEN...
THE TREES, THE SHRUBS, THE GRASS...
WHAT IF YOU DON'T **LIKE** GREEN?
SCHULZ

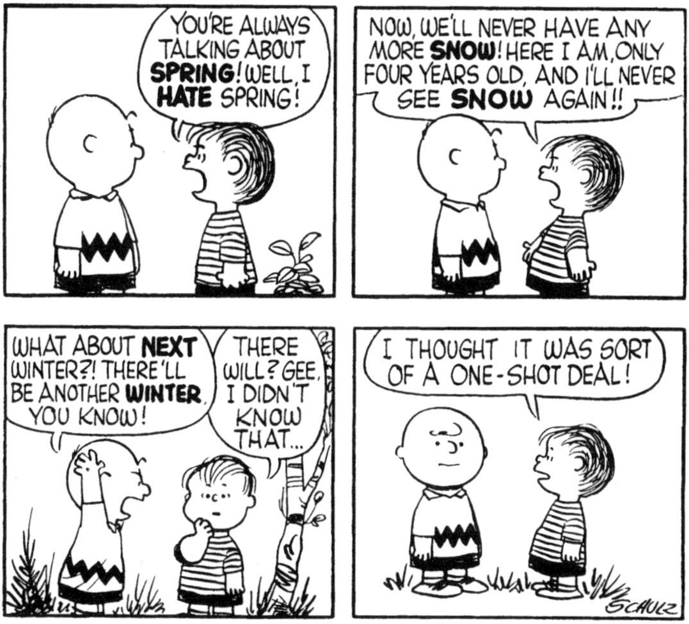
YOU'RE ALWAYS TALKING ABOUT **SPRING**! WELL, I **HATE** SPRING!
NOW, WE'LL NEVER HAVE ANY MORE **SNOW**! HERE I AM, ONLY FOUR YEARS OLD, AND I'LL NEVER SEE **SNOW** AGAIN!!
WHAT ABOUT **NEXT** WINTER?! THERE'LL BE ANOTHER **WINTER**, YOU KNOW!
THERE WILL? GEE, I DIDN'T KNOW THAT...
I THOUGHT IT WAS SORT OF A ONE-SHOT DEAL!
SCHULZ

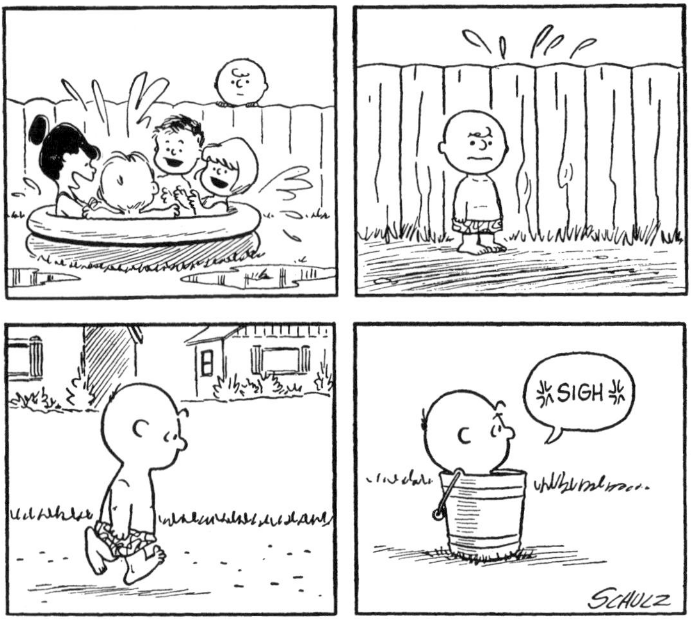
SIGH
SCHULZ

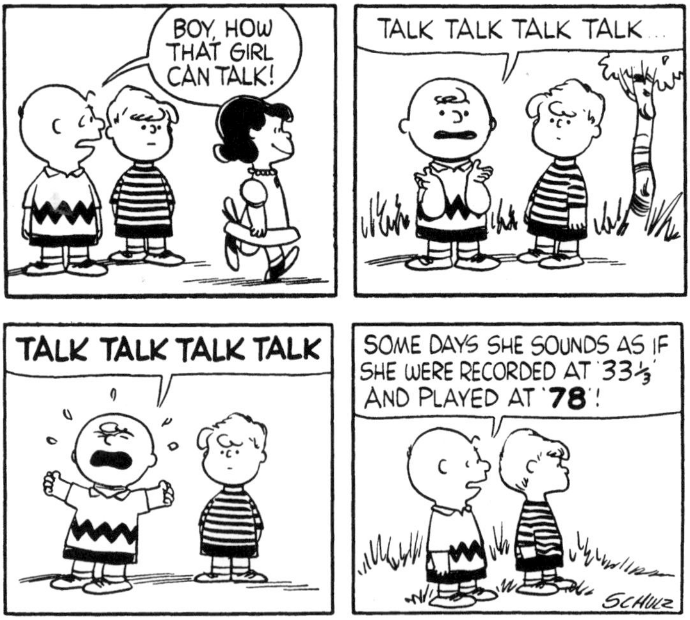
BOY, HOW THAT GIRL CAN TALK!
TALK TALK TALK TALK...
TALK TALK TALK TALK
SOME DAYS SHE SOUNDS AS IF SHE WERE RECORDED AT '33⅓' AND PLAYED AT '78'!
SCHULZ

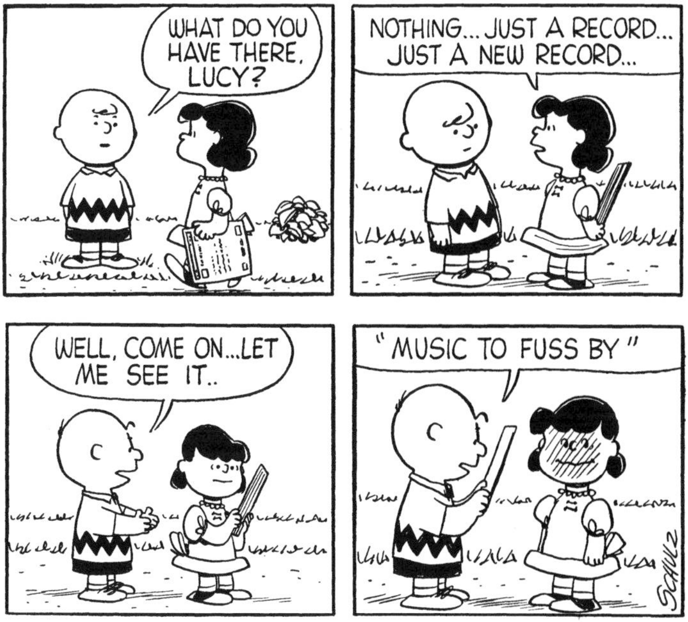
WHAT DO YOU HAVE THERE, LUCY?
NOTHING... JUST A RECORD... JUST A NEW RECORD...
WELL, COME ON...LET ME SEE IT..
"MUSIC TO FUSS BY"
SCHULZ

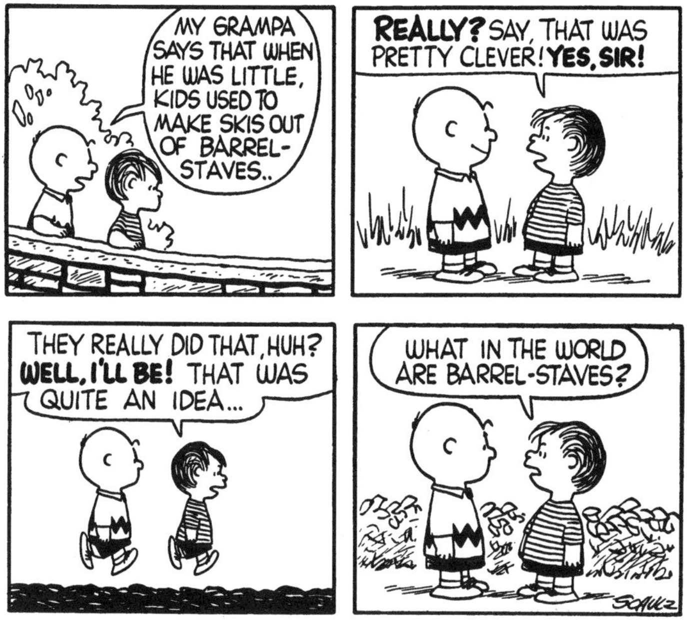
MY GRAMPA SAYS THAT WHEN HE WAS LITTLE, KIDS USED TO MAKE SKIS OUT OF BARREL-STAVES..
REALLY? SAY, THAT WAS PRETTY CLEVER! YES, SIR!
THEY REALLY DID THAT, HUH? WELL, I'LL BE! THAT WAS QUITE AN IDEA...
WHAT IN THE WORLD ARE BARREL-STAVES?
SCHULZ

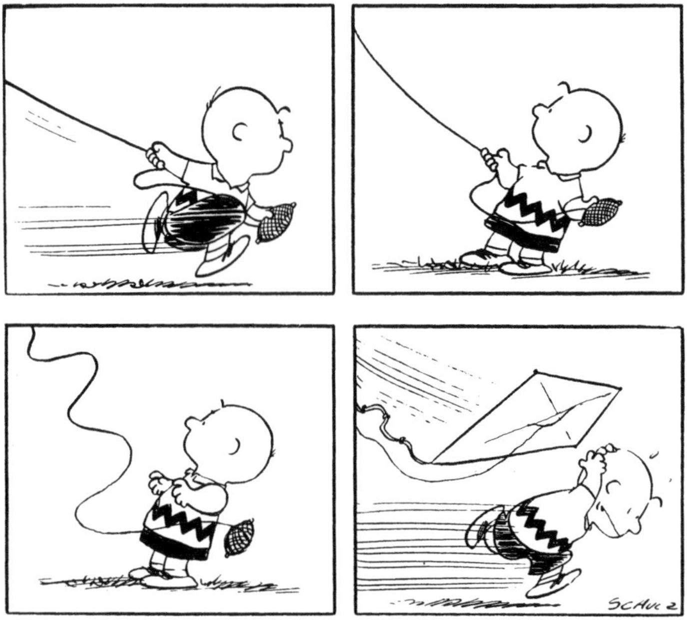

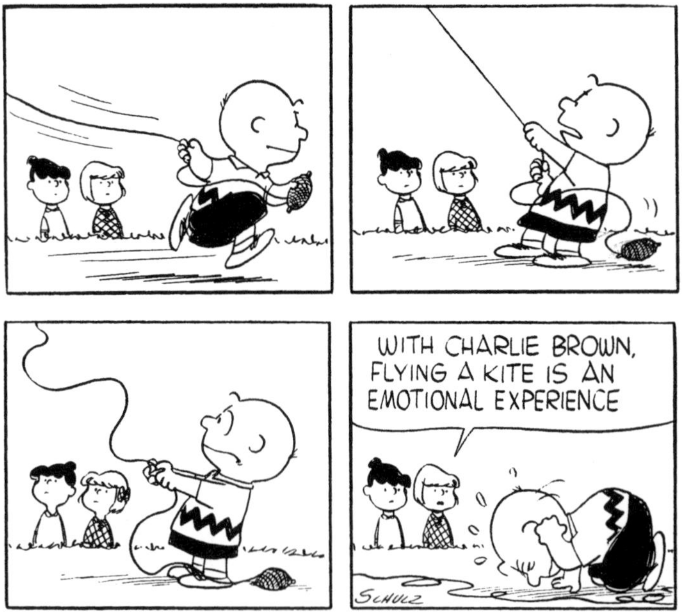
WITH CHARLIE BROWN, FLYING A KITE IS AN EMOTIONAL EXPERIENCE
SCHULZ

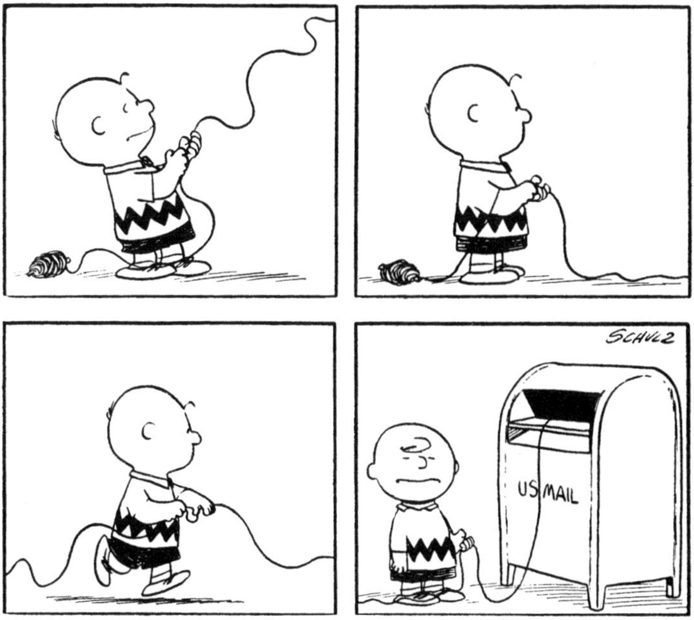
SCHULZ
US MAIL

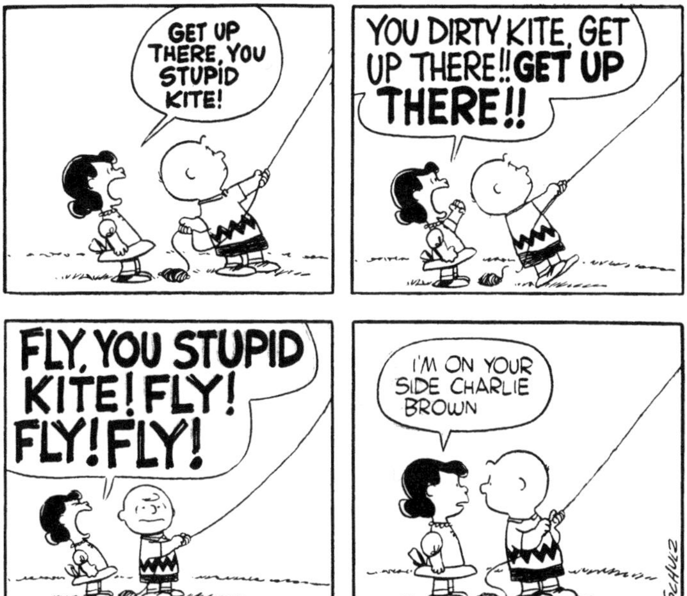
GET UP THERE, YOU STUPID KITE!
YOU DIRTY KITE, GET UP THERE!! GET UP THERE!!
FLY, YOU STUPID KITE! FLY! FLY! FLY!
I'M ON YOUR SIDE CHARLIE BROWN
SCHULZ

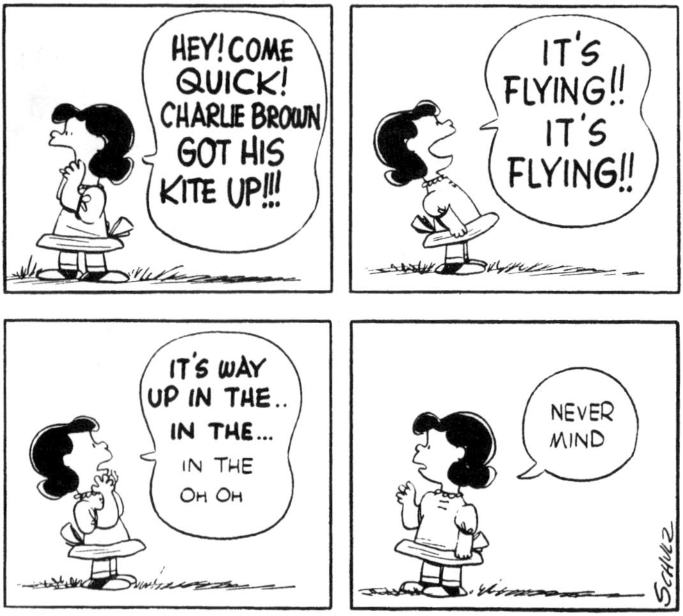
HEY! COME QUICK! CHARLIE BROWN GOT HIS KITE UP!!!
IT'S FLYING!! IT'S FLYING!!
IT'S WAY UP IN THE.. IN THE... IN THE OH OH
NEVER MIND
SCHULZ

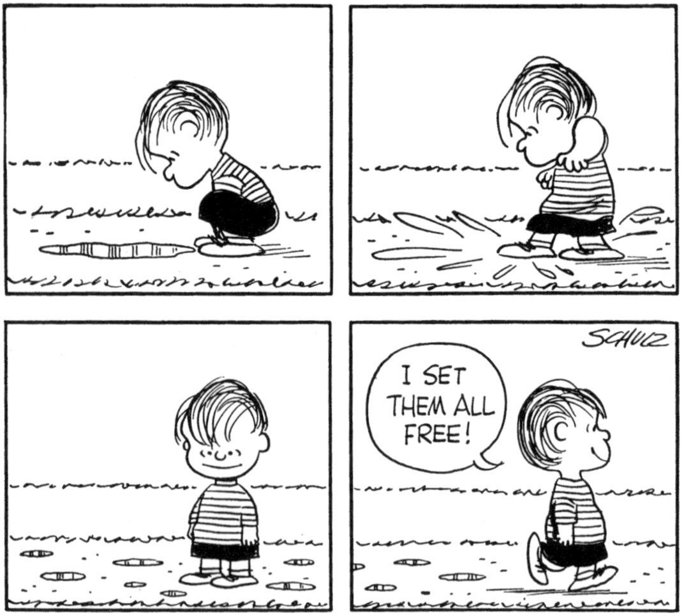
SCHULZ
I SET THEM ALL FREE!

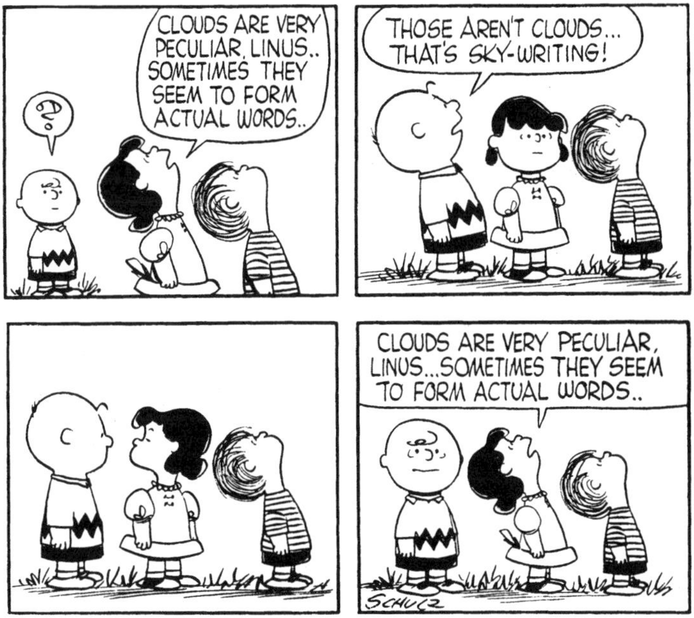
CLOUDS ARE VERY PECULIAR, LINUS.. SOMETIMES THEY SEEM TO FORM ACTUAL WORDS..
?
THOSE AREN'T CLOUDS... THAT'S SKY-WRITING!
CLOUDS ARE VERY PECULIAR, LINUS...SOMETIMES THEY SEEM TO FORM ACTUAL WORDS..
SCHULZ

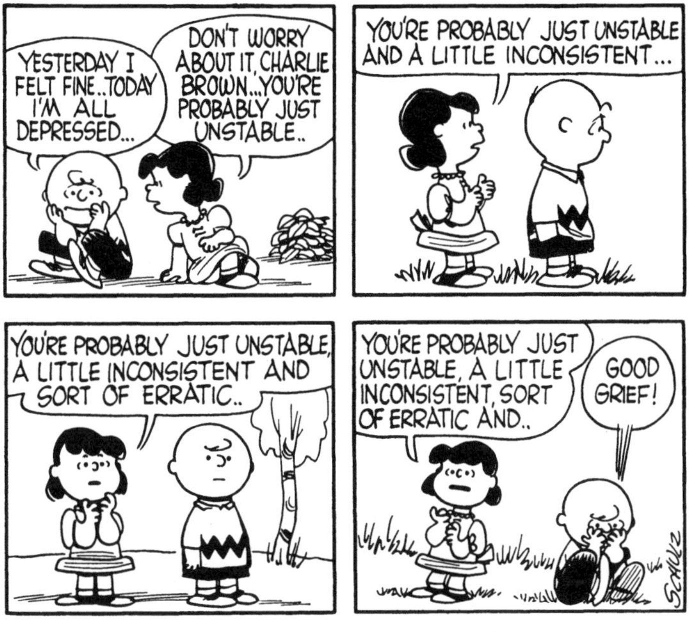
YESTERDAY I FELT FINE..TODAY I'M ALL DEPRESSED...
DON'T WORRY ABOUT IT, CHARLIE BROWN...YOU'RE PROBABLY JUST UNSTABLE..
YOU'RE PROBABLY JUST UNSTABLE AND A LITTLE INCONSISTENT...
YOU'RE PROBABLY JUST UNSTABLE, A LITTLE INCONSISTENT AND SORT OF ERRATIC..
YOU'RE PROBABLY JUST UNSTABLE, A LITTLE INCONSISTENT, SORT OF ERRATIC AND..
GOOD GRIEF!
SCHULZ

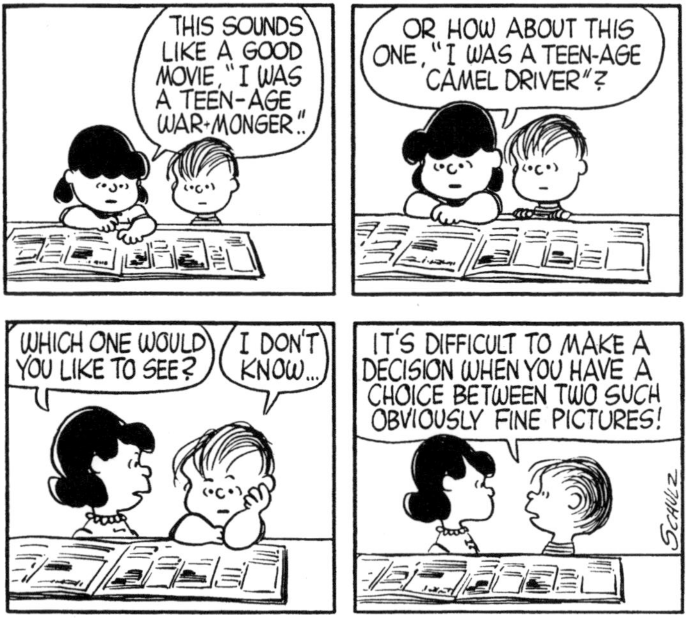
THIS SOUNDS LIKE A GOOD MOVIE, "I WAS A TEEN-AGE WAR-MONGER".
OR HOW ABOUT THIS ONE, "I WAS A TEEN-AGE CAMEL DRIVER"?
WHICH ONE WOULD YOU LIKE TO SEE?
I DON'T KNOW...
IT'S DIFFICULT TO MAKE A DECISION WHEN YOU HAVE A CHOICE BETWEEN TWO SUCH OBVIOUSLY FINE PICTURES!
SCHULZ

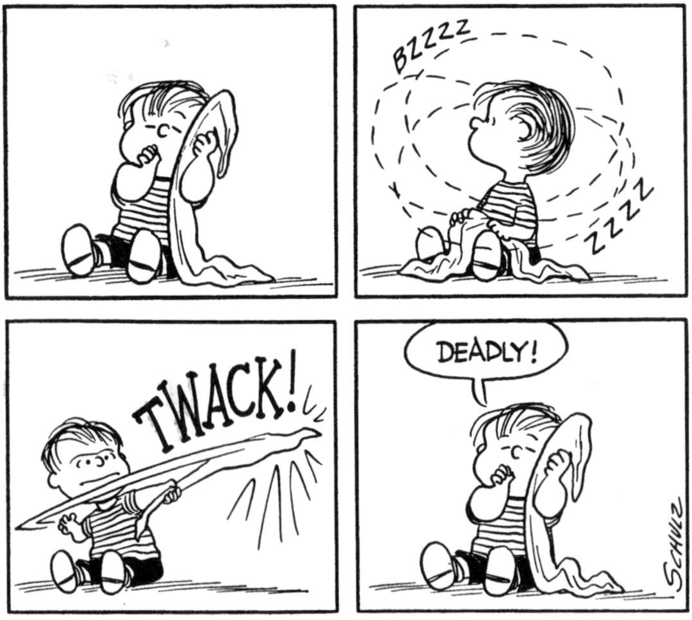
BZZZZ
ZZZZ
TWACK!
DEADLY!
SCHULZ

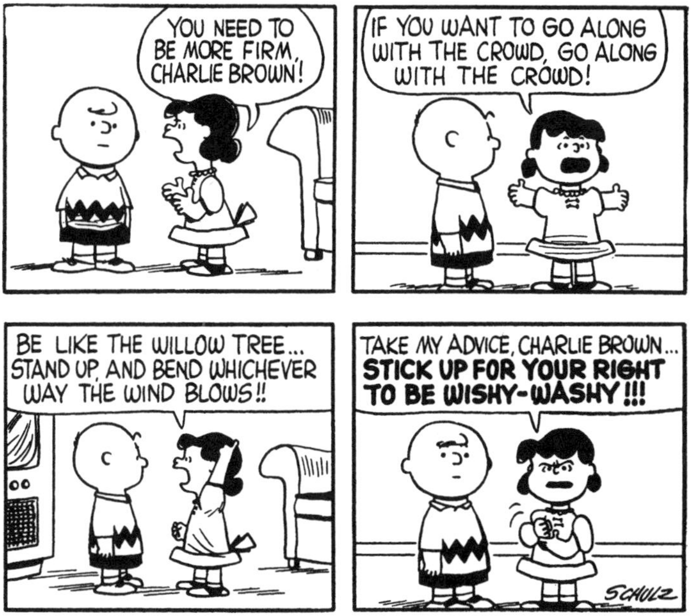
YOU NEED TO BE MORE FIRM, CHARLIE BROWN!
IF YOU WANT TO GO ALONG WITH THE CROWD, GO ALONG WITH THE CROWD!
BE LIKE THE WILLOW TREE... STAND UP, AND BEND WHICHEVER WAY THE WIND BLOWS!!
TAKE MY ADVICE, CHARLIE BROWN... STICK UP FOR YOUR RIGHT TO BE WISHY-WASHY!!!
SCHULZ

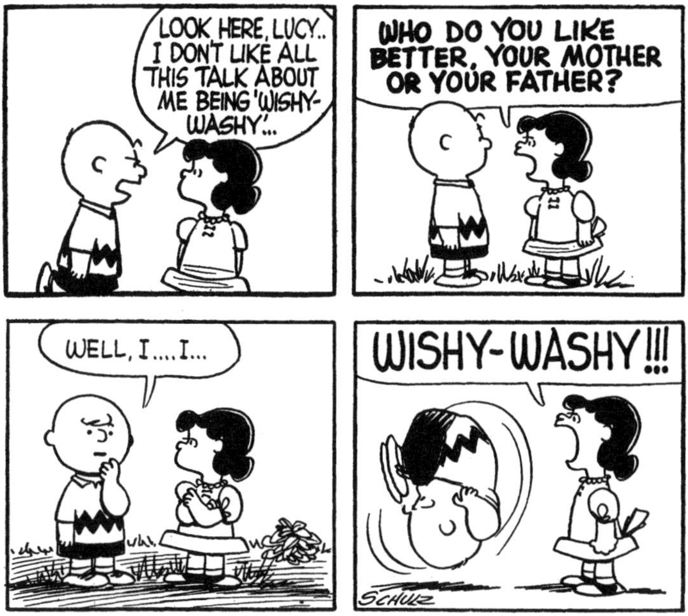
LOOK HERE, LUCY.. I DON'T LIKE ALL THIS TALK ABOUT ME BEING 'WISHY-WASHY'...
WHO DO YOU LIKE BETTER, YOUR MOTHER OR YOUR FATHER?
WELL, I.... I...
WISHY-WASHY!!!
SCHULZ

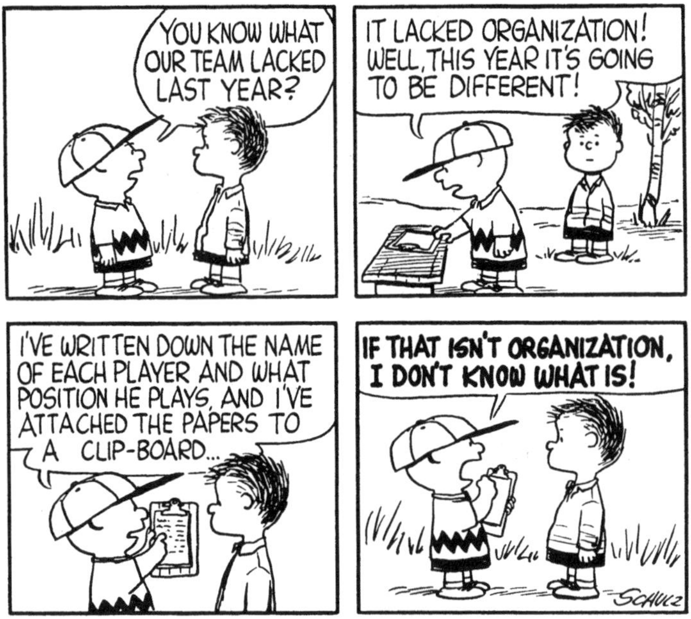
YOU KNOW WHAT OUR TEAM LACKED LAST YEAR?
IT LACKED ORGANIZATION! WELL, THIS YEAR IT'S GOING TO BE DIFFERENT!
I'VE WRITTEN DOWN THE NAME OF EACH PLAYER AND WHAT POSITION HE PLAYS, AND I'VE ATTACHED THE PAPERS TO A CLIP-BOARD...
IF THAT ISN'T ORGANIZATION, I DON'T KNOW WHAT IS!
SCHULZ

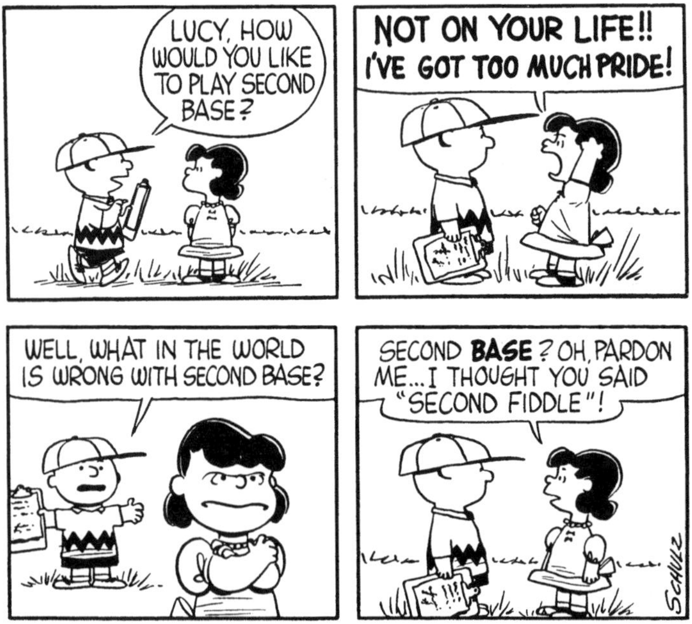
LUCY, HOW WOULD YOU LIKE TO PLAY SECOND BASE?
NOT ON YOUR LIFE!! I'VE GOT TOO MUCH PRIDE!
WELL, WHAT IN THE WORLD IS WRONG WITH SECOND BASE?
SECOND BASE? OH, PARDON ME...I THOUGHT YOU SAID "SECOND FIDDLE"!
SCHULZ

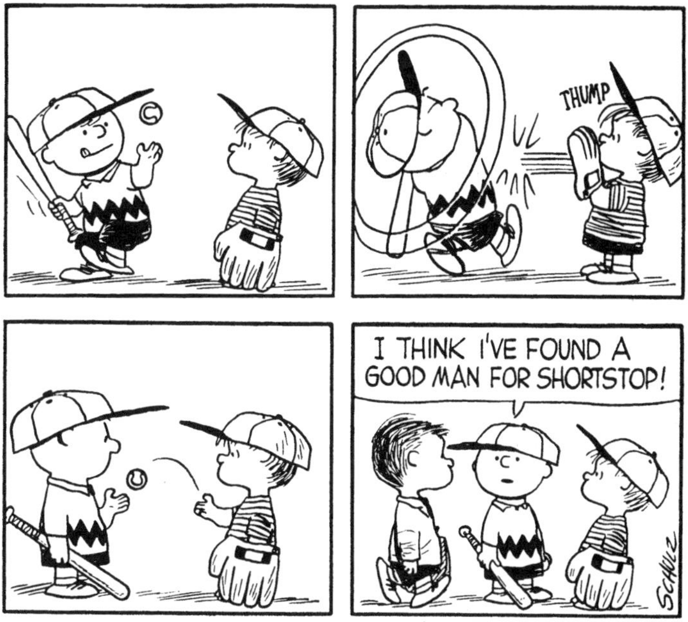
THUMP
I THINK I'VE FOUND A GOOD MAN FOR SHORTSTOP!
SCHULZ

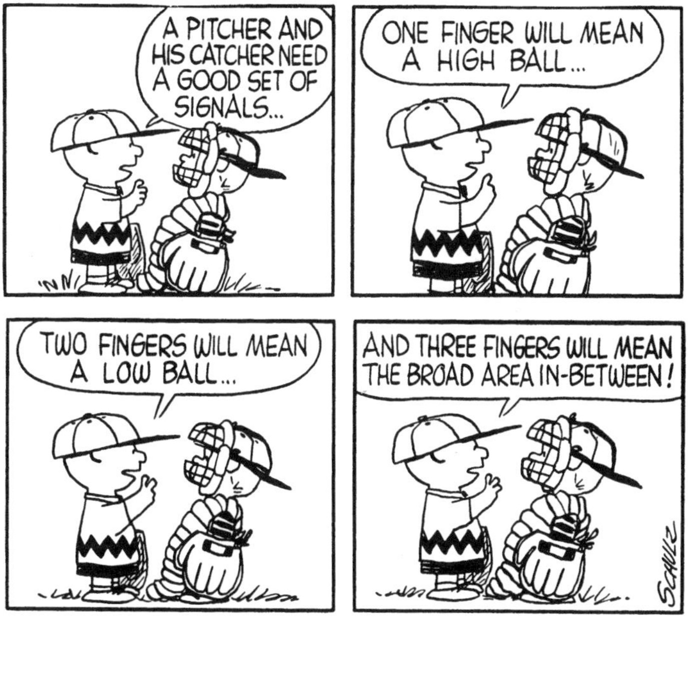
A PITCHER AND HIS CATCHER NEED A GOOD SET OF SIGNALS...
ONE FINGER WILL MEAN A HIGH BALL...
TWO FINGERS WILL MEAN A LOW BALL...
AND THREE FINGERS WILL MEAN THE BROAD AREA IN-BETWEEN!
SCHULZ

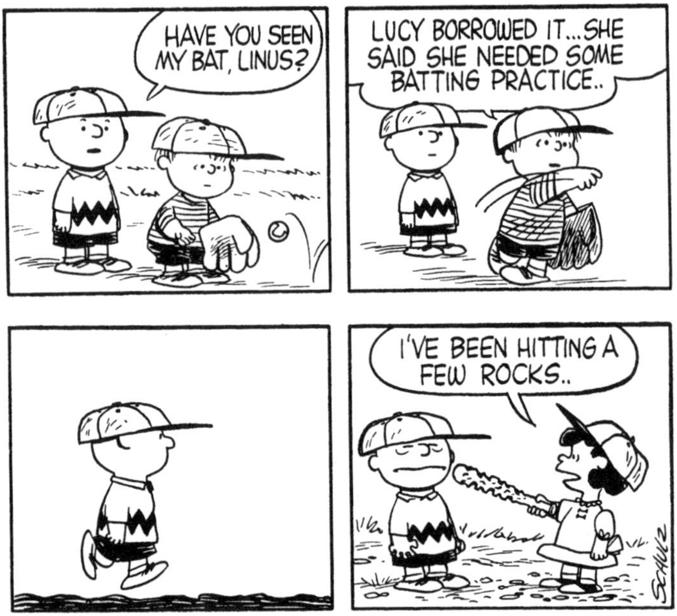
HAVE YOU SEEN MY BAT, LINUS?
LUCY BORROWED IT...SHE SAID SHE NEEDED SOME BATTING PRACTICE..
I'VE BEEN HITTING A FEW ROCKS..
SCHULZ

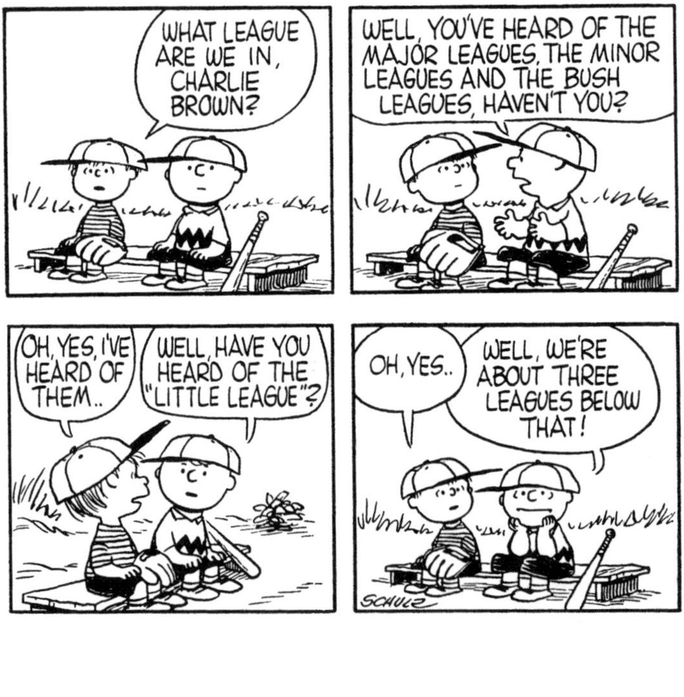
WHAT LEAGUE ARE WE IN, CHARLIE BROWN?
WELL, YOU'VE HEARD OF THE MAJOR LEAGUES, THE MINOR LEAGUES AND THE BUSH LEAGUES, HAVEN'T YOU?
OH, YES, I'VE HEARD OF THEM..
WELL, HAVE YOU HEARD OF THE "LITTLE LEAGUE"?
OH, YES..
WELL, WE'RE ABOUT THREE LEAGUES BELOW THAT!
SCHULZ

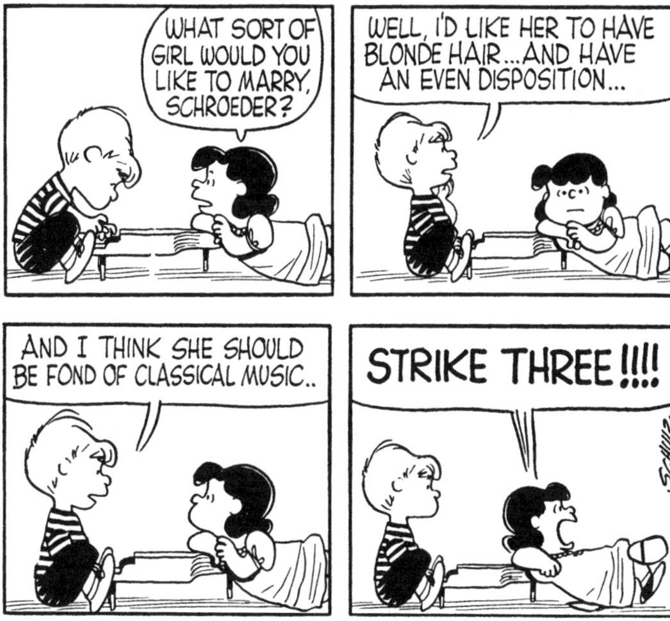
WHAT SORT OF GIRL WOULD YOU LIKE TO MARRY, SCHROEDER?
WELL, I'D LIKE HER TO HAVE BLONDE HAIR...AND HAVE AN EVEN DISPOSITION...
AND I THINK SHE SHOULD BE FOND OF CLASSICAL MUSIC..
STRIKE THREE!!!!
SCHULZ

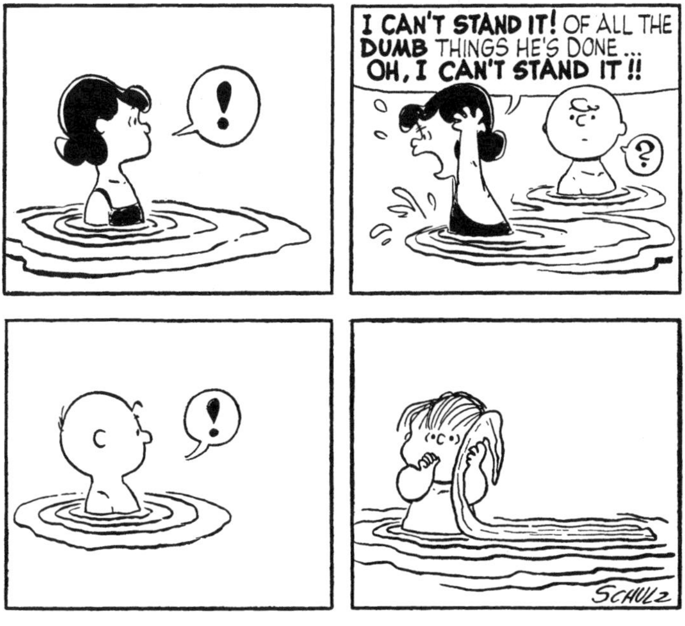
!
I CAN'T STAND IT! OF ALL THE DUMB THINGS HE'S DONE... OH, I CAN'T STAND IT!!
?
!
SCHULZ

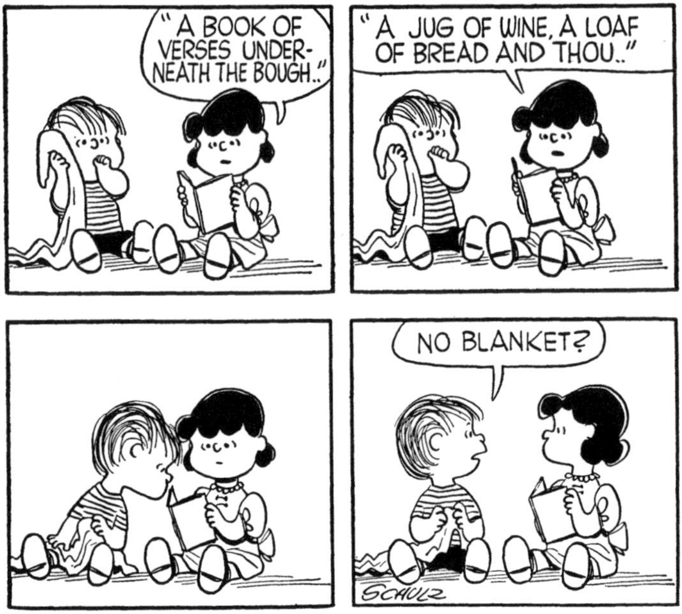
"A BOOK OF VERSES UNDERNEATH THE BOUGH.."
"A JUG OF WINE, A LOAF OF BREAD AND THOU.."
NO BLANKET?
SCHULZ

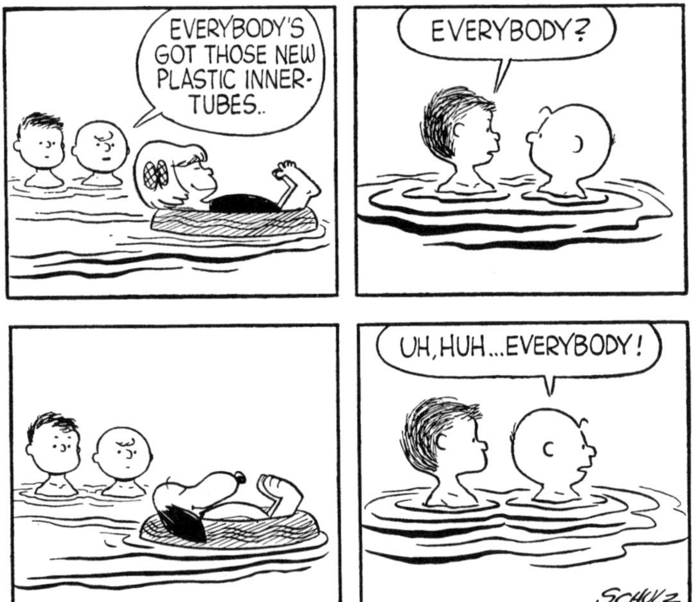
EVERYBODY'S GOT THOSE NEW PLASTIC INNER-TUBES..
EVERYBODY?
UH, HUH...EVERYBODY!
SCHULZ

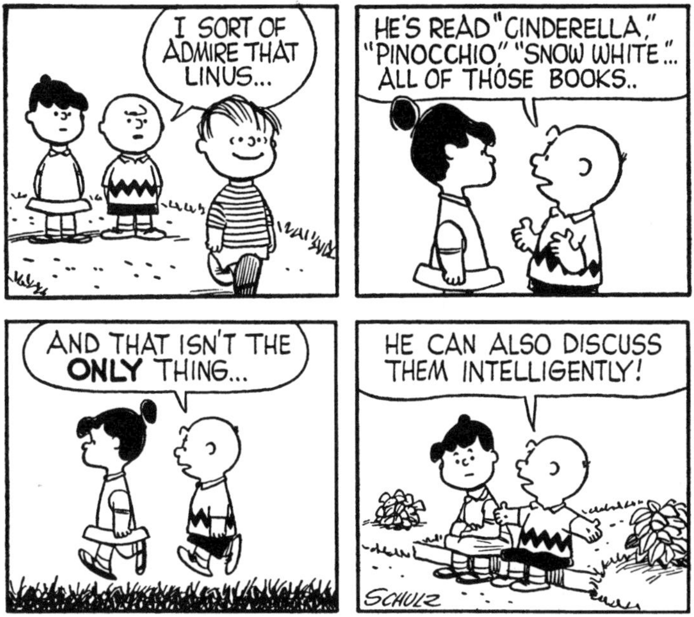
I SORT OF ADMIRE THAT LINUS...
HE'S READ "CINDERELLA," "PINOCCHIO," "SNOW WHITE."... ALL OF THOSE BOOKS..
AND THAT ISN'T THE **ONLY** THING...
HE CAN ALSO DISCUSS THEM INTELLIGENTLY!
SCHULZ

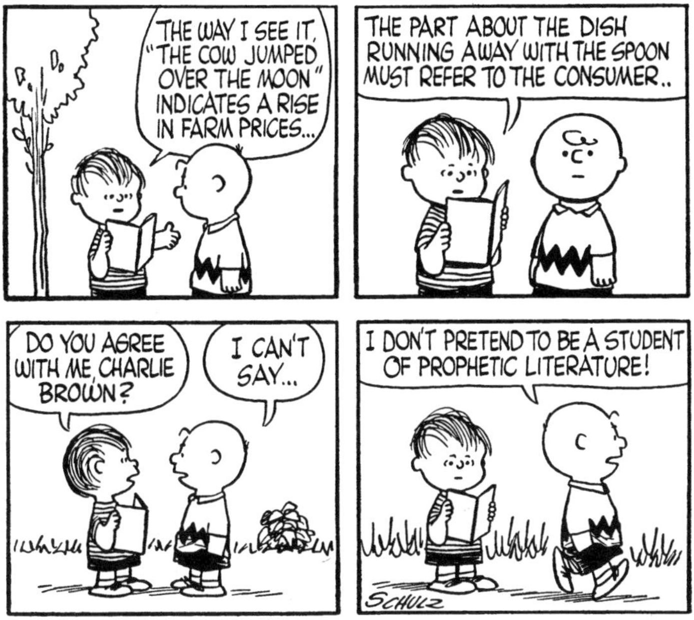
THE WAY I SEE IT, "THE COW JUMPED OVER THE MOON" INDICATES A RISE IN FARM PRICES...
THE PART ABOUT THE DISH RUNNING AWAY WITH THE SPOON MUST REFER TO THE CONSUMER..
DO YOU AGREE WITH ME, CHARLIE BROWN?
I CAN'T SAY...
I DON'T PRETEND TO BE A STUDENT OF PROPHETIC LITERATURE!
SCHULZ

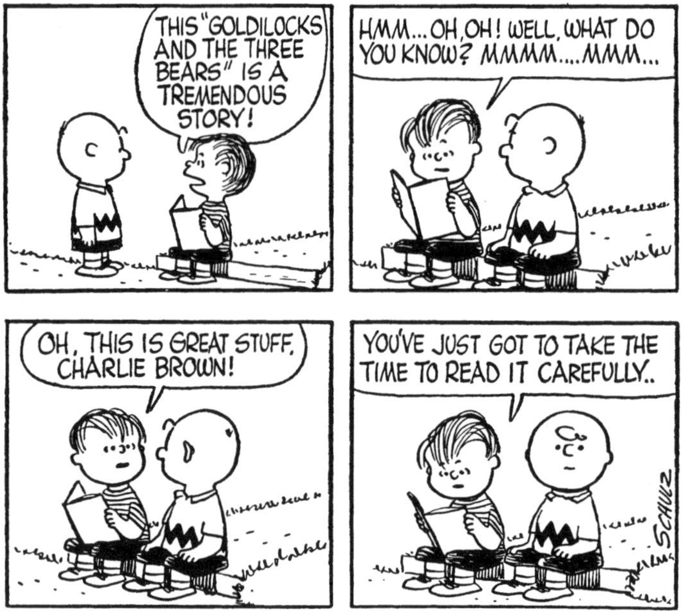
THIS "GOLDILOCKS AND THE THREE BEARS" IS A TREMENDOUS STORY!
HMM...OH, OH! WELL, WHAT DO YOU KNOW? MMMM....MMM...
OH, THIS IS GREAT STUFF, CHARLIE BROWN!
YOU'VE JUST GOT TO TAKE THE TIME TO READ IT CAREFULLY..
SCHULZ

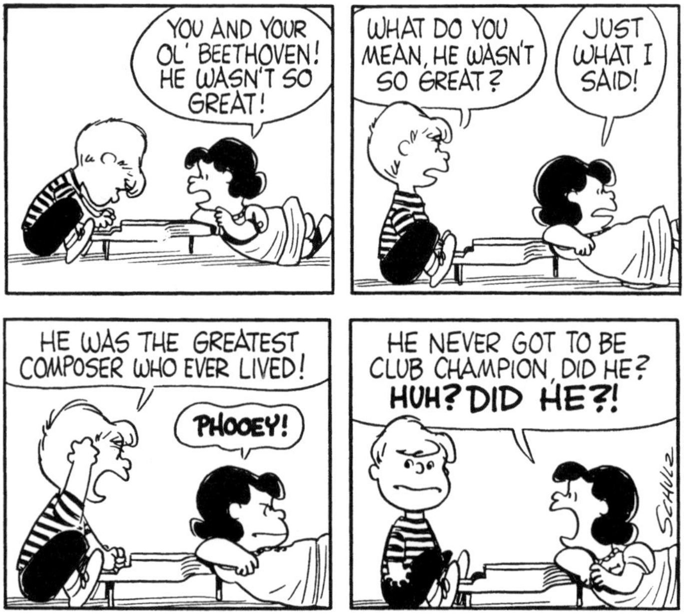
YOU AND YOUR OL' BEETHOVEN! HE WASN'T SO GREAT!
WHAT DO YOU MEAN, HE WASN'T SO GREAT?
JUST WHAT I SAID!
HE WAS THE GREATEST COMPOSER WHO EVER LIVED!
PHOOEY!
HE NEVER GOT TO BE CLUB CHAMPION, DID HE? HUH? DID HE?!
SCHULZ

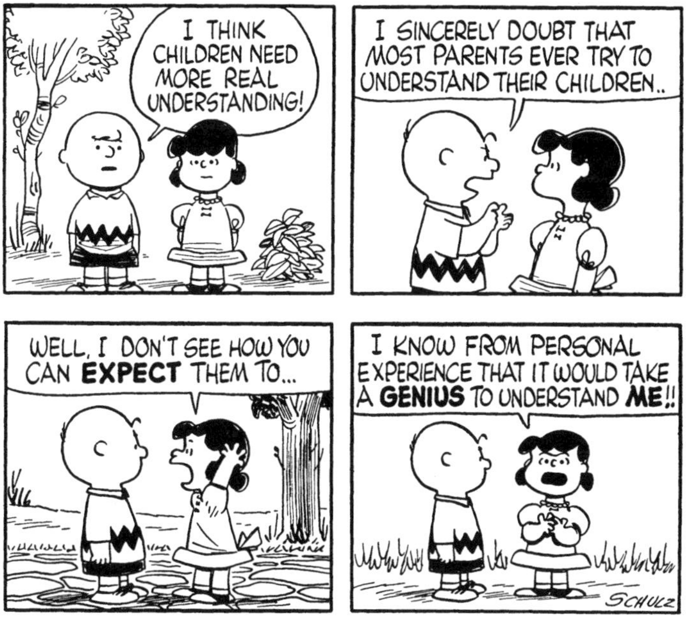

I THINK CHILDREN NEED MORE REAL UNDERSTANDING!
I SINCERELY DOUBT THAT MOST PARENTS EVER TRY TO UNDERSTAND THEIR CHILDREN..
WELL, I DON'T SEE HOW YOU CAN **EXPECT** THEM TO...
I KNOW FROM PERSONAL EXPERIENCE THAT IT WOULD TAKE A **GENIUS** TO UNDERSTAND **ME**!!
SCHULZ

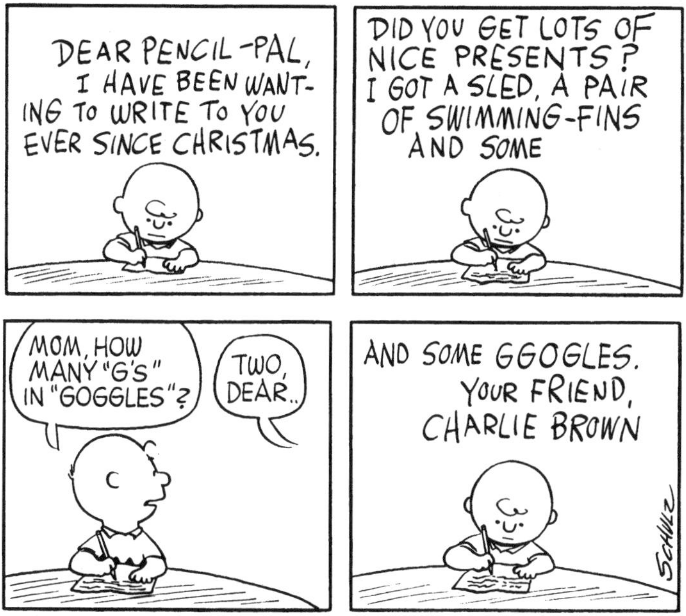

DEAR PENCIL-PAL, I HAVE BEEN WANTING TO WRITE TO YOU EVER SINCE CHRISTMAS.
DID YOU GET LOTS OF NICE PRESENTS? I GOT A SLED, A PAIR OF SWIMMING-FINS AND SOME
MOM, HOW MANY "G'S" IN "GOGGLES"?
TWO, DEAR..
AND SOME GGOGLES. YOUR FRIEND, CHARLIE BROWN
SCHULZ

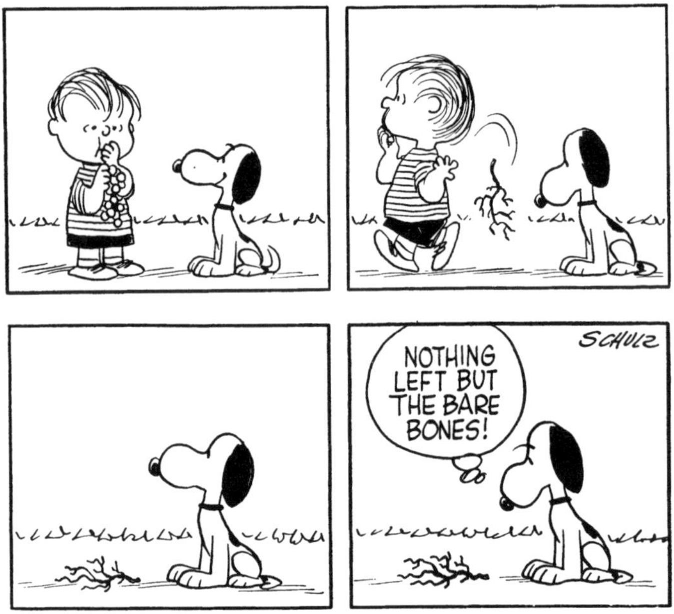
NOTHING LEFT BUT THE BARE BONES!
SCHULZ

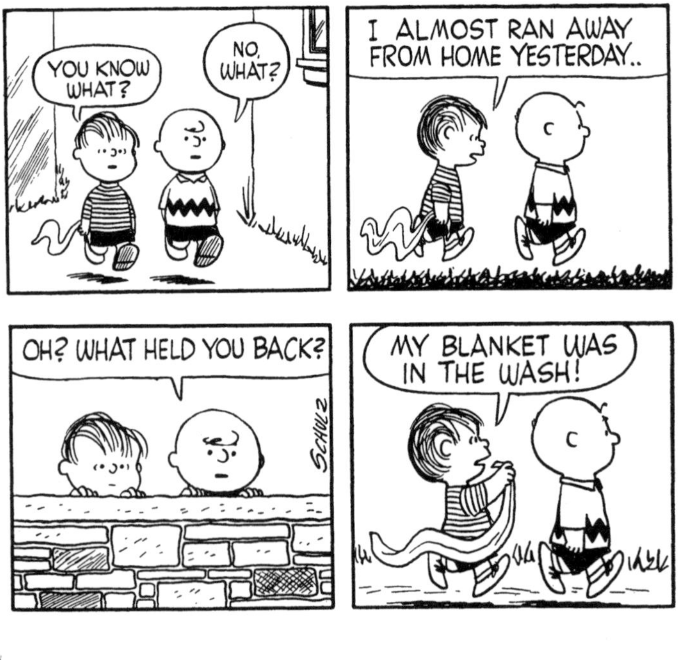
YOU KNOW WHAT?
NO, WHAT?
I ALMOST RAN AWAY FROM HOME YESTERDAY..
OH? WHAT HELD YOU BACK?
SCHULZ
MY BLANKET WAS IN THE WASH!

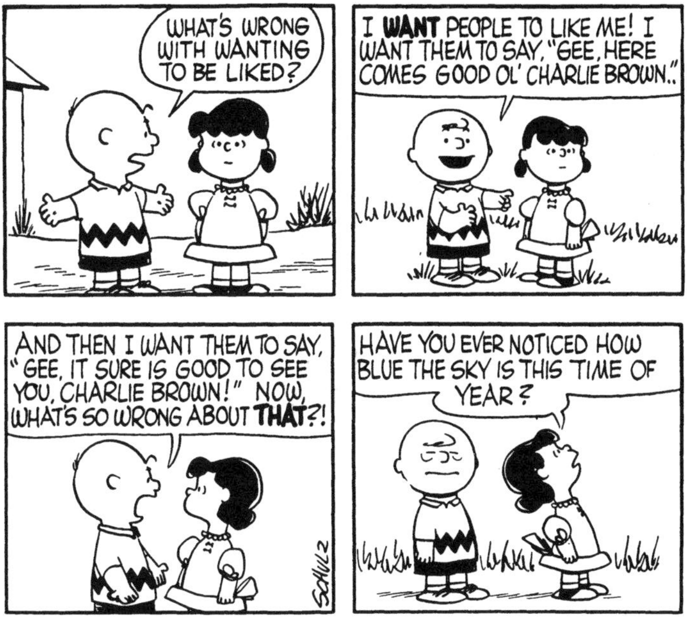
WHAT'S WRONG WITH WANTING TO BE LIKED?
I **WANT** PEOPLE TO LIKE ME! I WANT THEM TO SAY, "GEE, HERE COMES GOOD OL' CHARLIE BROWN."
AND THEN I WANT THEM TO SAY, "GEE, IT SURE IS GOOD TO SEE YOU, CHARLIE BROWN!" NOW, WHAT'S SO WRONG ABOUT **THAT**?!
SCHULZ
HAVE YOU EVER NOTICED HOW BLUE THE SKY IS THIS TIME OF YEAR?

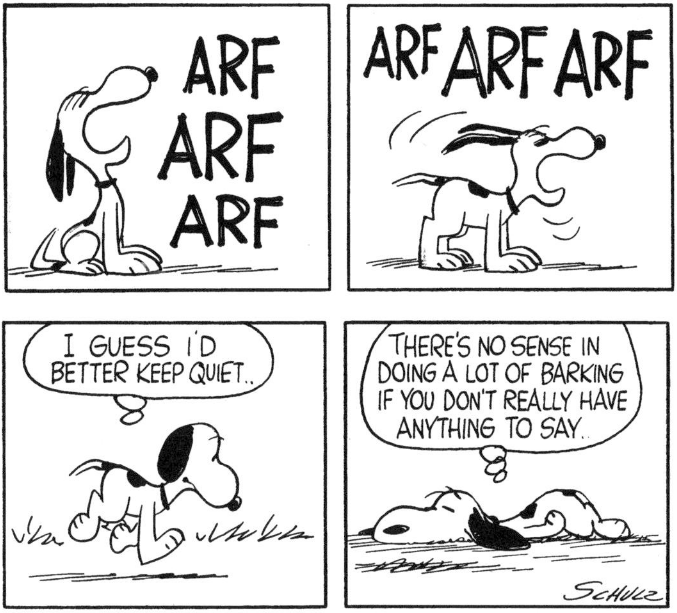
ARF ARF ARF
ARF ARF ARF
I GUESS I'D BETTER KEEP QUIET..
THERE'S NO SENSE IN DOING A LOT OF BARKING IF YOU DON'T REALLY HAVE ANYTHING TO SAY..
SCHULZ

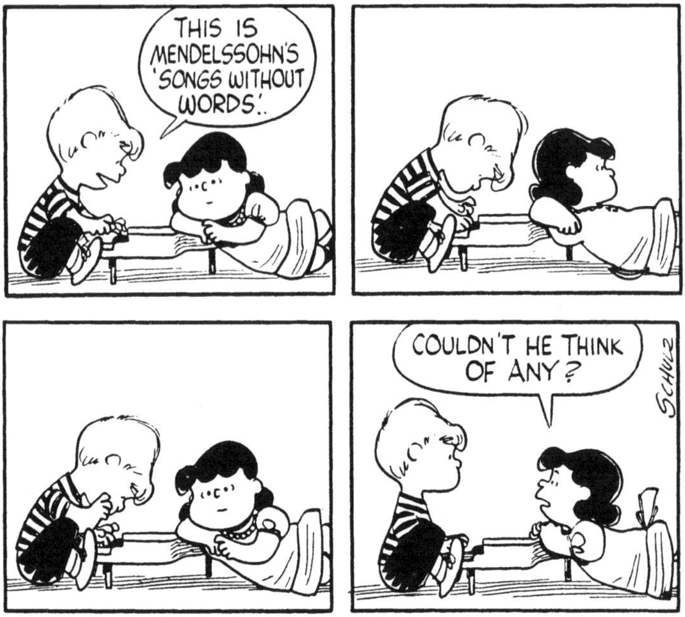
THIS IS MENDELSSOHN'S 'SONGS WITHOUT WORDS'.
COULDN'T HE THINK OF ANY?
SCHULZ

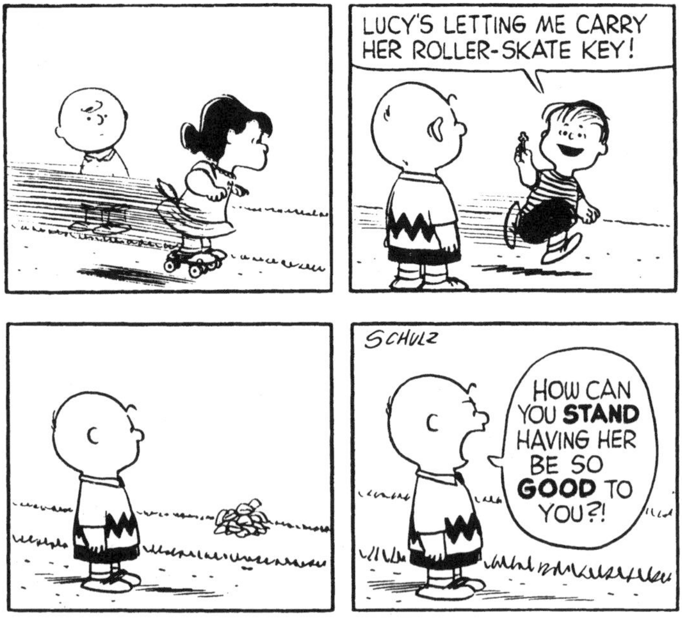
LUCY'S LETTING ME CARRY HER ROLLER-SKATE KEY!
SCHULZ
HOW CAN YOU **STAND** HAVING HER BE SO **GOOD** TO YOU?!

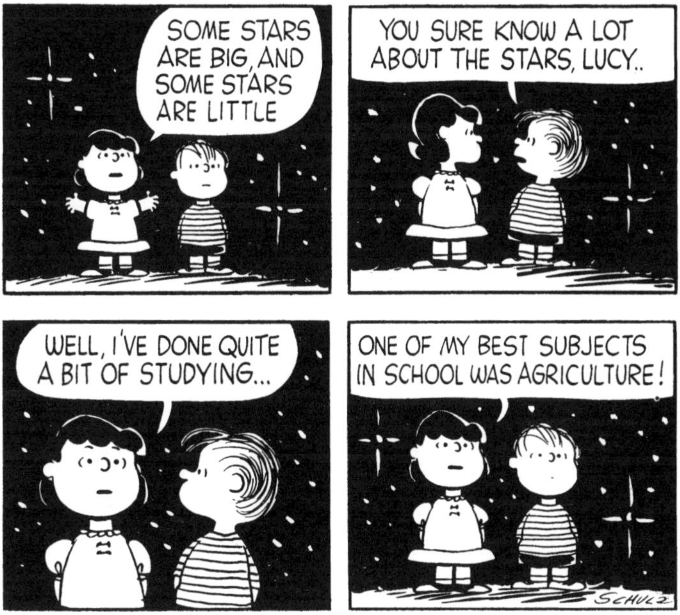
SOME STARS ARE BIG, AND SOME STARS ARE LITTLE
YOU SURE KNOW A LOT ABOUT THE STARS, LUCY..
WELL, I'VE DONE QUITE A BIT OF STUDYING...
ONE OF MY BEST SUBJECTS IN SCHOOL WAS AGRICULTURE!
SCHULZ

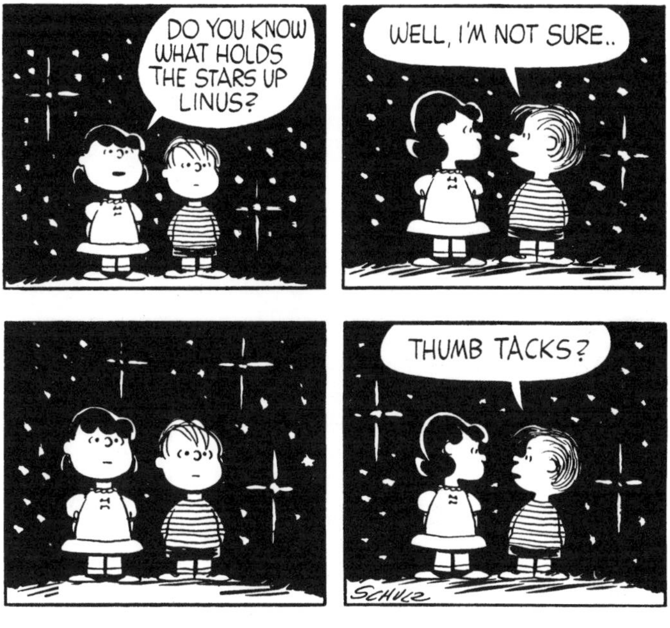
DO YOU KNOW WHAT HOLDS THE STARS UP LINUS?
WELL, I'M NOT SURE..
THUMB TACKS?
SCHULZ

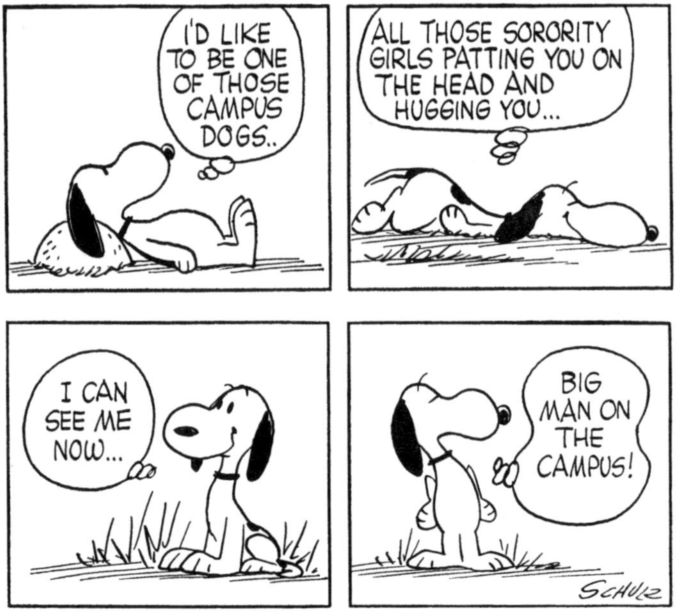
I'D LIKE TO BE ONE OF THOSE CAMPUS DOGS..
ALL THOSE SORORITY GIRLS PATTING YOU ON THE HEAD AND HUGGING YOU...
I CAN SEE ME NOW...
BIG MAN ON THE CAMPUS!
SCHULZ

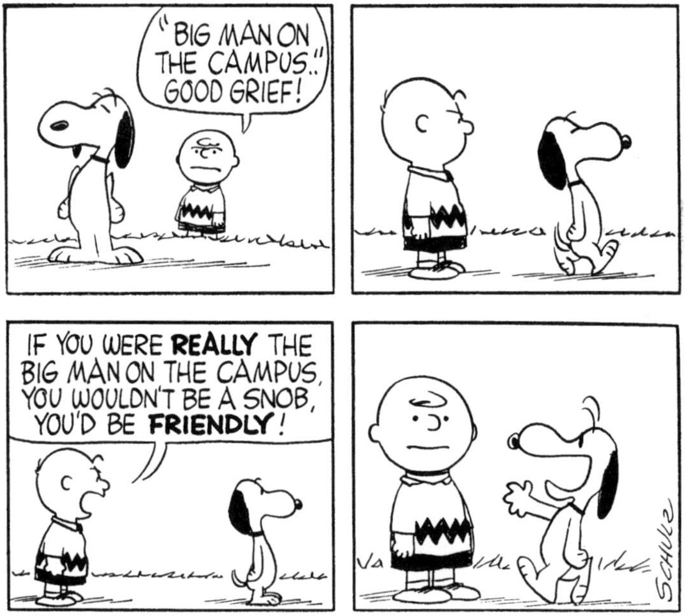
"BIG MAN ON THE CAMPUS.." GOOD GRIEF!
IF YOU WERE **REALLY** THE BIG MAN ON THE CAMPUS, YOU WOULDN'T BE A SNOB, YOU'D BE **FRIENDLY**!
SCHULZ

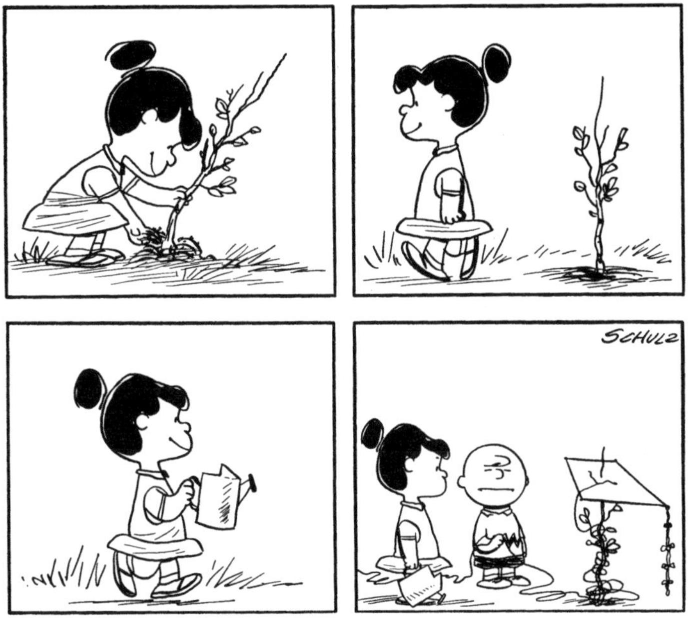
SCHULZ

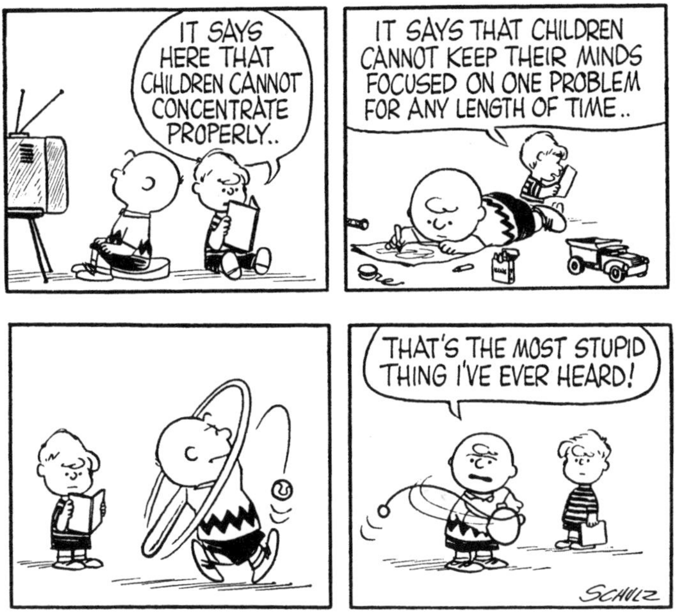
IT SAYS HERE THAT CHILDREN CANNOT CONCENTRATE PROPERLY..
IT SAYS THAT CHILDREN CANNOT KEEP THEIR MINDS FOCUSED ON ONE PROBLEM FOR ANY LENGTH OF TIME..
THAT'S THE MOST STUPID THING I'VE EVER HEARD!
SCHULZ

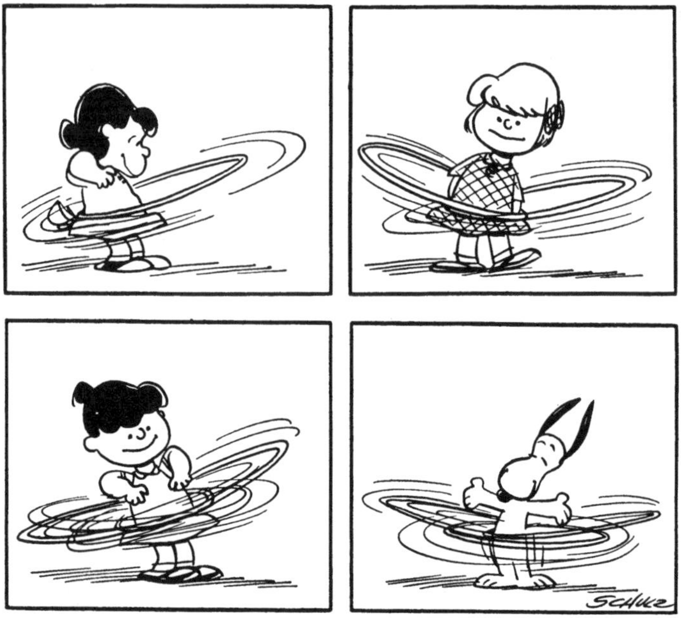

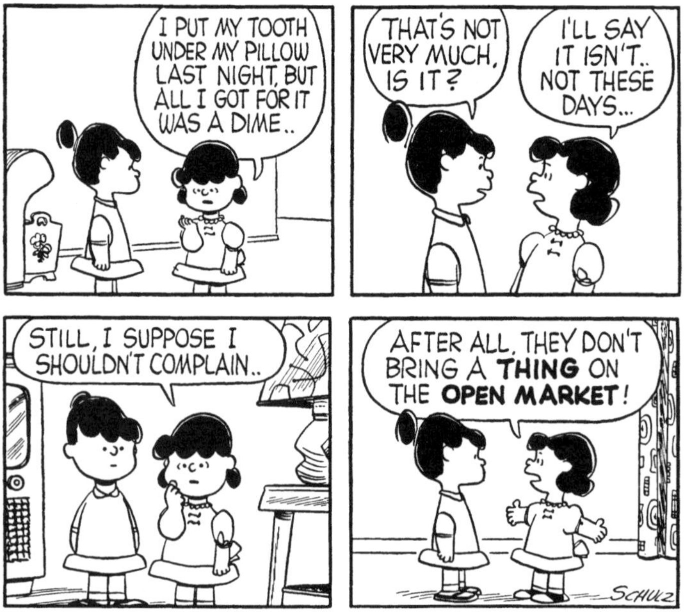
I PUT MY TOOTH UNDER MY PILLOW LAST NIGHT, BUT ALL I GOT FOR IT WAS A DIME..
THAT'S NOT VERY MUCH, IS IT?
I'LL SAY IT ISN'T.. NOT THESE DAYS...
STILL, I SUPPOSE I SHOULDN'T COMPLAIN..
AFTER ALL, THEY DON'T BRING A **THING** ON THE **OPEN MARKET**!
SCHULZ

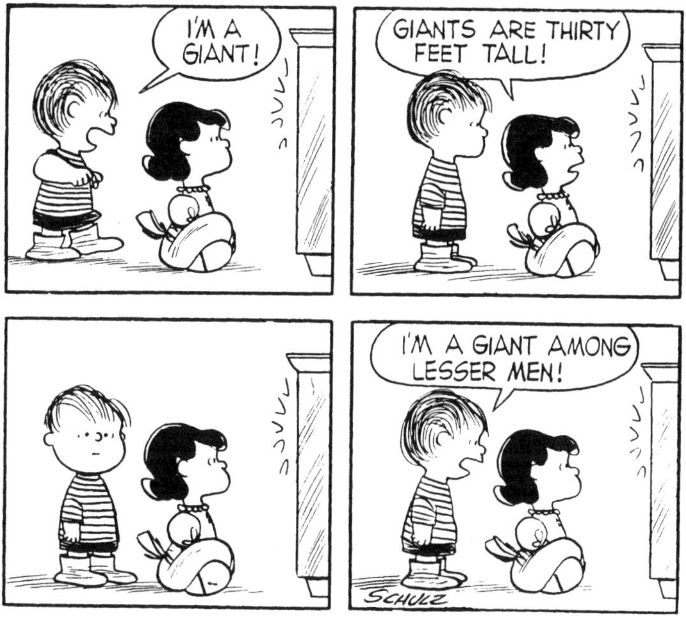
I'M A GIANT!
GIANTS ARE THIRTY FEET TALL!
I'M A GIANT AMONG LESSER MEN!
SCHULZ

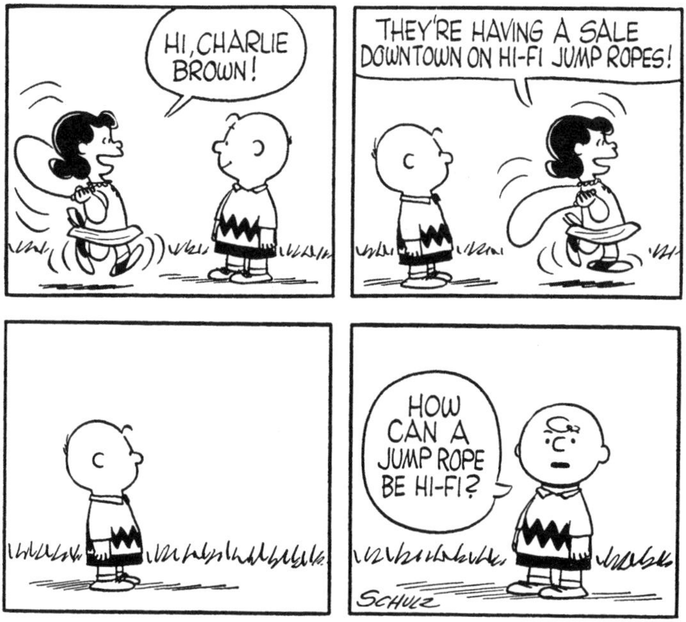
HI, CHARLIE BROWN!
THEY'RE HAVING A SALE DOWNTOWN ON HI-FI JUMP ROPES!
HOW CAN A JUMP ROPE BE HI-FI?
SCHULZ

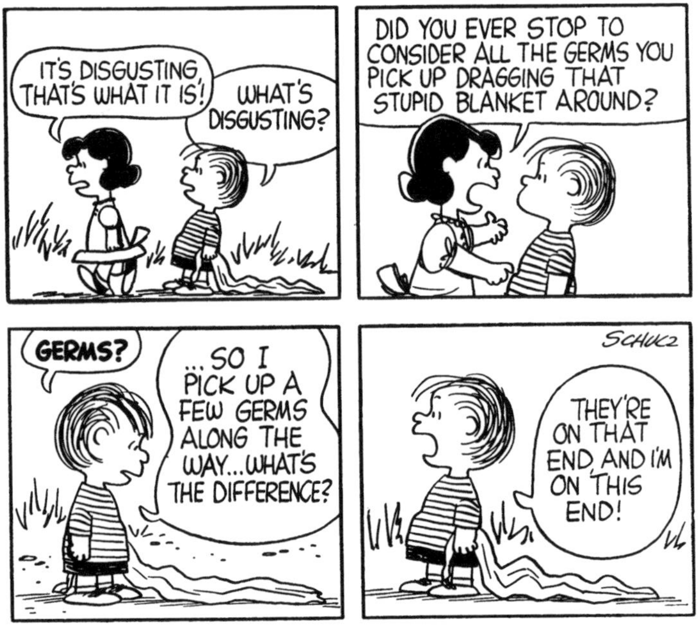
IT'S DISGUSTING, THAT'S WHAT IT IS!
WHAT'S DISGUSTING?
DID YOU EVER STOP TO CONSIDER ALL THE GERMS YOU PICK UP DRAGGING THAT STUPID BLANKET AROUND?
GERMS?
...SO I PICK UP A FEW GERMS ALONG THE WAY...WHAT'S THE DIFFERENCE?
SCHULZ
THEY'RE ON THAT END AND I'M ON THIS END!

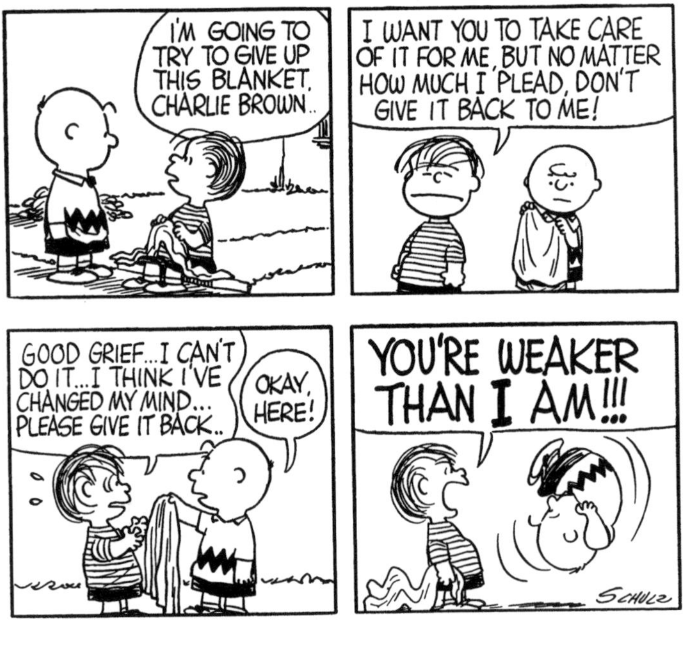
I'M GOING TO TRY TO GIVE UP THIS BLANKET, CHARLIE BROWN..
I WANT YOU TO TAKE CARE OF IT FOR ME, BUT NO MATTER HOW MUCH I PLEAD, DON'T GIVE IT BACK TO ME!
GOOD GRIEF...I CAN'T DO IT...I THINK I'VE CHANGED MY MIND... PLEASE GIVE IT BACK..
OKAY, HERE!
YOU'RE WEAKER THAN I AM!!!
SCHULZ

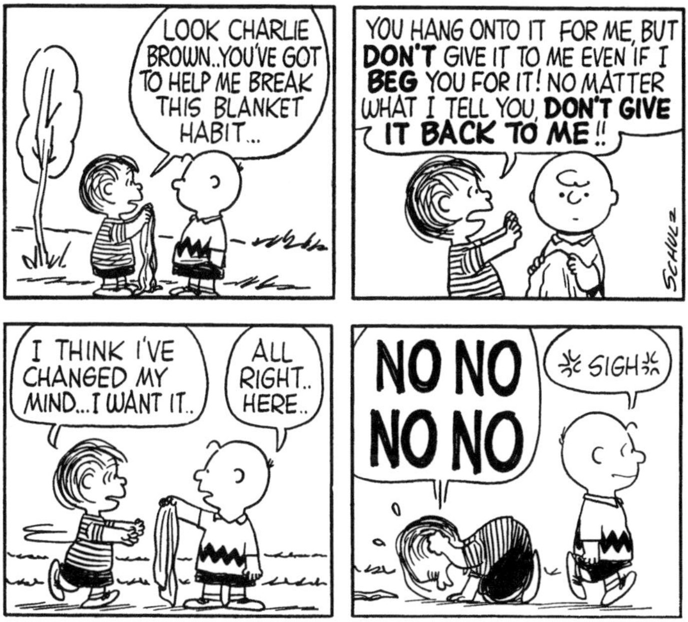
LOOK CHARLIE BROWN..YOU'VE GOT TO HELP ME BREAK THIS BLANKET HABIT...
YOU HANG ONTO IT FOR ME, BUT **DON'T** GIVE IT TO ME EVEN IF I **BEG** YOU FOR IT! NO MATTER WHAT I TELL YOU, **DON'T GIVE IT BACK TO ME**!!
SCHULZ
I THINK I'VE CHANGED MY MIND...I WANT IT..
ALL RIGHT.. HERE..
NO NO NO NO
SIGH

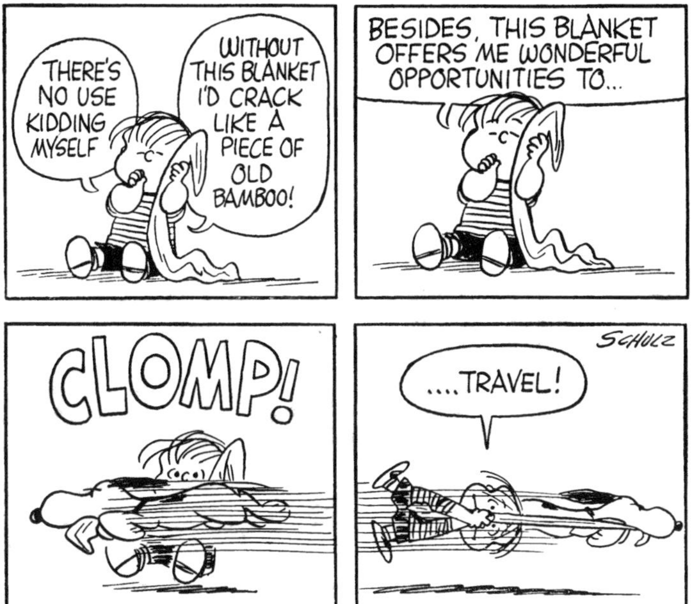
THERE'S NO USE KIDDING MYSELF
WITHOUT THIS BLANKET I'D CRACK LIKE A PIECE OF OLD BAMBOO!
BESIDES, THIS BLANKET OFFERS ME WONDERFUL OPPORTUNITIES TO...
CLOMP!
SCHULZ
....TRAVEL!

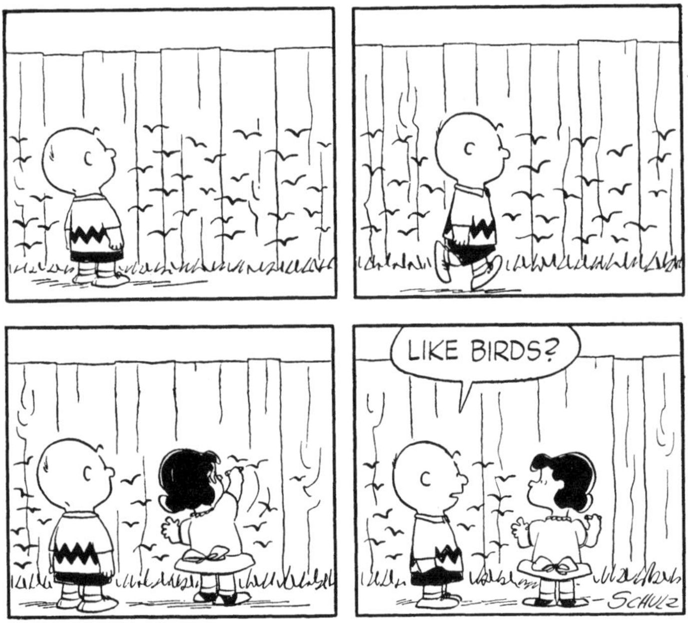
LIKE BIRDS?
SCHULZ

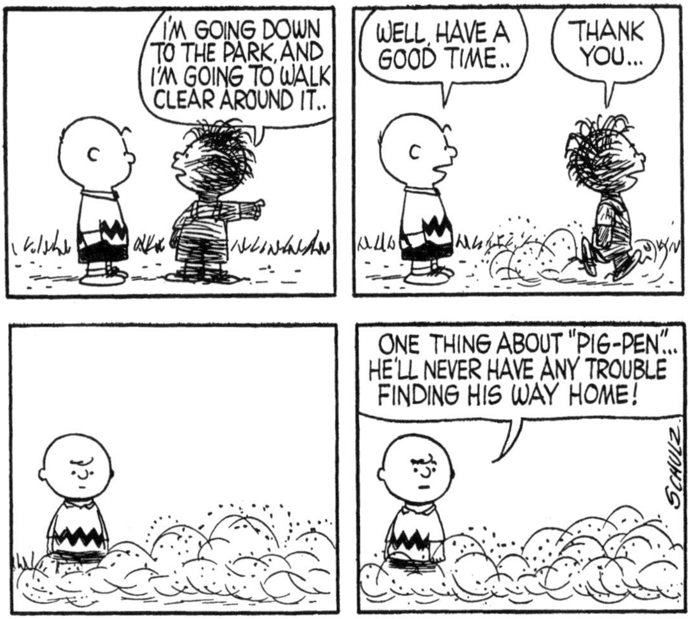
I'M GOING DOWN TO THE PARK, AND I'M GOING TO WALK CLEAR AROUND IT..
WELL, HAVE A GOOD TIME..
THANK YOU...
ONE THING ABOUT "PIG-PEN"... HE'LL NEVER HAVE ANY TROUBLE FINDING HIS WAY HOME!
SCHULZ

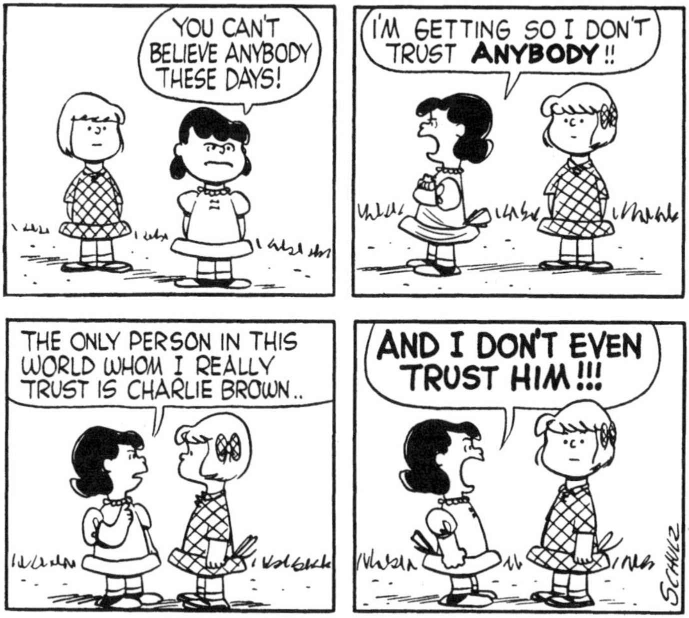
YOU CAN'T BELIEVE ANYBODY THESE DAYS!
I'M GETTING SO I DON'T TRUST **ANYBODY**!!
THE ONLY PERSON IN THIS WORLD WHOM I REALLY TRUST IS CHARLIE BROWN..
AND I DON'T EVEN TRUST HIM!!!
SCHULZ

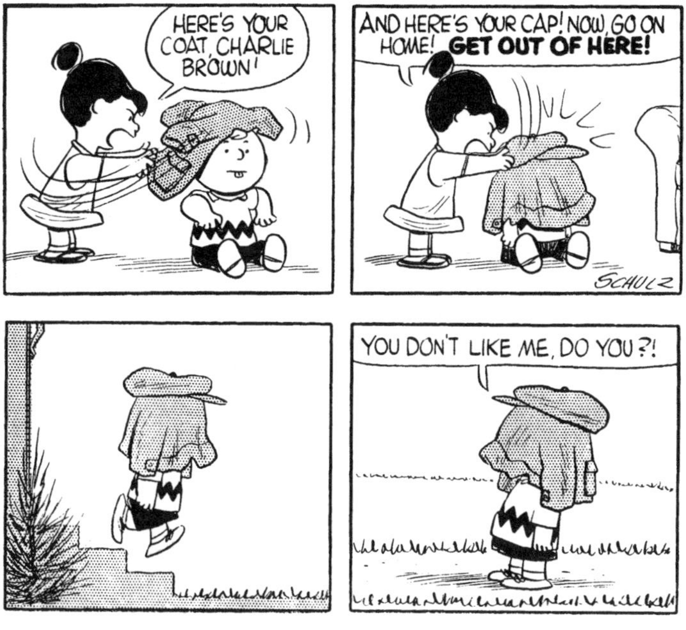
HERE'S YOUR COAT, CHARLIE BROWN!
AND HERE'S YOUR CAP! NOW, GO ON HOME! **GET OUT OF HERE!**
SCHULZ
YOU DON'T LIKE ME, DO YOU?!

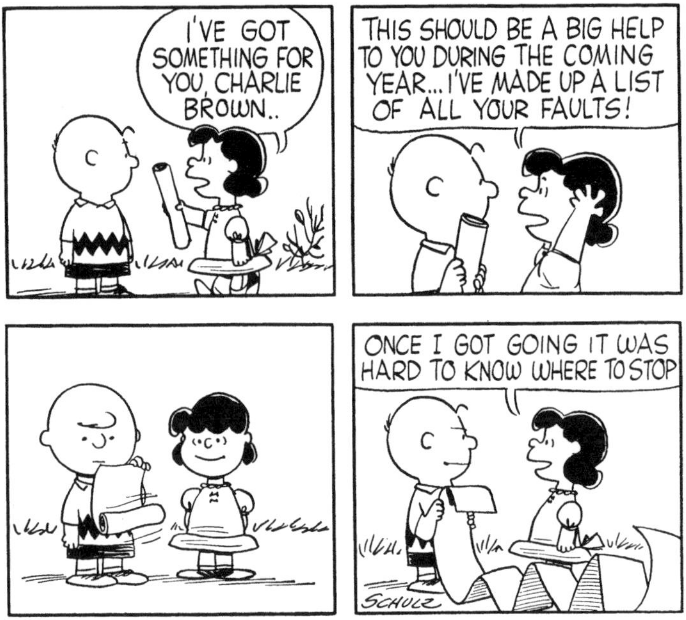
I'VE GOT SOMETHING FOR YOU, CHARLIE BROWN..
THIS SHOULD BE A BIG HELP TO YOU DURING THE COMING YEAR... I'VE MADE UP A LIST OF ALL YOUR FAULTS!
ONCE I GOT GOING IT WAS HARD TO KNOW WHERE TO STOP
SCHULZ

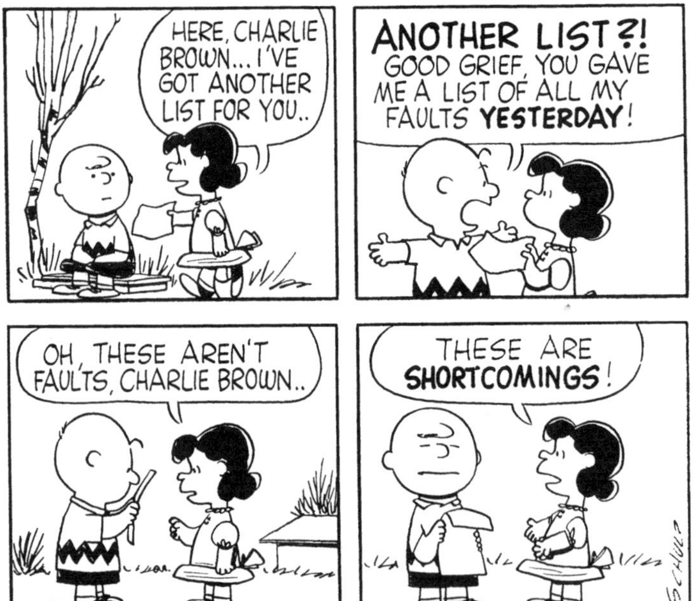
HERE, CHARLIE BROWN... I'VE GOT ANOTHER LIST FOR YOU..
ANOTHER LIST?! GOOD GRIEF, YOU GAVE ME A LIST OF ALL MY FAULTS YESTERDAY!
OH, THESE AREN'T FAULTS, CHARLIE BROWN..
THESE ARE SHORTCOMINGS!
SCHULZ

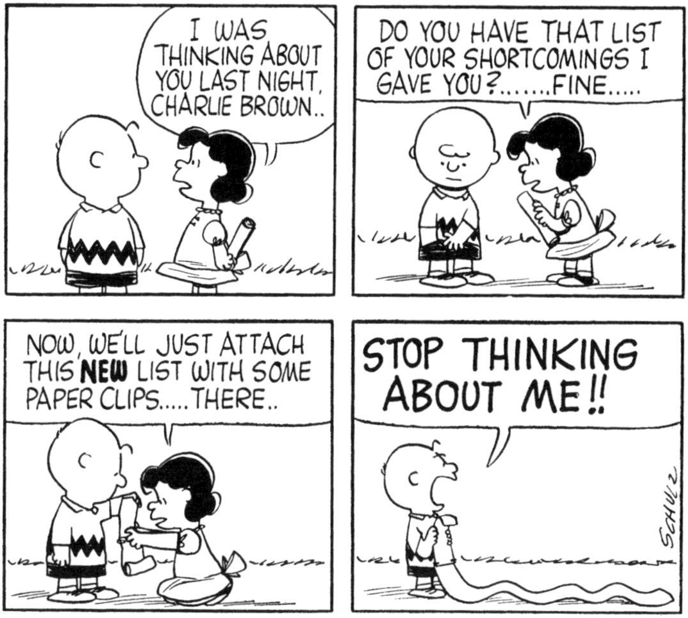
I WAS THINKING ABOUT YOU LAST NIGHT, CHARLIE BROWN..
DO YOU HAVE THAT LIST OF YOUR SHORTCOMINGS I GAVE YOU?.......FINE.....
NOW, WE'LL JUST ATTACH THIS **NEW** LIST WITH SOME PAPER CLIPS.....THERE..
STOP THINKING ABOUT ME!!
SCHULZ

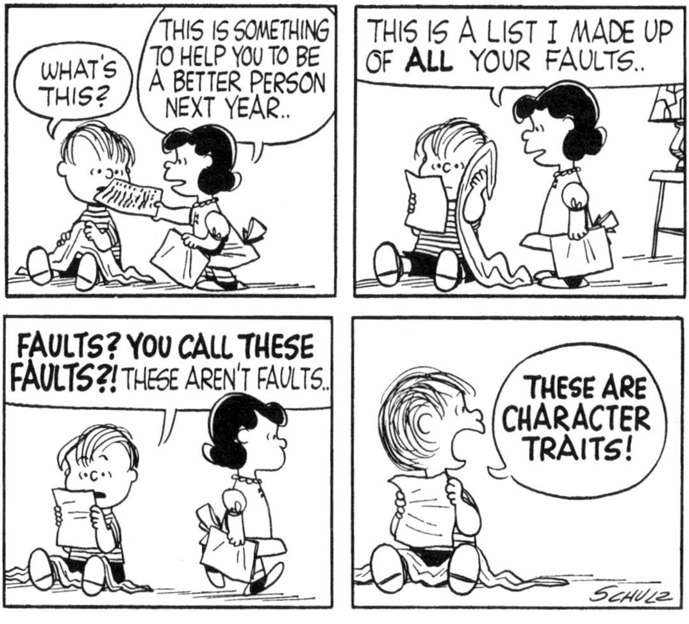
WHAT'S THIS?
THIS IS SOMETHING TO HELP YOU TO BE A BETTER PERSON NEXT YEAR..
THIS IS A LIST I MADE UP OF **ALL** YOUR FAULTS..
FAULTS? YOU CALL THESE FAULTS?! THESE AREN'T FAULTS..
THESE ARE CHARACTER TRAITS!
SCHULZ

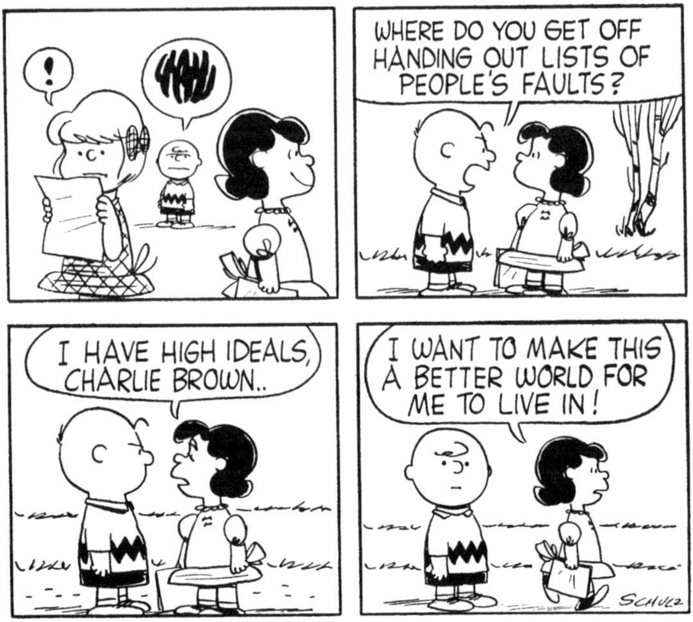
!
WHERE DO YOU GET OFF HANDING OUT LISTS OF PEOPLE'S FAULTS?
I HAVE HIGH IDEALS, CHARLIE BROWN..
I WANT TO MAKE THIS A BETTER WORLD FOR ME TO LIVE IN!
SCHULZ

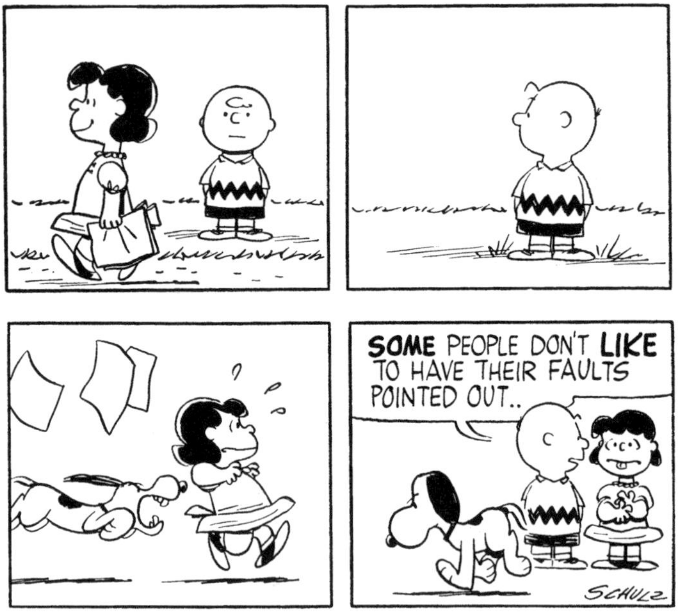
SOME PEOPLE DON'T LIKE TO HAVE THEIR FAULTS POINTED OUT..
SCHULZ

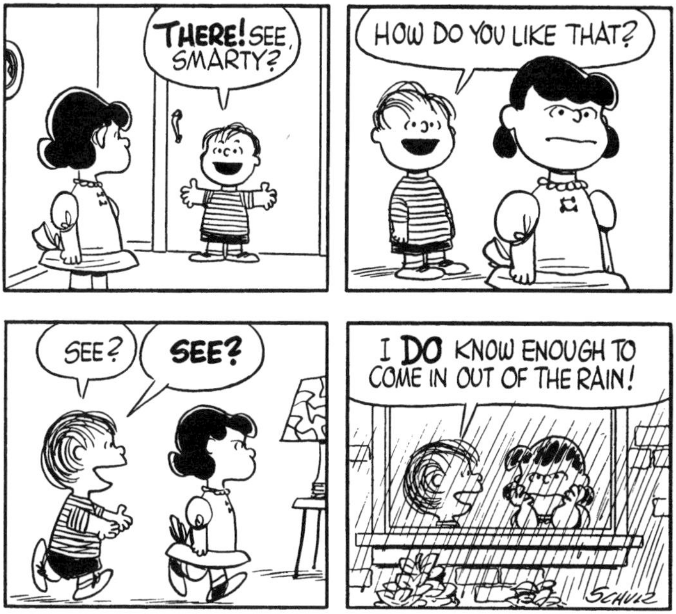
THERE! SEE, SMARTY?
HOW DO YOU LIKE THAT?
SEE?
SEE?
I DO KNOW ENOUGH TO COME IN OUT OF THE RAIN!
SCHULZ

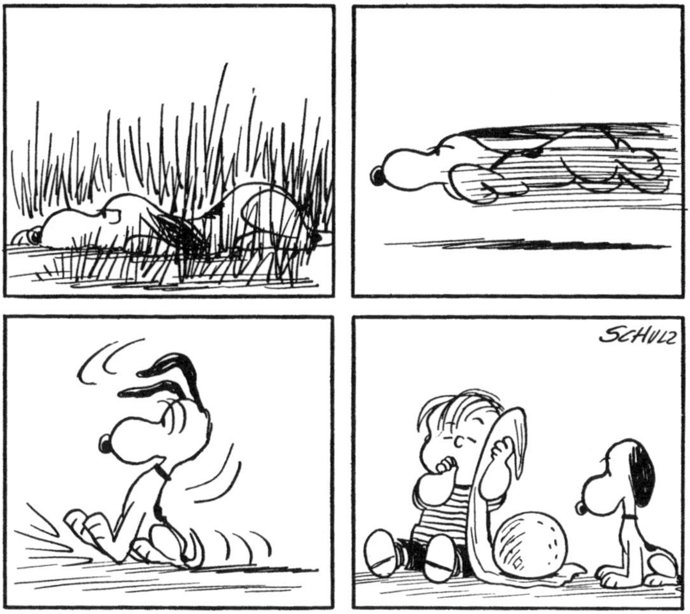
SCHULZ

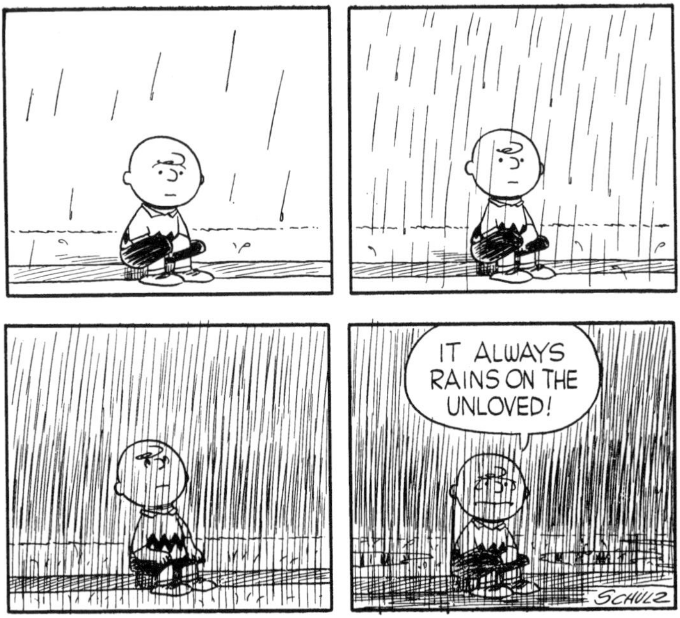
IT ALWAYS RAINS ON THE UNLOVED!
SCHULZ

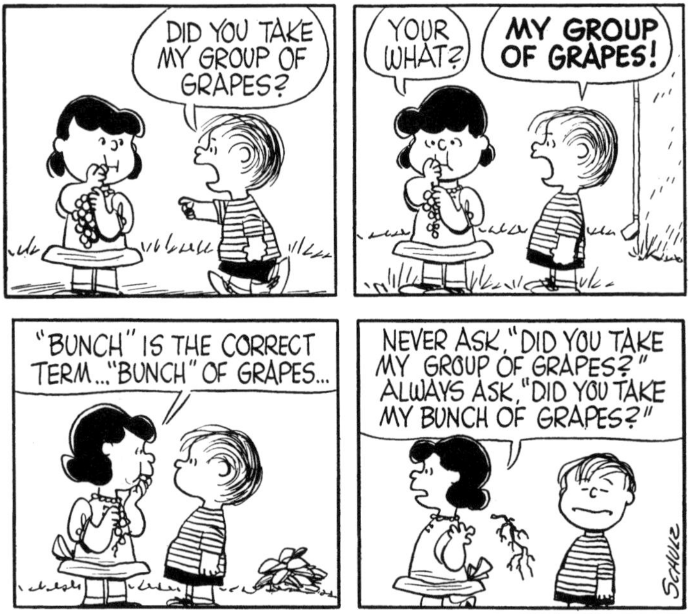
DID YOU TAKE MY GROUP OF GRAPES?
YOUR WHAT?
MY GROUP OF GRAPES!
"BUNCH" IS THE CORRECT TERM..."BUNCH" OF GRAPES...
NEVER ASK, "DID YOU TAKE MY GROUP OF GRAPES?" ALWAYS ASK, "DID YOU TAKE MY BUNCH OF GRAPES?"
SCHULZ

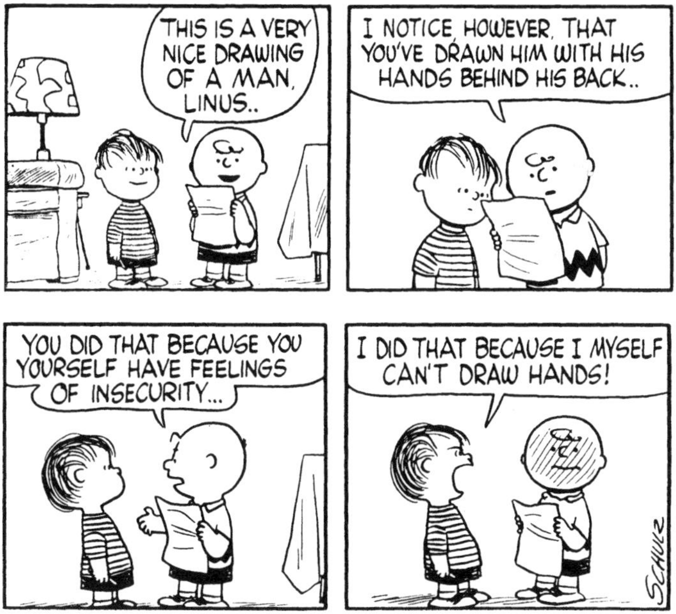
THIS IS A VERY NICE DRAWING OF A MAN, LINUS..
I NOTICE, HOWEVER, THAT YOU'VE DRAWN HIM WITH HIS HANDS BEHIND HIS BACK..
YOU DID THAT BECAUSE YOU YOURSELF HAVE FEELINGS OF INSECURITY...
I DID THAT BECAUSE I MYSELF CAN'T DRAW HANDS!
SCHULZ

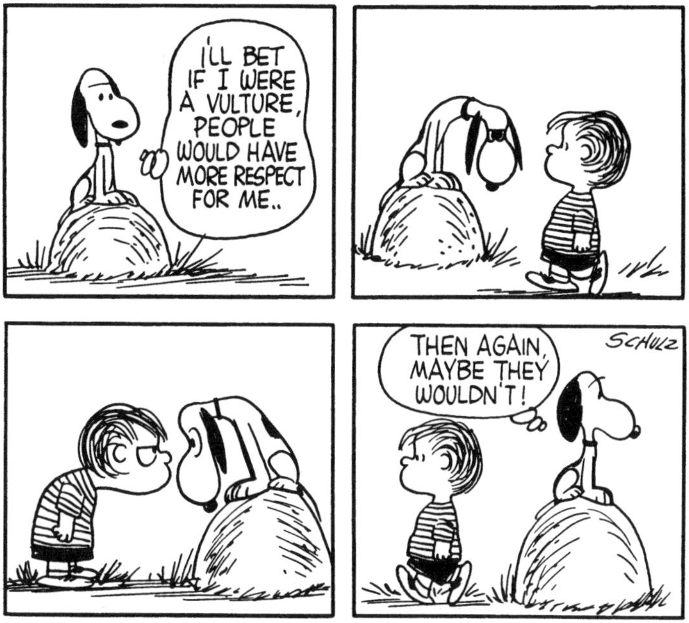
I'LL BET IF I WERE A VULTURE, PEOPLE WOULD HAVE MORE RESPECT FOR ME..
THEN AGAIN, MAYBE THEY WOULDN'T!
SCHULZ

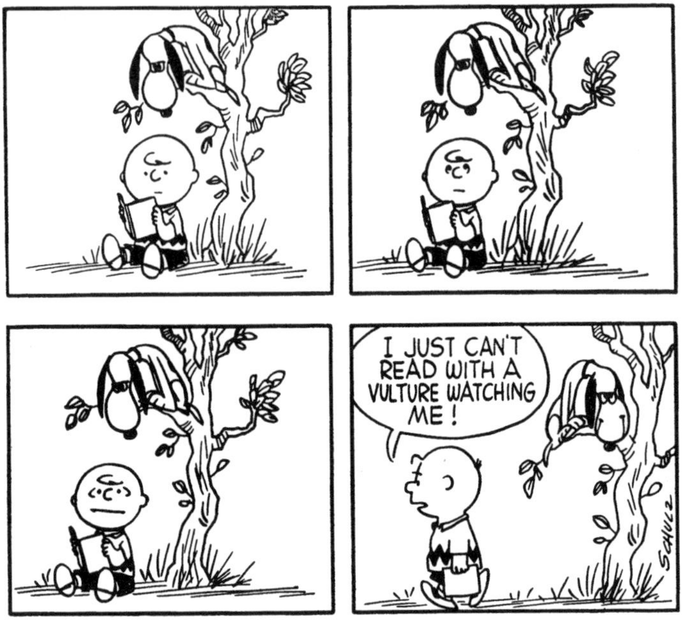
I JUST CAN'T READ WITH A VULTURE WATCHING ME !
SCHULZ

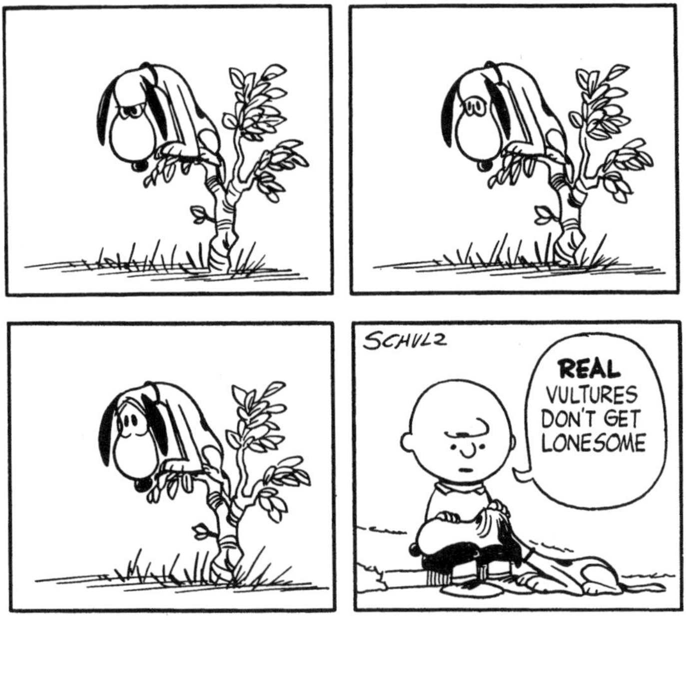
SCHULZ
REAL VULTURES DON'T GET LONESOME

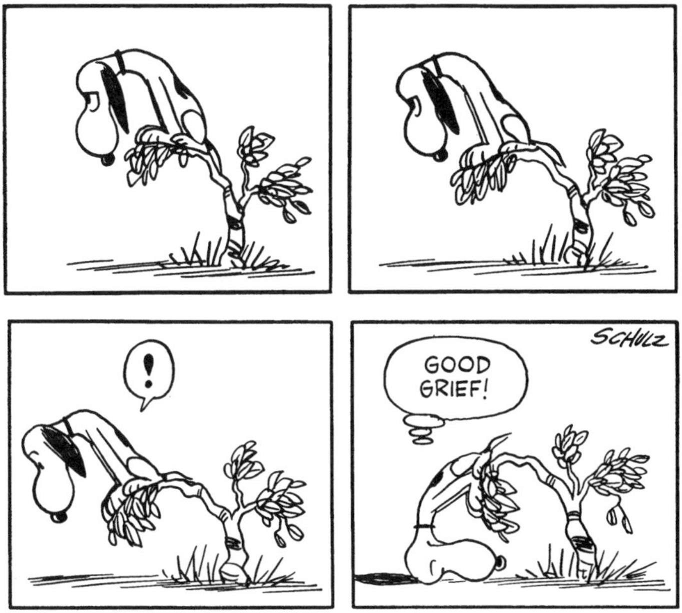
SCHULZ
!
GOOD GRIEF!

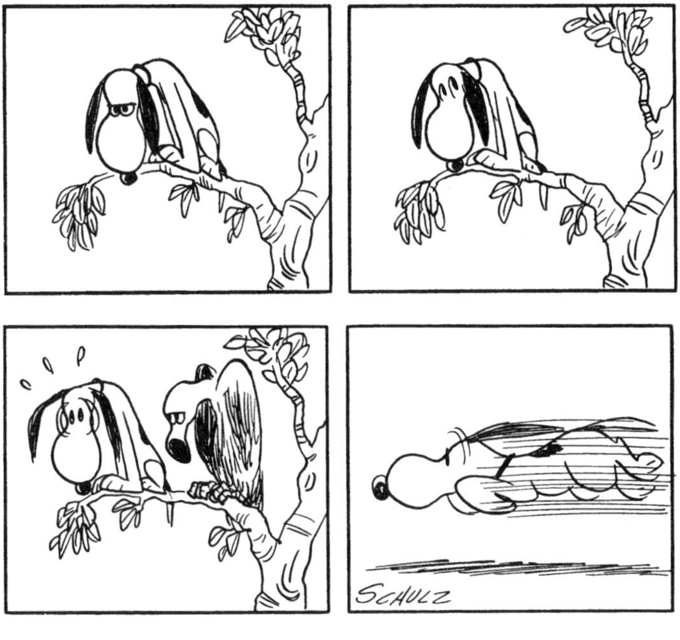
SCHULZ

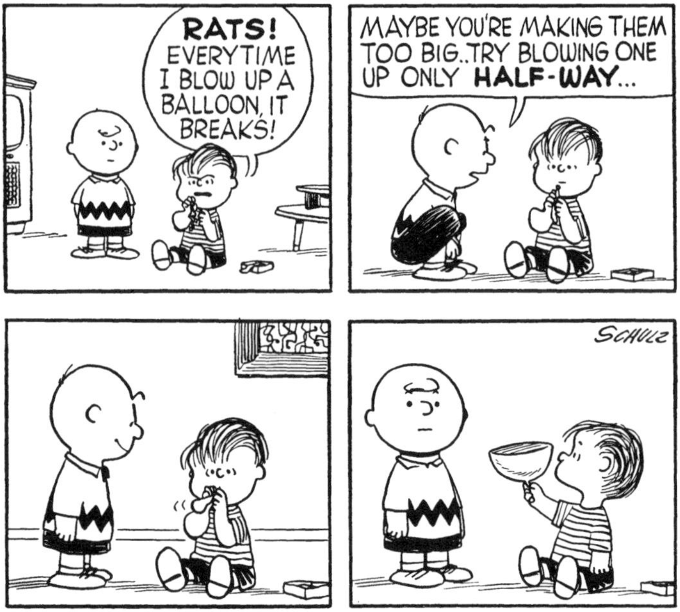
RATS! EVERYTIME I BLOW UP A BALLOON, IT BREAKS!
MAYBE YOU'RE MAKING THEM TOO BIG..TRY BLOWING ONE UP ONLY HALF-WAY...
SCHULZ

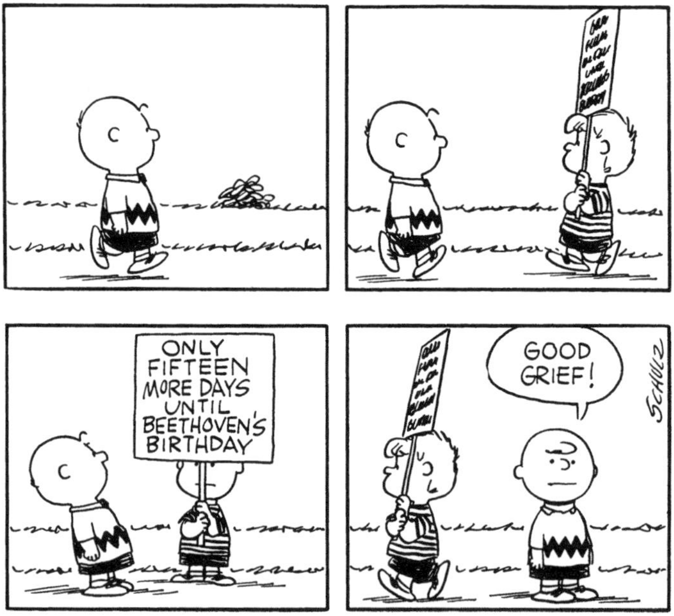
ONLY FIFTEEN MORE DAYS UNTIL BEETHOVEN'S BIRTHDAY
GOOD GRIEF!
SCHULZ

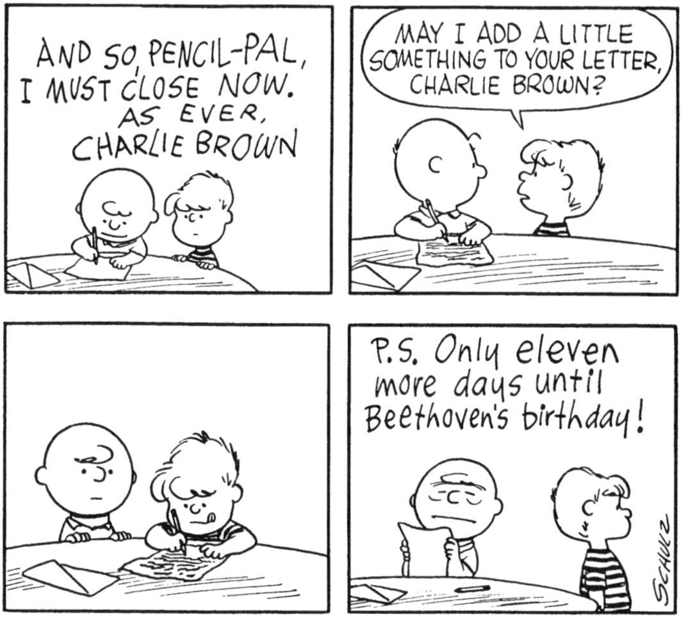
AND SO, PENCIL-PAL, I MUST CLOSE NOW. AS EVER, CHARLIE BROWN
MAY I ADD A LITTLE SOMETHING TO YOUR LETTER, CHARLIE BROWN?
P.S. Only eleven more days until Beethoven's birthday!
SCHULZ

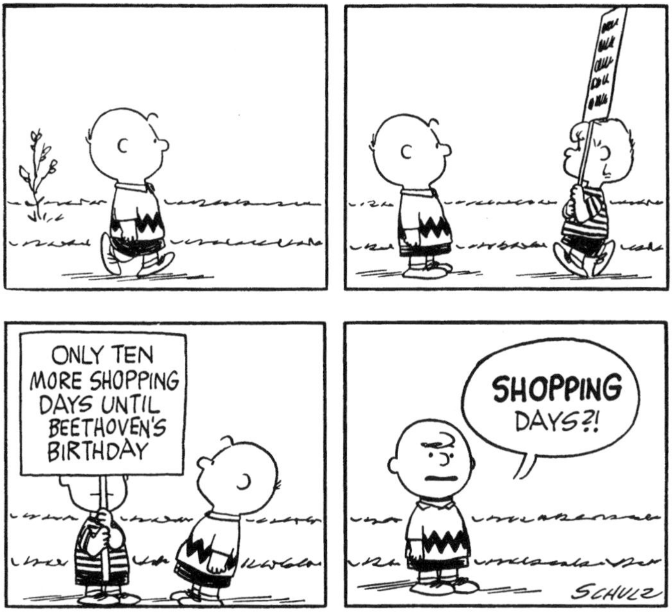
ONLY TEN MORE SHOPPING DAYS UNTIL BEETHOVEN'S BIRTHDAY
SHOPPING DAYS?!
SCHULZ

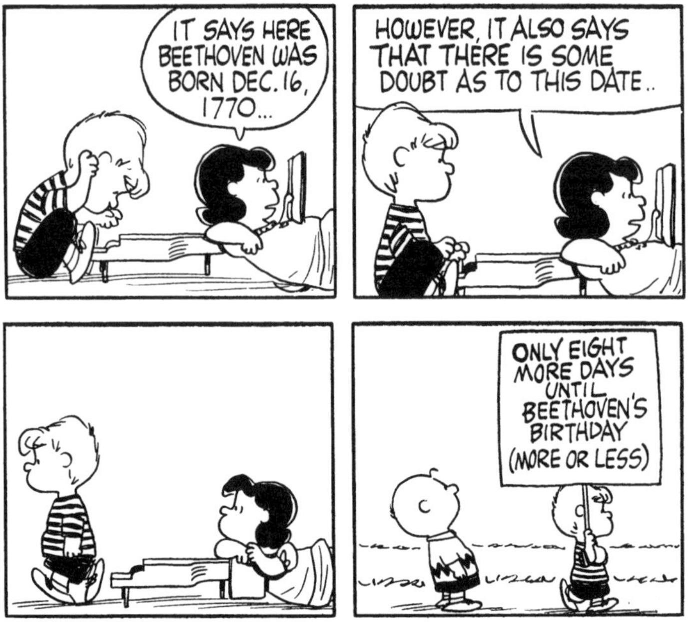
IT SAYS HERE BEETHOVEN WAS BORN DEC. 16, 1770...
HOWEVER, IT ALSO SAYS THAT THERE IS SOME DOUBT AS TO THIS DATE..
ONLY EIGHT MORE DAYS UNTIL BEETHOVEN'S BIRTHDAY (MORE OR LESS)

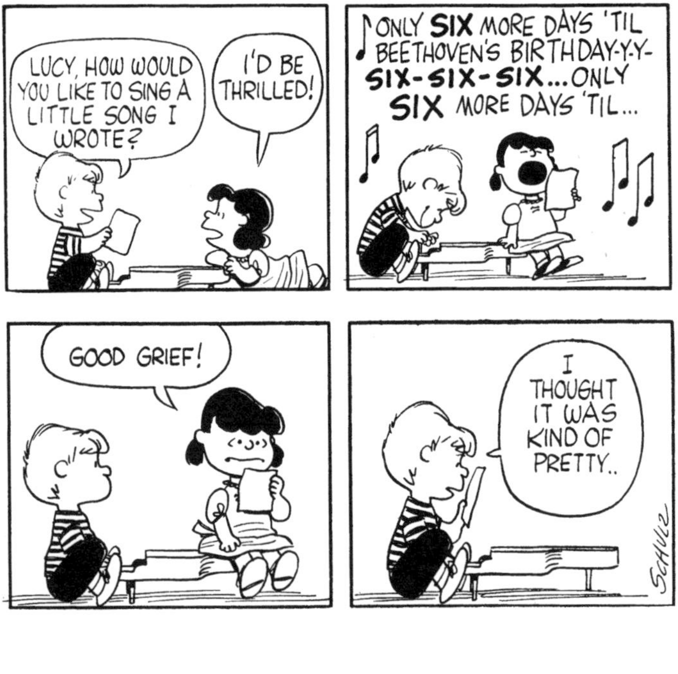
LUCY, HOW WOULD YOU LIKE TO SING A LITTLE SONG I WROTE?
I'D BE THRILLED!
ONLY SIX MORE DAYS 'TIL BEETHOVEN'S BIRTHDAY-Y-Y-SIX-SIX-SIX...ONLY SIX MORE DAYS 'TIL...
GOOD GRIEF!
I THOUGHT IT WAS KIND OF PRETTY..
SCHULZ

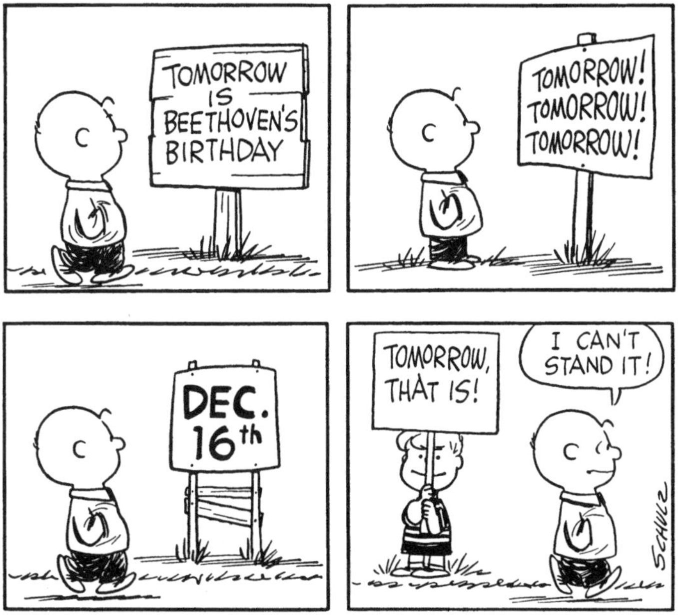
TOMORROW IS BEETHOVEN'S BIRTHDAY
TOMORROW! TOMORROW! TOMORROW!
DEC. 16th
TOMORROW, THAT IS!
I CAN'T STAND IT!
SCHULZ

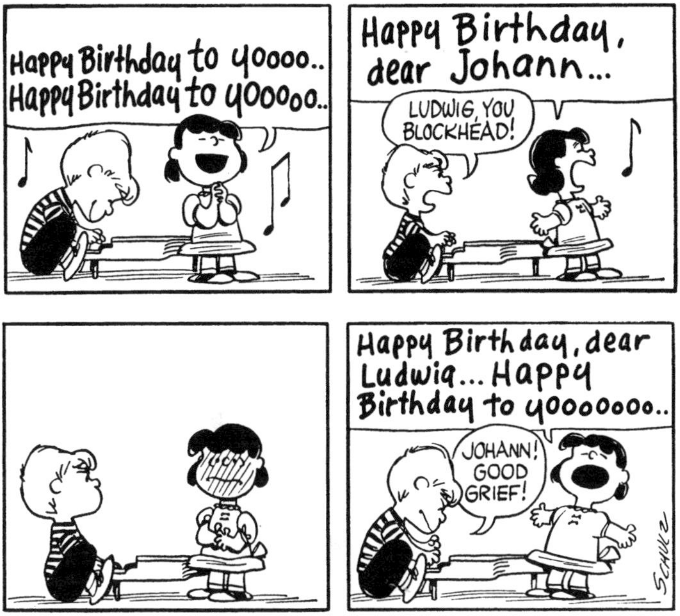
Happy Birthday to yoooo.. Happy Birthday to yoooo..
Happy Birthday, dear Johann...
LUDWIG, YOU BLOCKHEAD!
Happy Birthday, dear Ludwig... Happy Birthday to yooooooo..
JOHANN! GOOD GRIEF!
SCHULZ

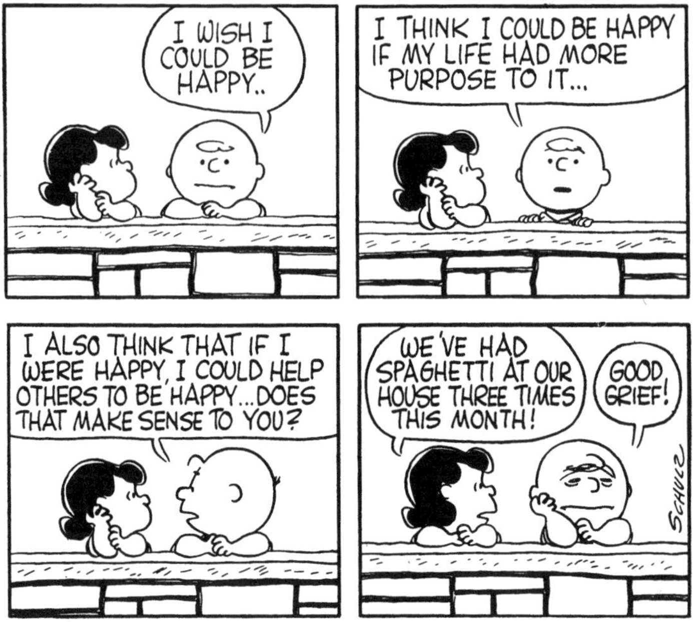
I WISH I COULD BE HAPPY..
I THINK I COULD BE HAPPY IF MY LIFE HAD MORE PURPOSE TO IT...
I ALSO THINK THAT IF I WERE HAPPY, I COULD HELP OTHERS TO BE HAPPY...DOES THAT MAKE SENSE TO YOU?
WE'VE HAD SPAGHETTI AT OUR HOUSE THREE TIMES THIS MONTH!
GOOD GRIEF!
SCHULZ

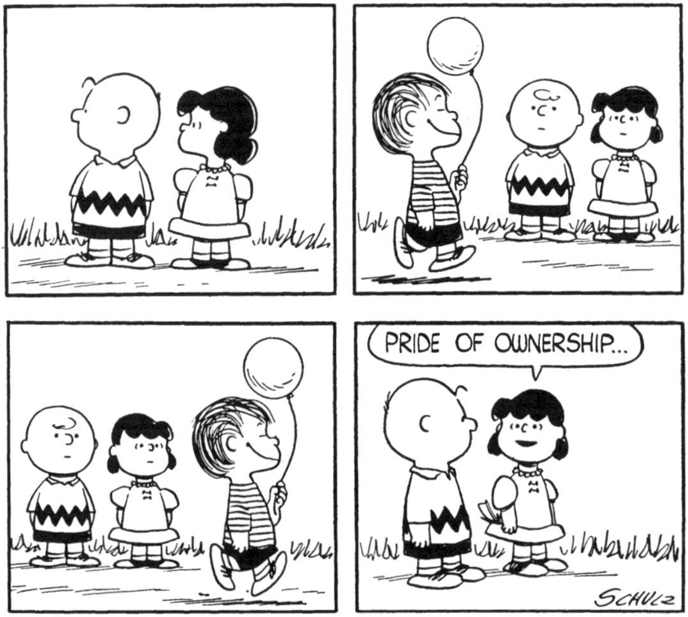
PRIDE OF OWNERSHIP...
SCHULZ

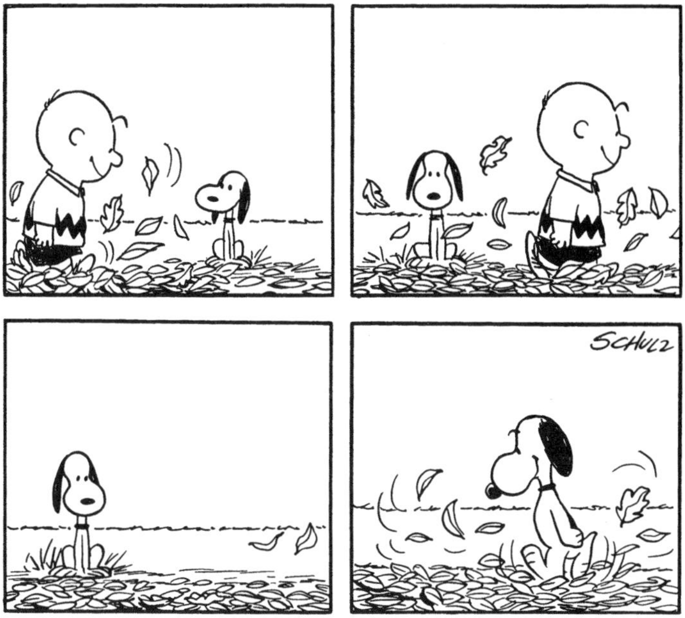
SCHULZ

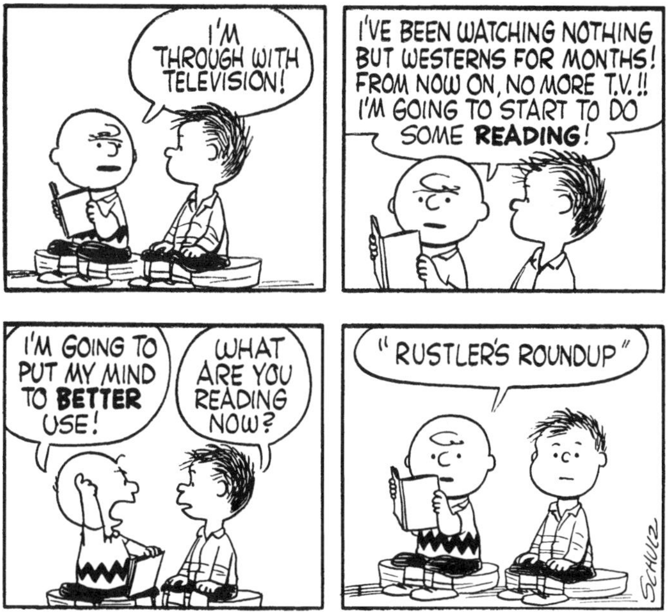
I'M THROUGH WITH TELEVISION!
I'VE BEEN WATCHING NOTHING BUT WESTERNS FOR MONTHS! FROM NOW ON, NO MORE T.V.!! I'M GOING TO START TO DO SOME **READING**!
I'M GOING TO PUT MY MIND TO **BETTER** USE!
WHAT ARE YOU READING NOW?
"RUSTLER'S ROUNDUP"
SCHULZ

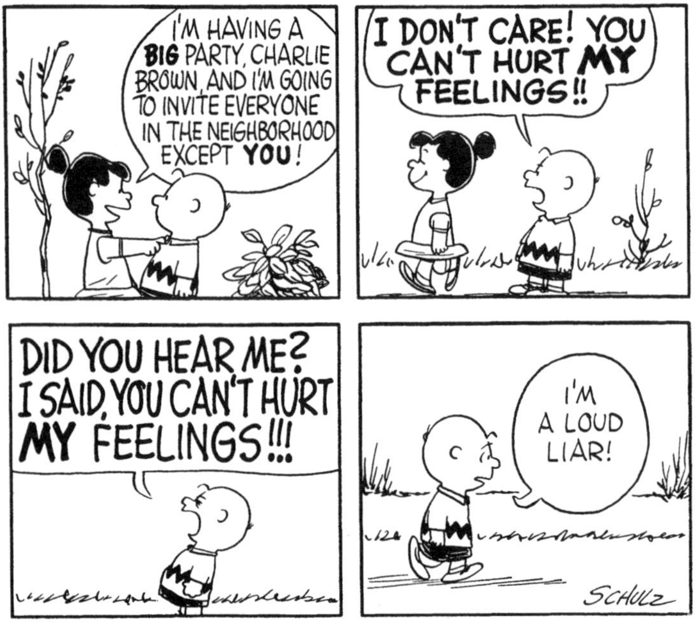
I'M HAVING A BIG PARTY, CHARLIE BROWN, AND I'M GOING TO INVITE EVERYONE IN THE NEIGHBORHOOD EXCEPT YOU!
I DON'T CARE! YOU CAN'T HURT MY FEELINGS!!
DID YOU HEAR ME? I SAID, YOU CAN'T HURT MY FEELINGS!!!
I'M A LOUD LIAR!
SCHULZ

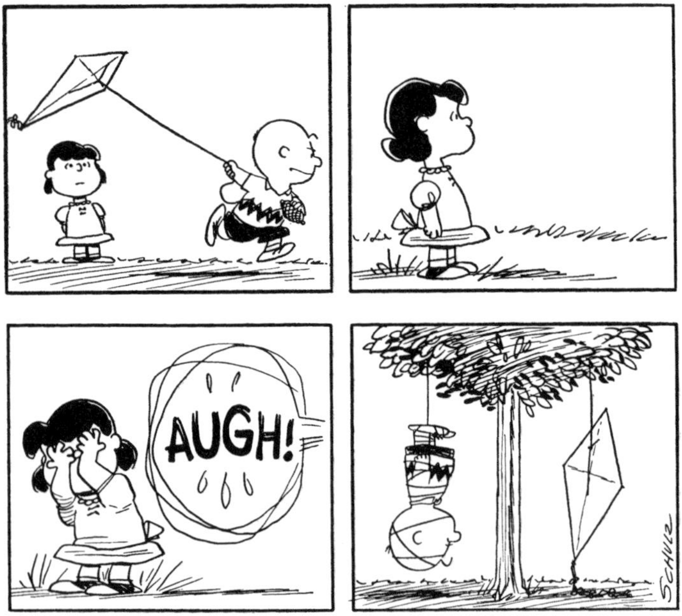
AUGH!
SCHULZ

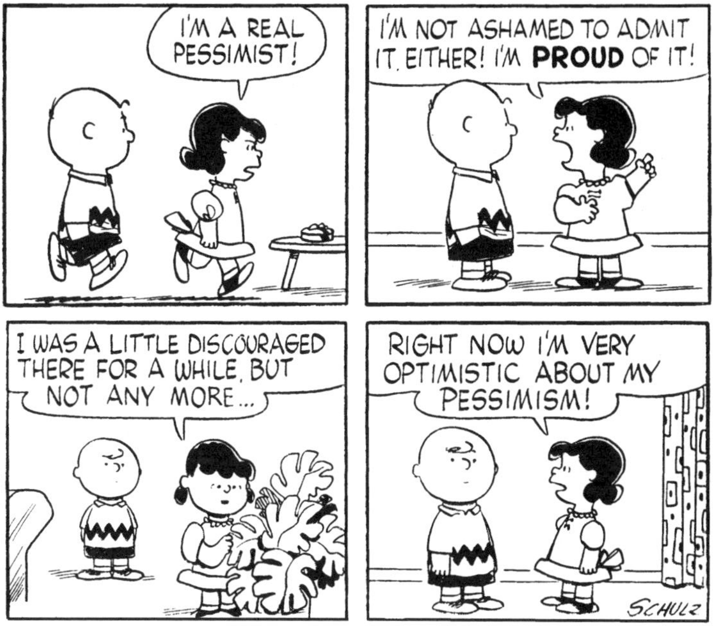
I'M A REAL PESSIMIST!
I'M NOT ASHAMED TO ADMIT IT, EITHER! I'M **PROUD** OF IT!
I WAS A LITTLE DISCOURAGED THERE FOR A WHILE, BUT NOT ANY MORE...
RIGHT NOW I'M VERY OPTIMISTIC ABOUT MY PESSIMISM!
SCHULZ

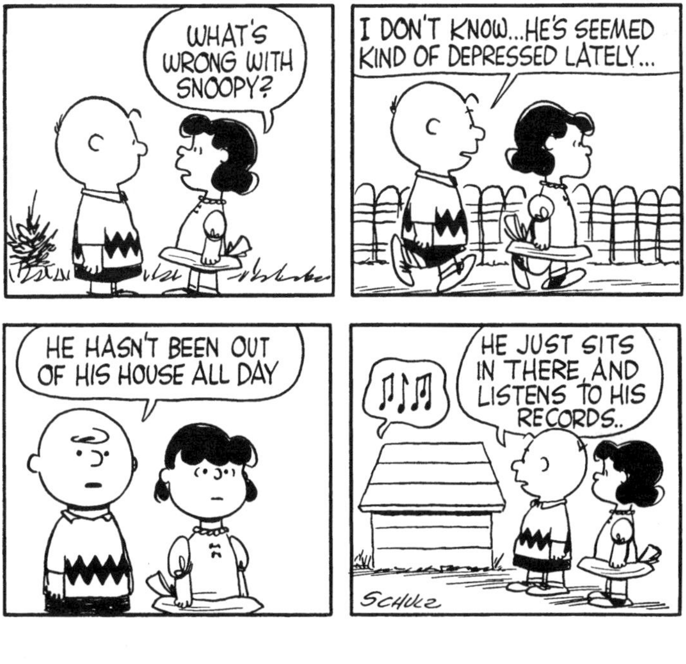
WHAT'S WRONG WITH SNOOPY?
I DON'T KNOW...HE'S SEEMED KIND OF DEPRESSED LATELY...
HE HASN'T BEEN OUT OF HIS HOUSE ALL DAY
HE JUST SITS IN THERE, AND LISTENS TO HIS RECORDS..
SCHULZ

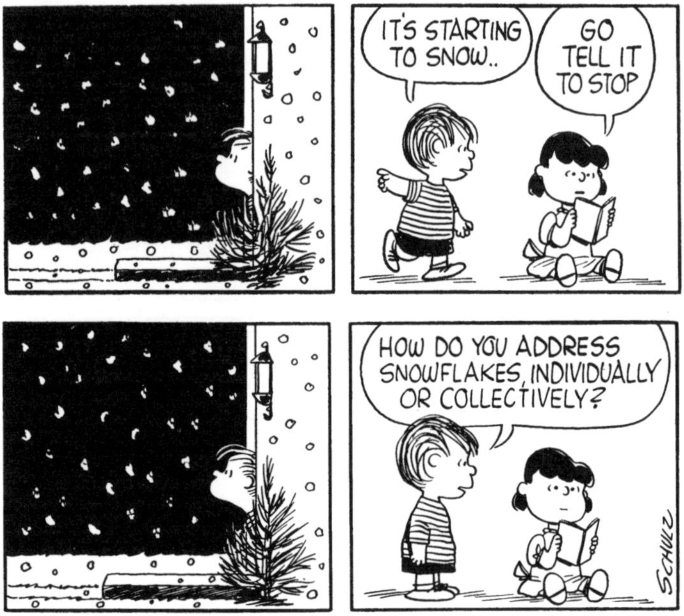
IT'S STARTING TO SNOW..
GO TELL IT TO STOP
HOW DO YOU ADDRESS SNOWFLAKES, INDIVIDUALLY OR COLLECTIVELY?
SCHULZ

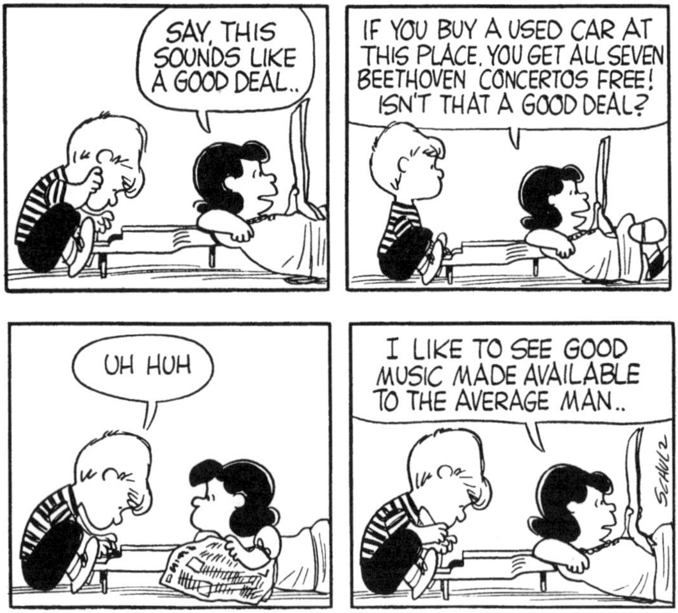
SAY, THIS SOUNDS LIKE A GOOD DEAL..
IF YOU BUY A USED CAR AT THIS PLACE, YOU GET ALL SEVEN BEETHOVEN CONCERTOS FREE! ISN'T THAT A GOOD DEAL?
UH HUH
I LIKE TO SEE GOOD MUSIC MADE AVAILABLE TO THE AVERAGE MAN..
SCHULZ

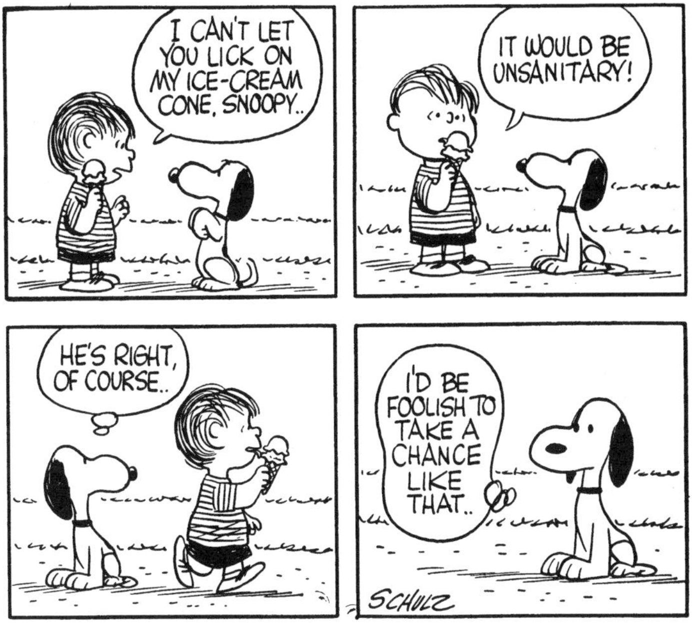
I CAN'T LET YOU LICK ON MY ICE-CREAM CONE, SNOOPY..
IT WOULD BE UNSANITARY!
HE'S RIGHT, OF COURSE..
I'D BE FOOLISH TO TAKE A CHANCE LIKE THAT..
SCHULZ

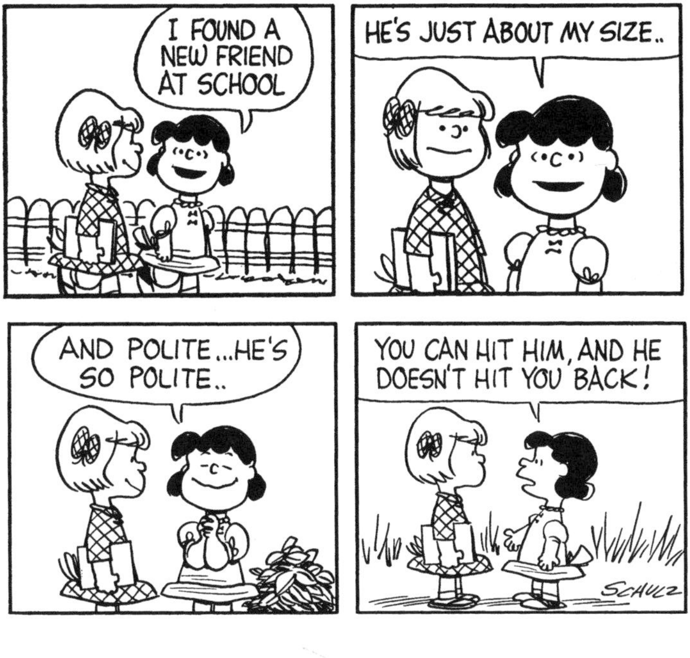
I FOUND A NEW FRIEND AT SCHOOL
HE'S JUST ABOUT MY SIZE..
AND POLITE...HE'S SO POLITE..
YOU CAN HIT HIM, AND HE DOESN'T HIT YOU BACK!
SCHULZ

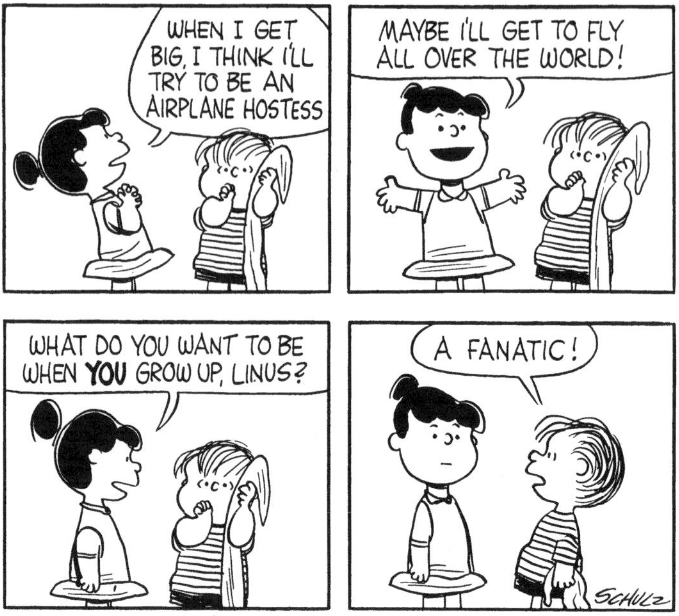
WHEN I GET BIG, I THINK I'LL TRY TO BE AN AIRPLANE HOSTESS
MAYBE I'LL GET TO FLY ALL OVER THE WORLD!
WHAT DO YOU WANT TO BE WHEN **YOU** GROW UP, LINUS?
A FANATIC!
SCHULZ

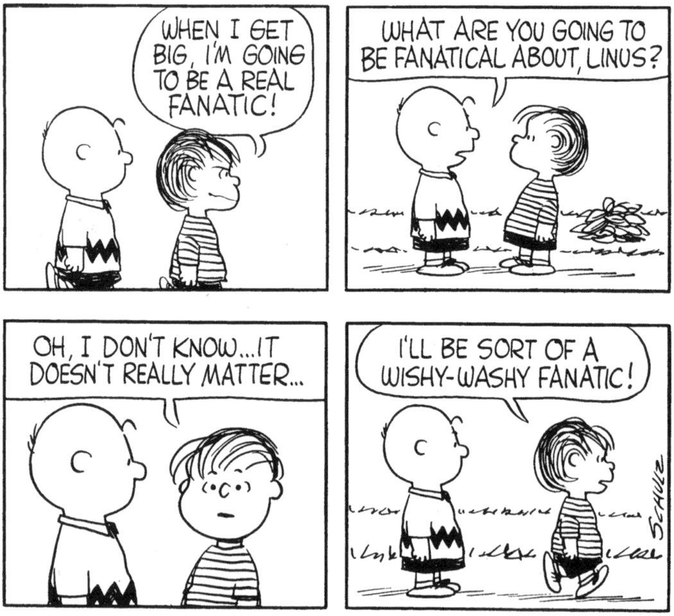
WHEN I GET BIG, I'M GOING TO BE A REAL FANATIC!
WHAT ARE YOU GOING TO BE FANATICAL ABOUT, LINUS?
OH, I DON'T KNOW...IT DOESN'T REALLY MATTER...
I'LL BE SORT OF A WISHY-WASHY FANATIC!
SCHULZ

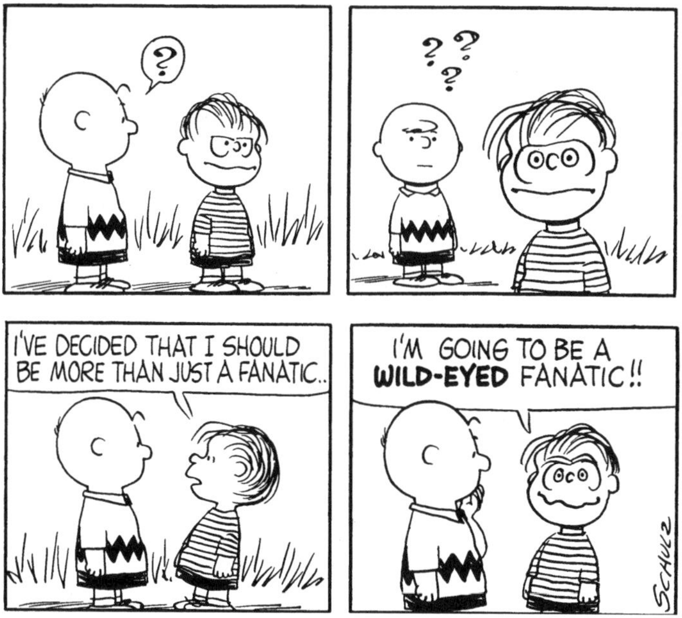
?
? ? ?
I'VE DECIDED THAT I SHOULD BE MORE THAN JUST A FANATIC..
I'M GOING TO BE A WILD-EYED FANATIC!!
SCHULZ

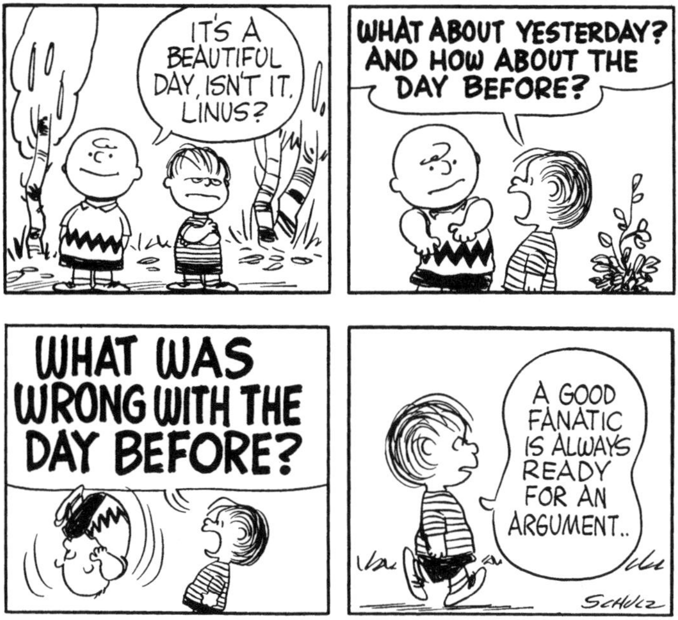
IT'S A BEAUTIFUL DAY, ISN'T IT, LINUS?
WHAT ABOUT YESTERDAY? AND HOW ABOUT THE DAY BEFORE?
WHAT WAS WRONG WITH THE DAY BEFORE?
A GOOD FANATIC IS ALWAYS READY FOR AN ARGUMENT..
SCHULZ

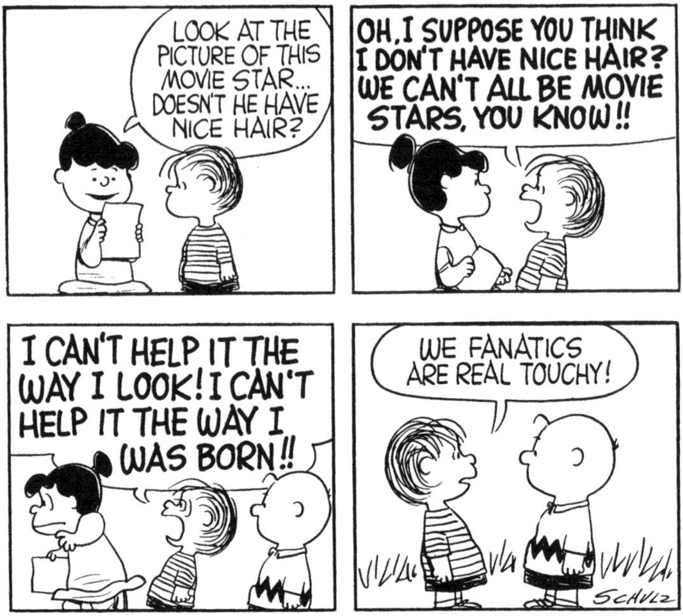
LOOK AT THE PICTURE OF THIS MOVIE STAR... DOESN'T HE HAVE NICE HAIR?
OH, I SUPPOSE YOU THINK I DON'T HAVE NICE HAIR? WE CAN'T ALL BE MOVIE STARS, YOU KNOW!!
I CAN'T HELP IT THE WAY I LOOK! I CAN'T HELP IT THE WAY I WAS BORN!!
WE FANATICS ARE REAL TOUCHY!
SCHULZ

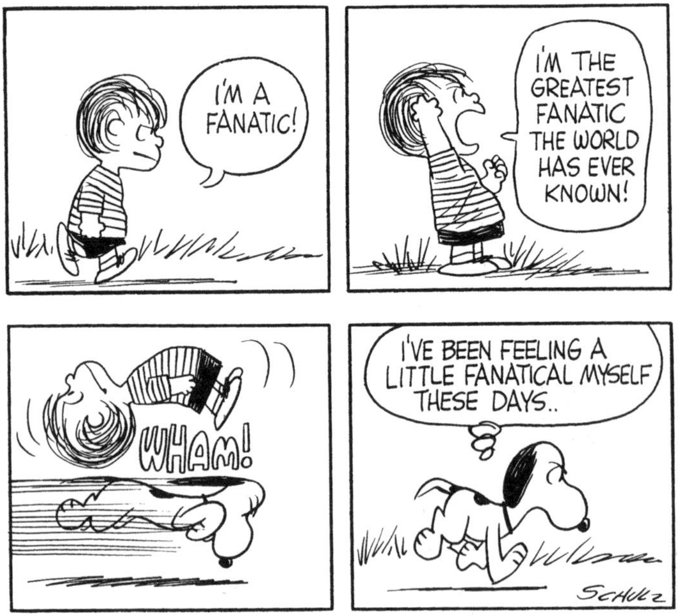
I'M A FANATIC!
I'M THE GREATEST FANATIC THE WORLD HAS EVER KNOWN!
WHAM!
I'VE BEEN FEELING A LITTLE FANATICAL MYSELF THESE DAYS..
SCHULZ

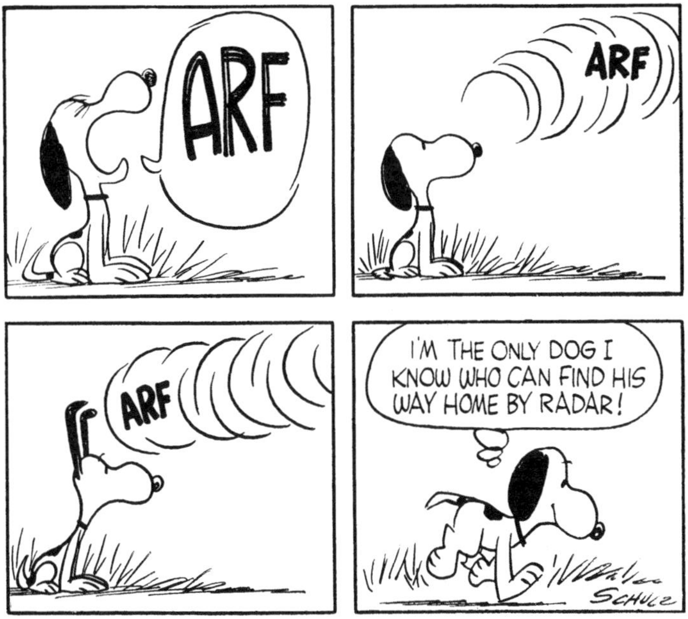
ARF
ARF
ARF
I'M THE ONLY DOG I KNOW WHO CAN FIND HIS WAY HOME BY RADAR!
SCHULZ

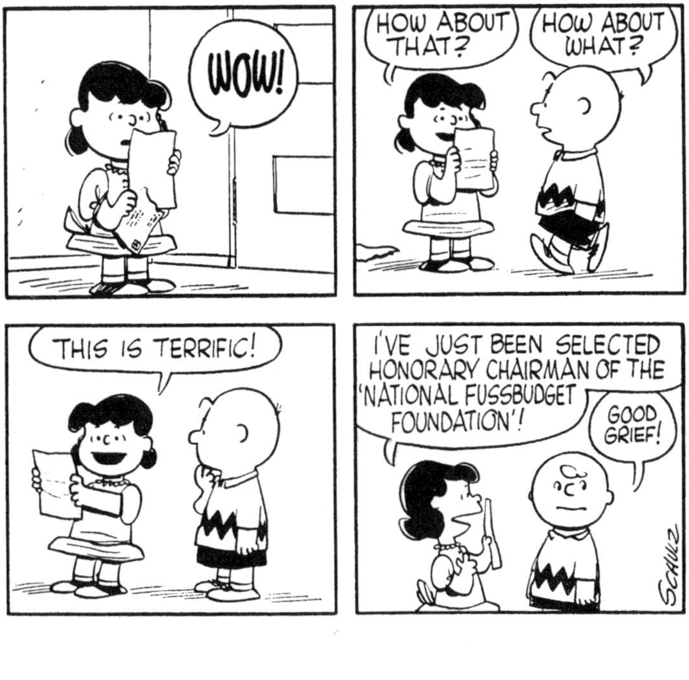
WOW!
HOW ABOUT THAT?
HOW ABOUT WHAT?
THIS IS TERRIFIC!
I'VE JUST BEEN SELECTED HONORARY CHAIRMAN OF THE 'NATIONAL FUSSBUDGET FOUNDATION'!
GOOD GRIEF!
SCHULZ

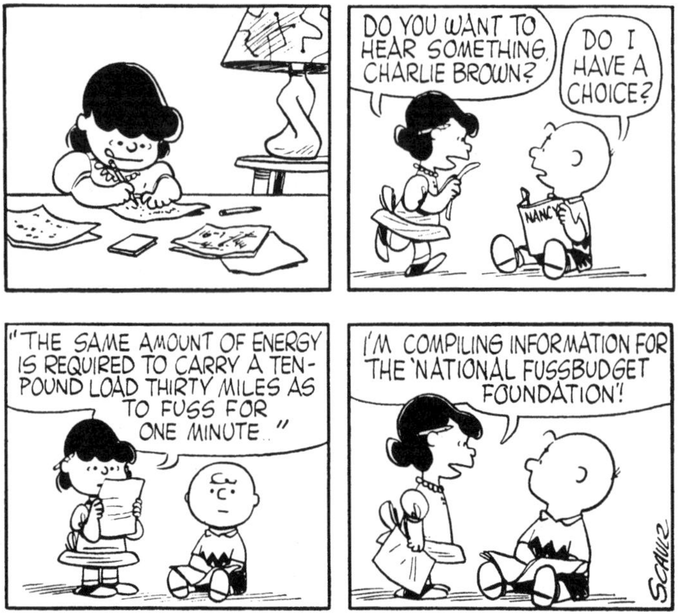
DO YOU WANT TO HEAR SOMETHING, CHARLIE BROWN?
DO I HAVE A CHOICE?
NANCY
"THE SAME AMOUNT OF ENERGY IS REQUIRED TO CARRY A TEN-POUND LOAD THIRTY MILES AS TO FUSS FOR ONE MINUTE..."
I'M COMPILING INFORMATION FOR THE 'NATIONAL FUSSBUDGET FOUNDATION'!
SCHULZ

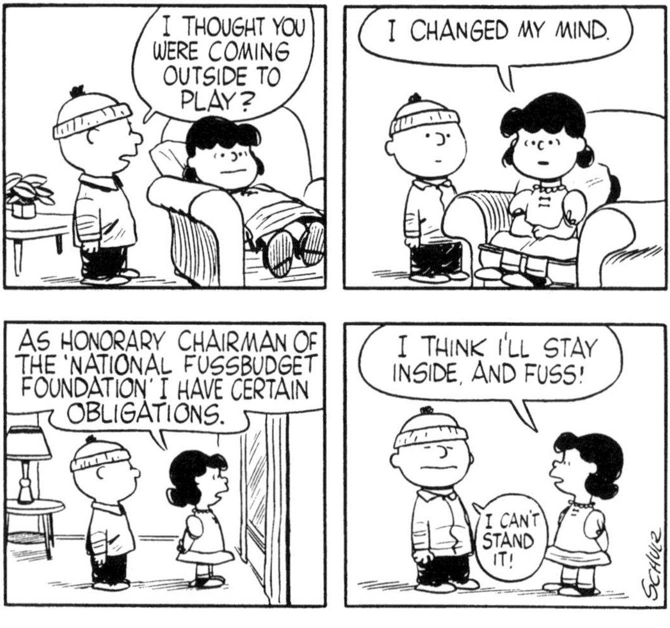
I THOUGHT YOU WERE COMING OUTSIDE TO PLAY?
I CHANGED MY MIND.
AS HONORARY CHAIRMAN OF THE 'NATIONAL FUSSBUDGET FOUNDATION' I HAVE CERTAIN OBLIGATIONS.
I THINK I'LL STAY INSIDE, AND FUSS!
I CAN'T STAND IT!
SCHULZ

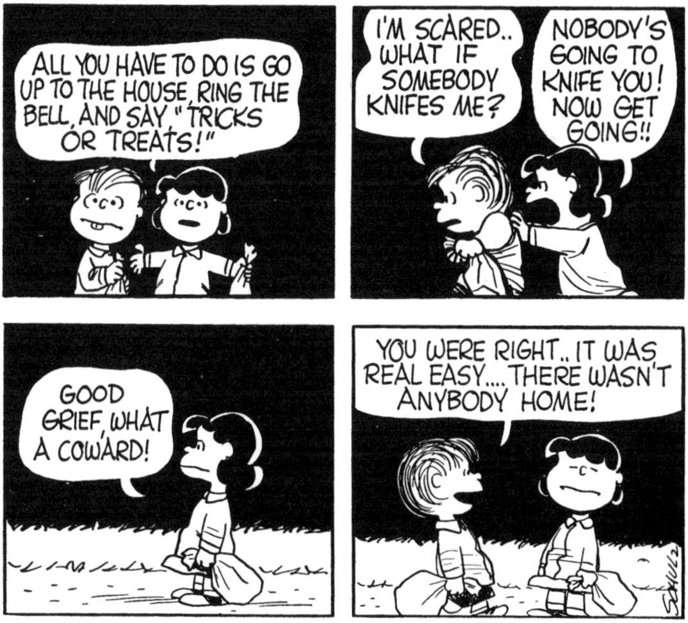
ALL YOU HAVE TO DO IS GO UP TO THE HOUSE, RING THE BELL, AND SAY, "TRICKS OR TREATS!"
I'M SCARED.. WHAT IF SOMEBODY KNIFES ME?
NOBODY'S GOING TO KNIFE YOU! NOW GET GOING!!
GOOD GRIEF, WHAT A COWARD!
YOU WERE RIGHT.. IT WAS REAL EASY.... THERE WASN'T ANYBODY HOME!
SCHULZ

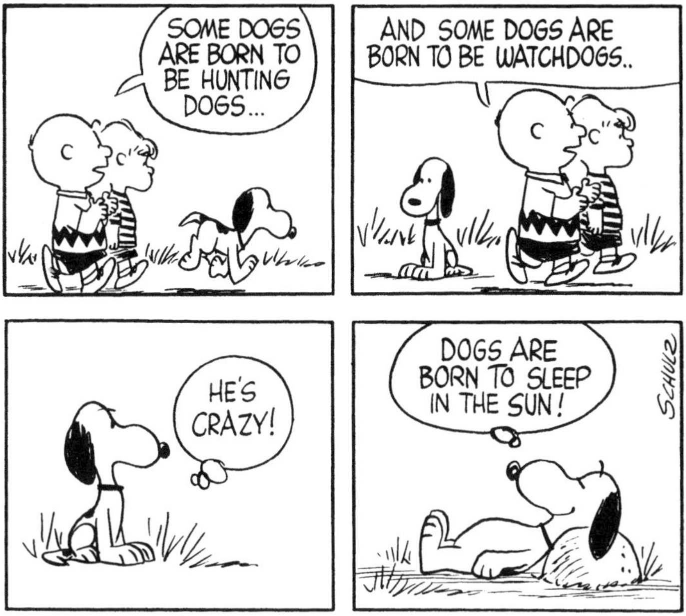
SOME DOGS ARE BORN TO BE HUNTING DOGS...
AND SOME DOGS ARE BORN TO BE WATCHDOGS..
HE'S CRAZY!
DOGS ARE BORN TO SLEEP IN THE SUN!
SCHULZ

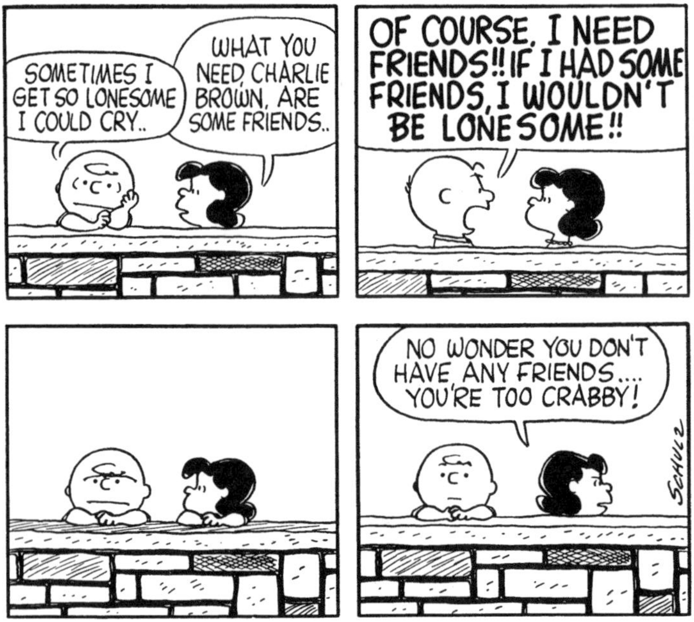
SOMETIMES I GET SO LONESOME I COULD CRY..
WHAT YOU NEED, CHARLIE BROWN, ARE SOME FRIENDS..
OF COURSE, I NEED FRIENDS!! IF I HAD SOME FRIENDS, I WOULDN'T BE LONESOME!!
NO WONDER YOU DON'T HAVE ANY FRIENDS.... YOU'RE TOO CRABBY!
SCHULZ

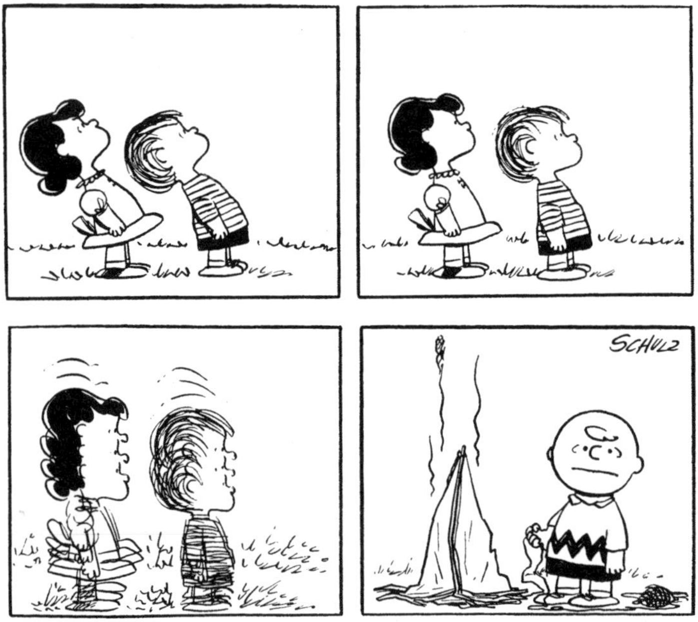
SCHULZ

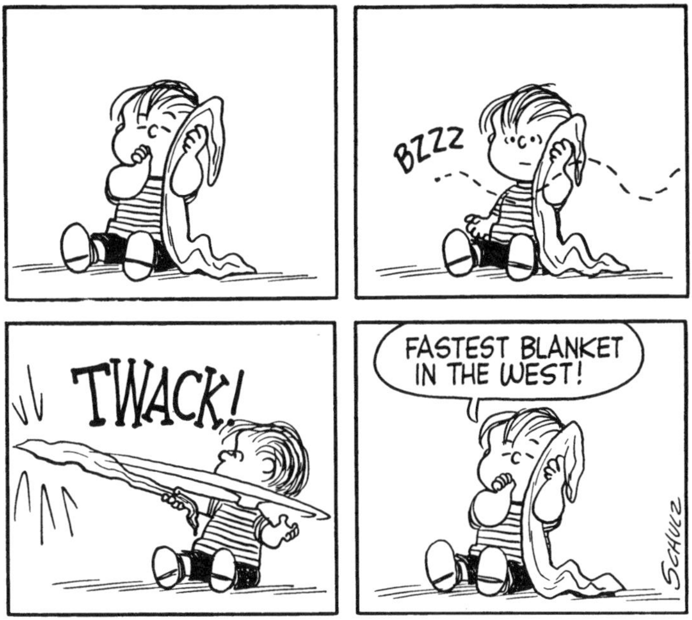
BZZZ
TWACK!
FASTEST BLANKET IN THE WEST!
SCHULZ

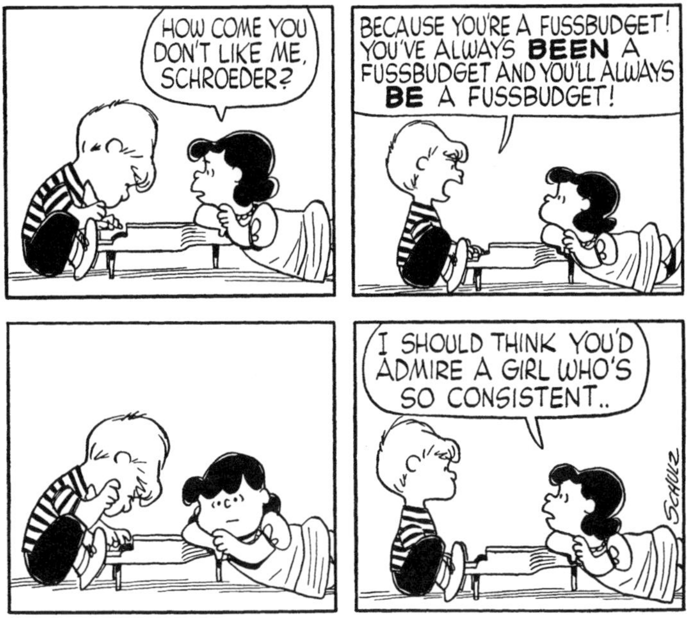
HOW COME YOU DON'T LIKE ME, SCHROEDER?
BECAUSE YOU'RE A FUSSBUDGET! YOU'VE ALWAYS **BEEN** A FUSSBUDGET AND YOU'LL ALWAYS **BE** A FUSSBUDGET!
I SHOULD THINK YOU'D ADMIRE A GIRL WHO'S SO CONSISTENT..
SCHULZ

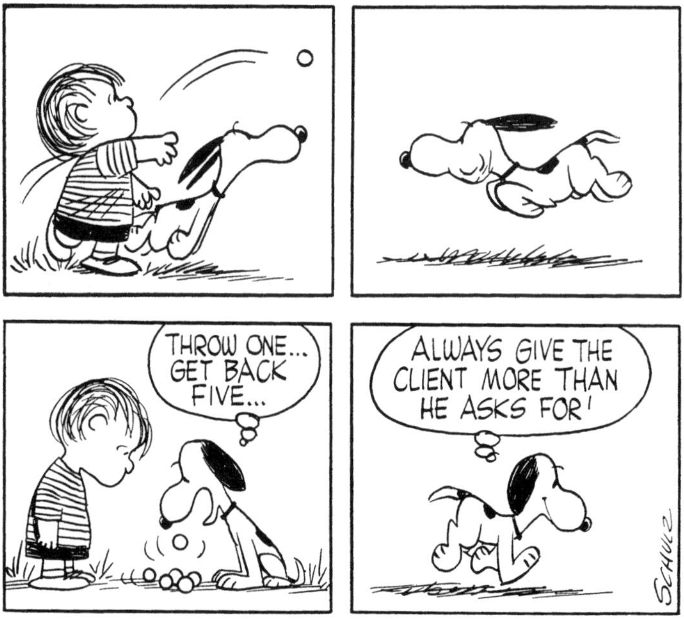
THROW ONE... GET BACK FIVE...
ALWAYS GIVE THE CLIENT MORE THAN HE ASKS FOR!
SCHULZ

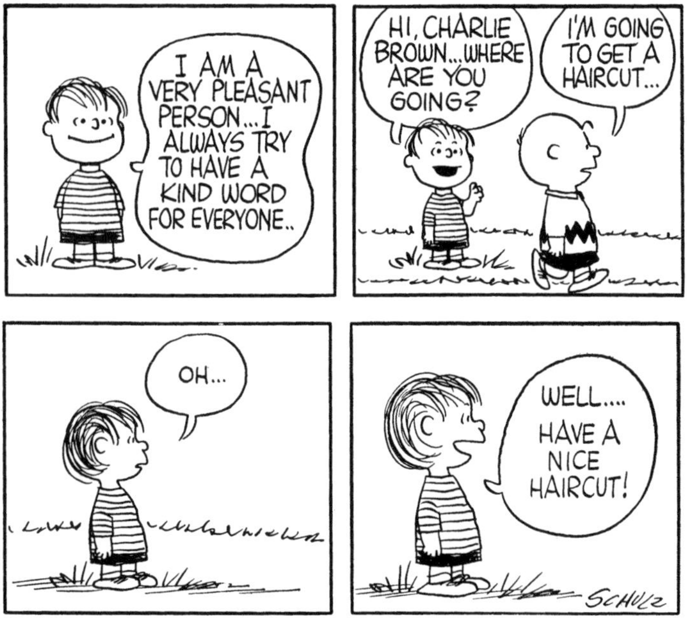
I AM A VERY PLEASANT PERSON... I ALWAYS TRY TO HAVE A KIND WORD FOR EVERYONE..
HI, CHARLIE BROWN... WHERE ARE YOU GOING?
I'M GOING TO GET A HAIRCUT...
OH...
WELL.... HAVE A NICE HAIRCUT!
SCHULZ

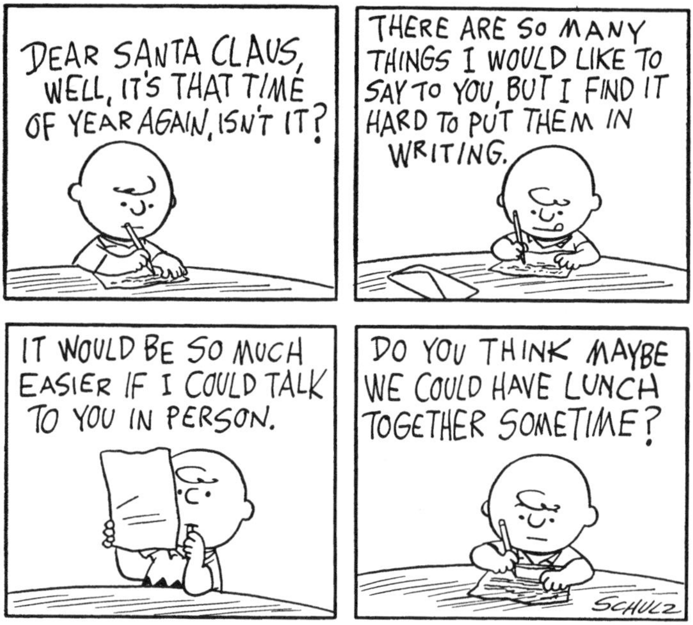
DEAR SANTA CLAUS, WELL, IT'S THAT TIME OF YEAR AGAIN, ISN'T IT?
THERE ARE SO MANY THINGS I WOULD LIKE TO SAY TO YOU, BUT I FIND IT HARD TO PUT THEM IN WRITING.
IT WOULD BE SO MUCH EASIER IF I COULD TALK TO YOU IN PERSON.
DO YOU THINK MAYBE WE COULD HAVE LUNCH TOGETHER SOMETIME?
SCHULZ

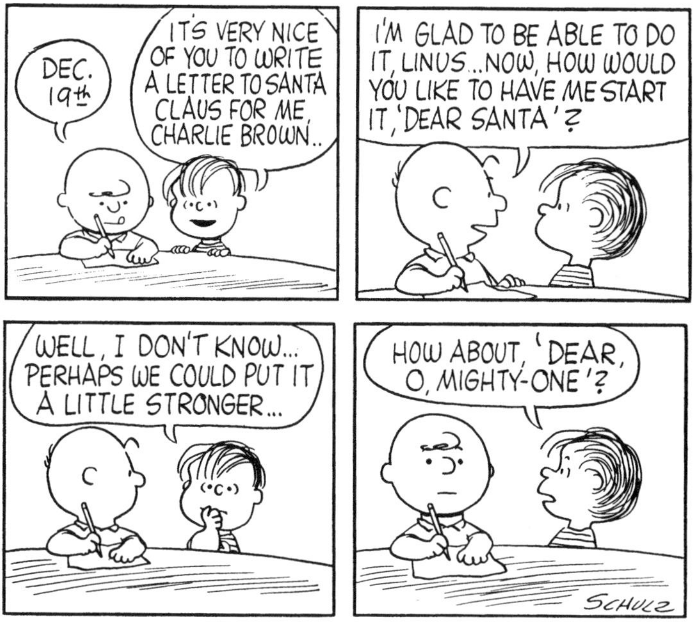
DEC. 19th
IT'S VERY NICE OF YOU TO WRITE A LETTER TO SANTA CLAUS FOR ME, CHARLIE BROWN..
I'M GLAD TO BE ABLE TO DO IT, LINUS...NOW, HOW WOULD YOU LIKE TO HAVE ME START IT, 'DEAR SANTA'?
WELL, I DON'T KNOW... PERHAPS WE COULD PUT IT A LITTLE STRONGER...
HOW ABOUT, 'DEAR, O, MIGHTY-ONE'?
SCHULZ

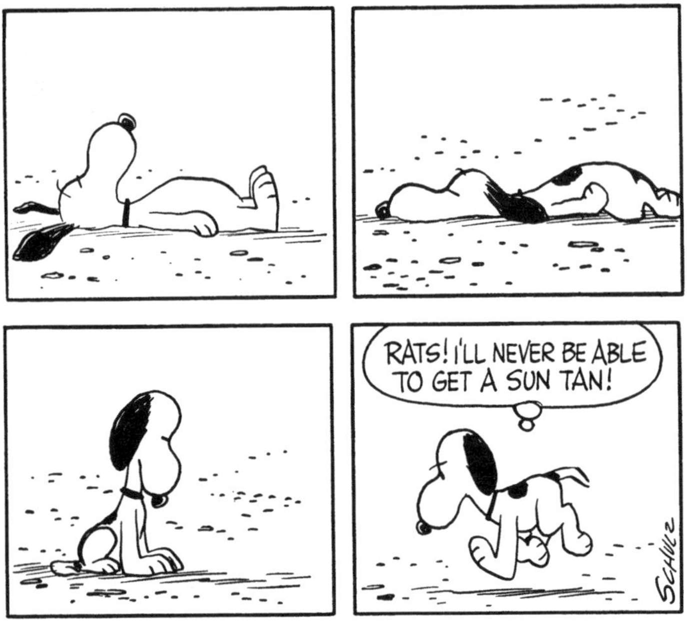
RATS! I'LL NEVER BE ABLE TO GET A SUN TAN!
SCHULZ

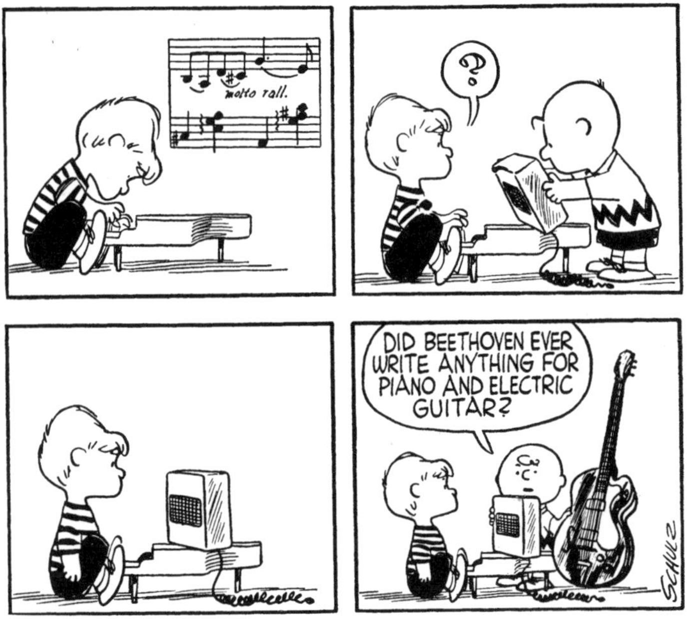
molto rall.
?
DID BEETHOVEN EVER WRITE ANYTHING FOR PIANO AND ELECTRIC GUITAR?
SCHULZ

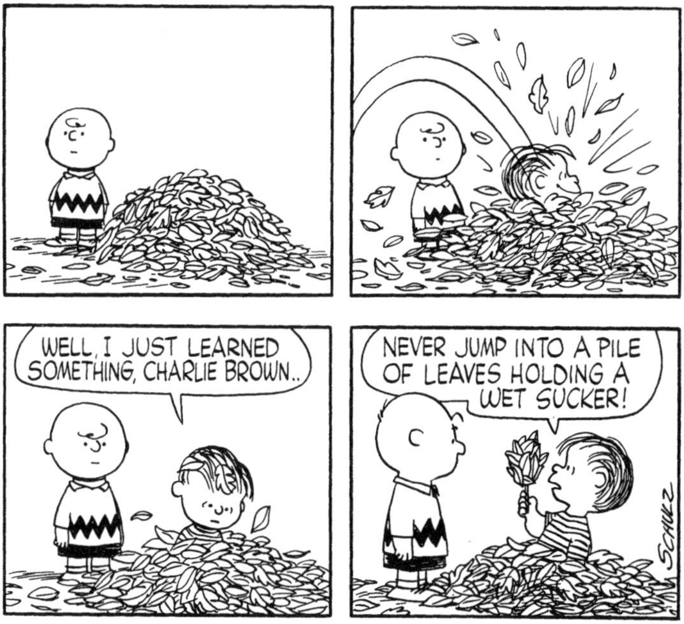
WELL, I JUST LEARNED SOMETHING, CHARLIE BROWN..
NEVER JUMP INTO A PILE OF LEAVES HOLDING A WET SUCKER!
SCHULZ

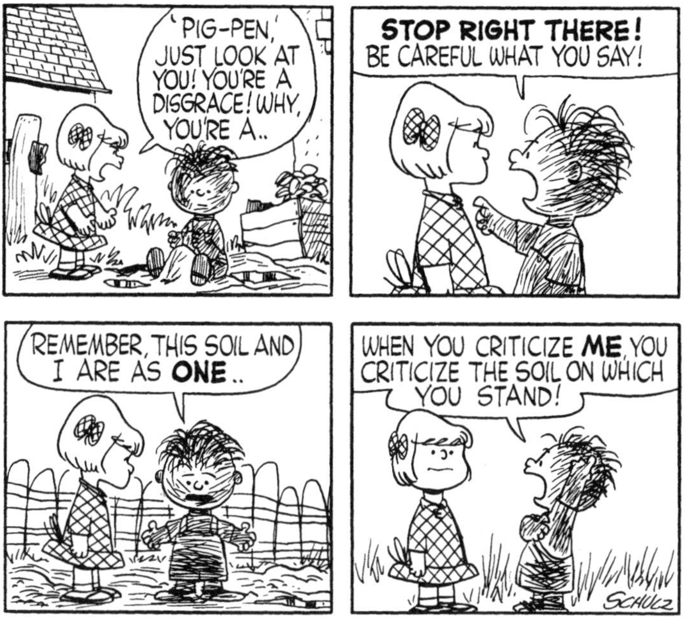
'PIG-PEN,' JUST LOOK AT YOU! YOU'RE A DISGRACE! WHY, YOU'RE A..
STOP RIGHT THERE! BE CAREFUL WHAT YOU SAY!
REMEMBER, THIS SOIL AND I ARE AS ONE..
WHEN YOU CRITICIZE ME, YOU CRITICIZE THE SOIL ON WHICH YOU STAND!
SCHULZ

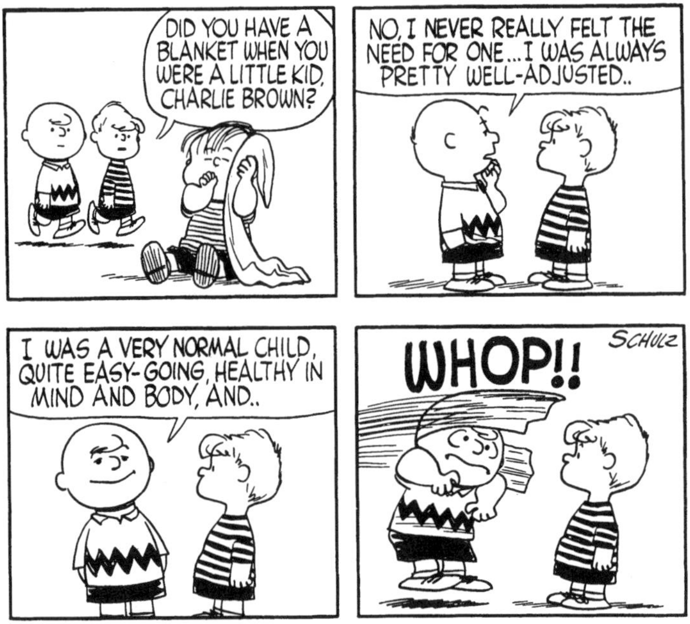
DID YOU HAVE A BLANKET WHEN YOU WERE A LITTLE KID, CHARLIE BROWN?
NO, I NEVER REALLY FELT THE NEED FOR ONE...I WAS ALWAYS PRETTY WELL-ADJUSTED..
I WAS A VERY NORMAL CHILD, QUITE EASY-GOING, HEALTHY IN MIND AND BODY, AND..
WHOP!!
SCHULZ

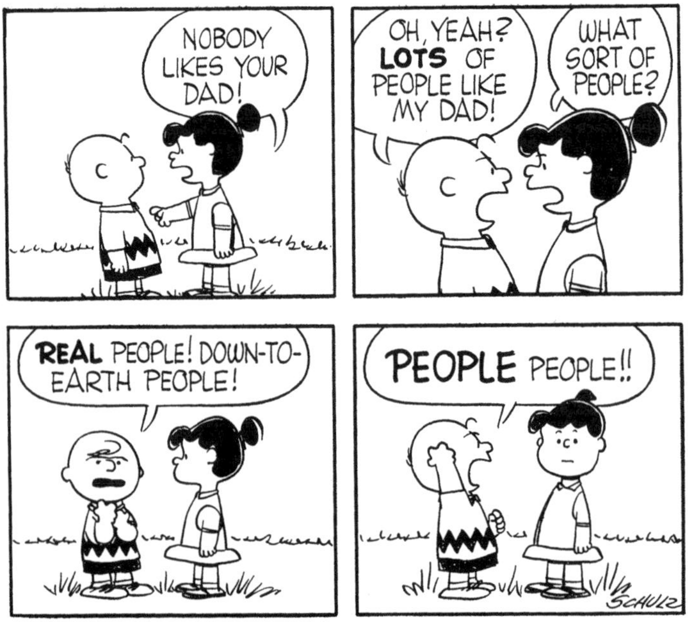
NOBODY LIKES YOUR DAD!
OH, YEAH? LOTS OF PEOPLE LIKE MY DAD!
WHAT SORT OF PEOPLE?
REAL PEOPLE! DOWN-TO-EARTH PEOPLE!
PEOPLE PEOPLE!!
SCHULZ

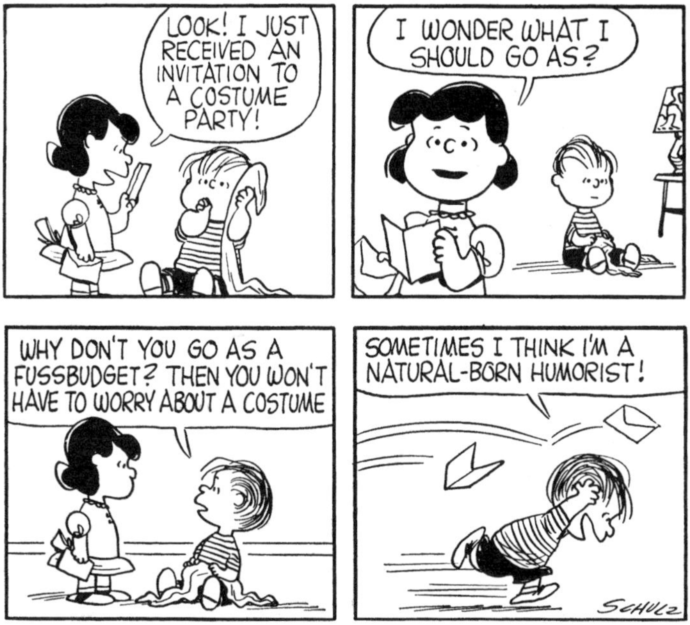
LOOK! I JUST RECEIVED AN INVITATION TO A COSTUME PARTY!
I WONDER WHAT I SHOULD GO AS?
WHY DON'T YOU GO AS A FUSSBUDGET? THEN YOU WON'T HAVE TO WORRY ABOUT A COSTUME
SOMETIMES I THINK I'M A NATURAL-BORN HUMORIST!
SCHULZ

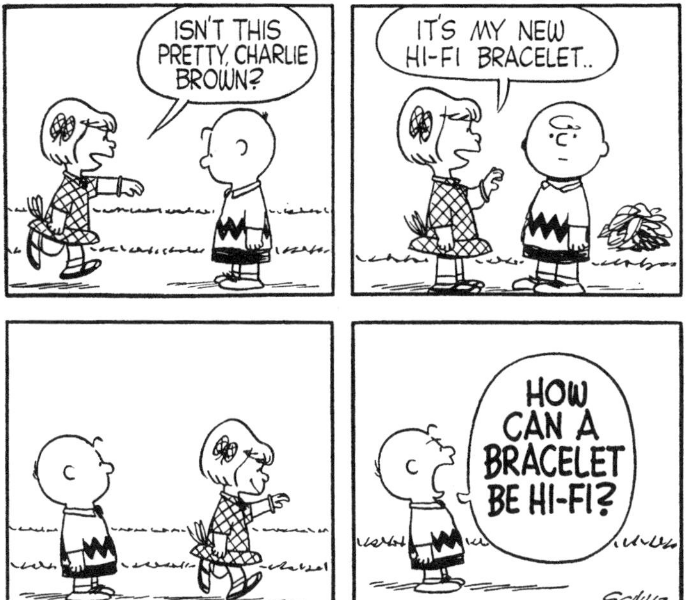
ISN'T THIS PRETTY, CHARLIE BROWN?
IT'S MY NEW HI-FI BRACELET..
HOW CAN A BRACELET BE HI-FI?
SCHULZ

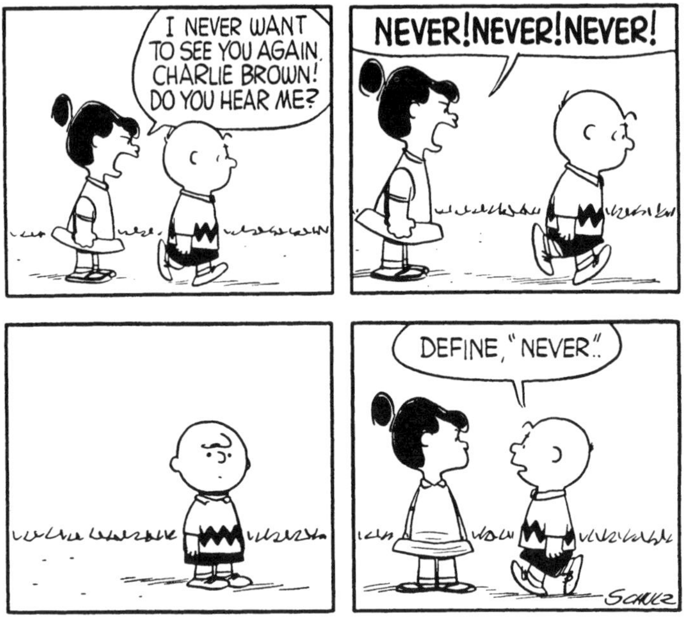
I NEVER WANT TO SEE YOU AGAIN, CHARLIE BROWN! DO YOU HEAR ME?
NEVER! NEVER! NEVER!
DEFINE, "NEVER"..
SCHULZ

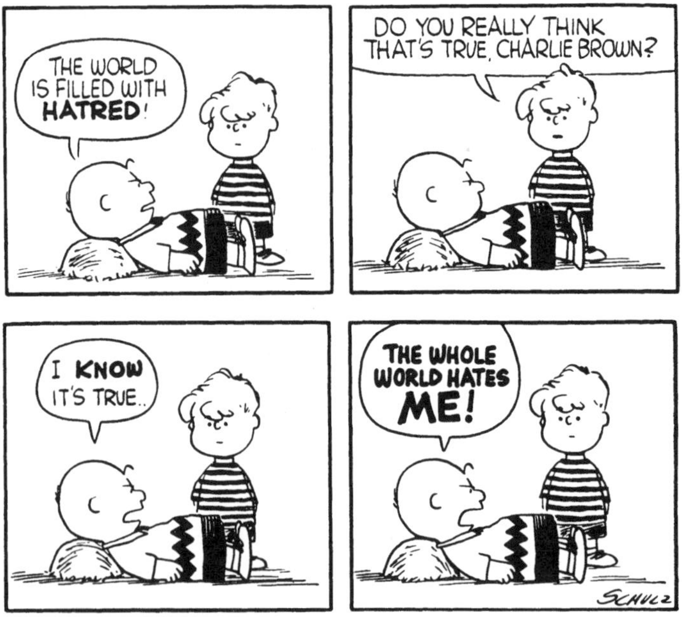
THE WORLD IS FILLED WITH HATRED!
DO YOU REALLY THINK THAT'S TRUE, CHARLIE BROWN?
I KNOW IT'S TRUE..
THE WHOLE WORLD HATES ME!
SCHULZ

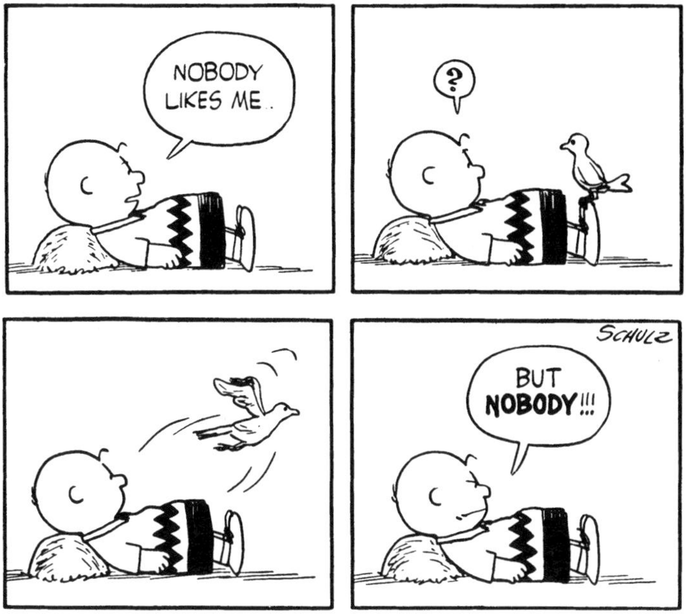
NOBODY LIKES ME..
?
SCHULZ
BUT NOBODY!!!

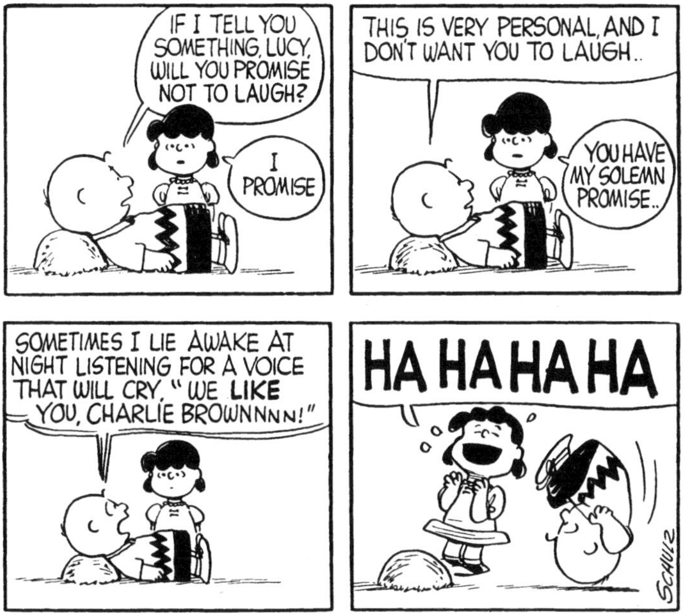
IF I TELL YOU SOMETHING, LUCY, WILL YOU PROMISE NOT TO LAUGH?
I PROMISE
THIS IS VERY PERSONAL, AND I DON'T WANT YOU TO LAUGH..
YOU HAVE MY SOLEMN PROMISE..
SOMETIMES I LIE AWAKE AT NIGHT LISTENING FOR A VOICE THAT WILL CRY, "WE LIKE YOU, CHARLIE BROWNNNNN!"
HA HA HA HA HA
SCHULZ

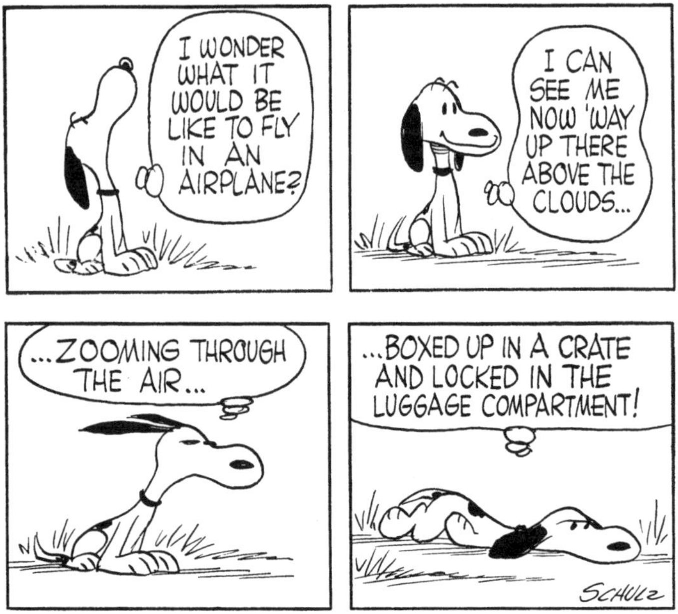
I WONDER WHAT IT WOULD BE LIKE TO FLY IN AN AIRPLANE?
I CAN SEE ME NOW 'WAY UP THERE ABOVE THE CLOUDS...
...ZOOMING THROUGH THE AIR...
...BOXED UP IN A CRATE AND LOCKED IN THE LUGGAGE COMPARTMENT!
SCHULZ

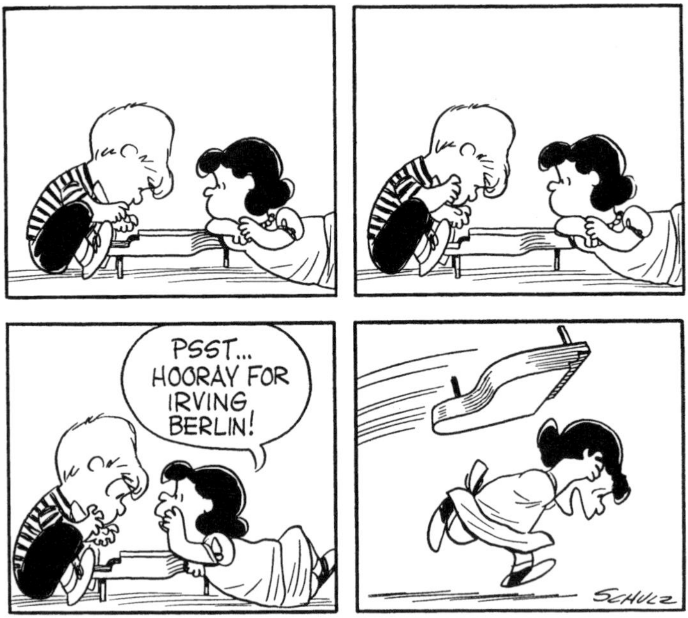
PSST... HOORAY FOR IRVING BERLIN!
SCHULZ

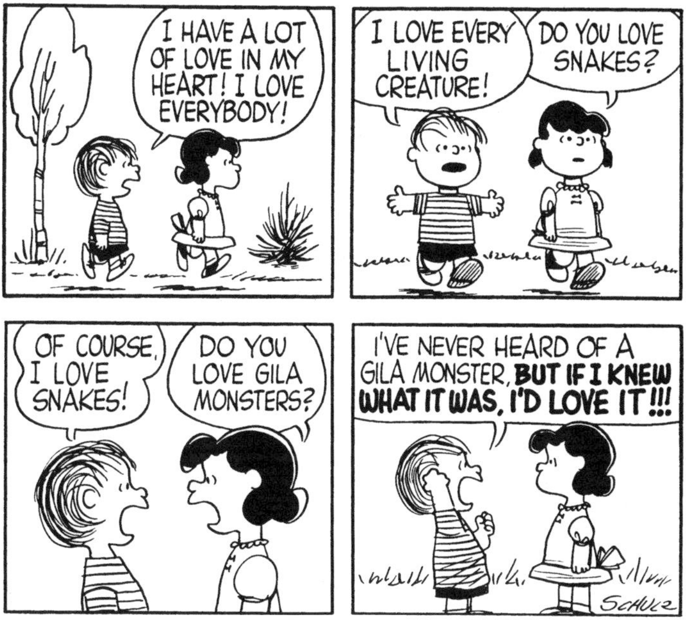
I HAVE A LOT OF LOVE IN MY HEART! I LOVE EVERYBODY!
I LOVE EVERY LIVING CREATURE!
DO YOU LOVE SNAKES?
OF COURSE, I LOVE SNAKES!
DO YOU LOVE GILA MONSTERS?
I'VE NEVER HEARD OF A GILA MONSTER, BUT IF I KNEW WHAT IT WAS, I'D LOVE IT!!!
SCHULZ

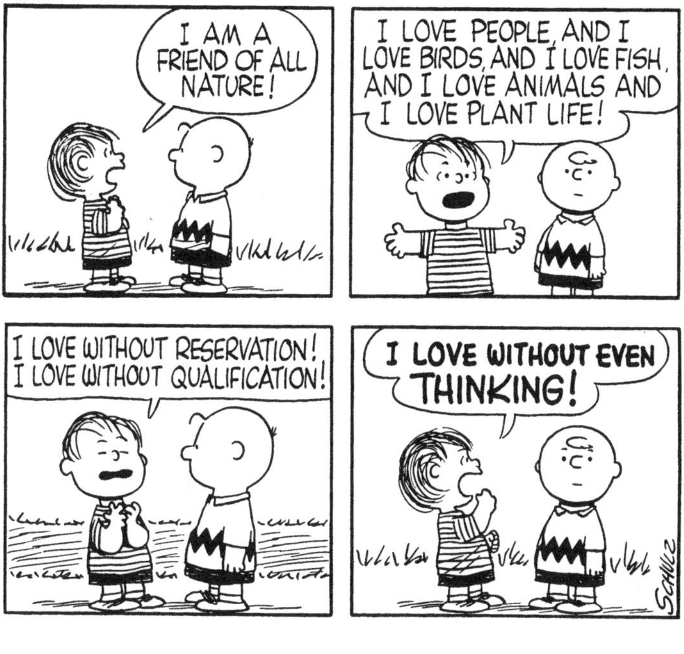
I AM A FRIEND OF ALL NATURE!
I LOVE PEOPLE, AND I LOVE BIRDS, AND I LOVE FISH, AND I LOVE ANIMALS AND I LOVE PLANT LIFE!
I LOVE WITHOUT RESERVATION! I LOVE WITHOUT QUALIFICATION!
I LOVE WITHOUT EVEN THINKING!
SCHULZ

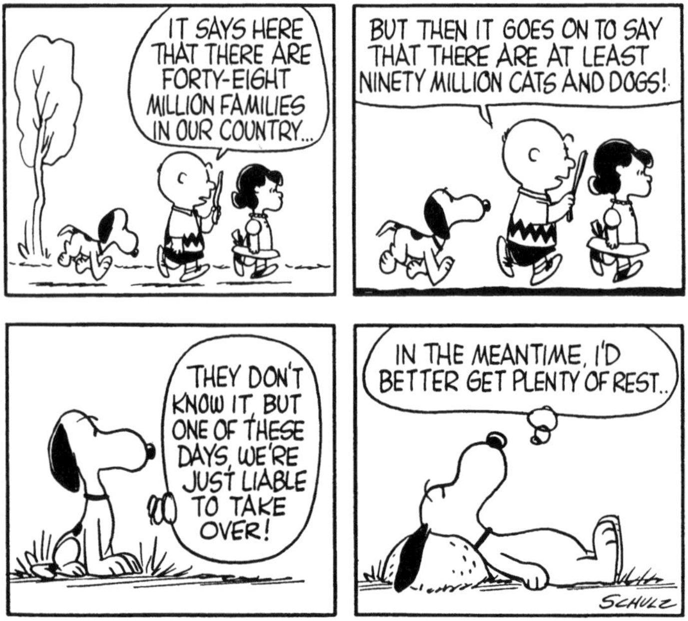
IT SAYS HERE THAT THERE ARE FORTY-EIGHT MILLION FAMILIES IN OUR COUNTRY...
BUT THEN IT GOES ON TO SAY THAT THERE ARE AT LEAST NINETY MILLION CATS AND DOGS!
THEY DON'T KNOW IT, BUT ONE OF THESE DAYS, WE'RE JUST LIABLE TO TAKE OVER!
IN THE MEANTIME, I'D BETTER GET PLENTY OF REST..
SCHULZ

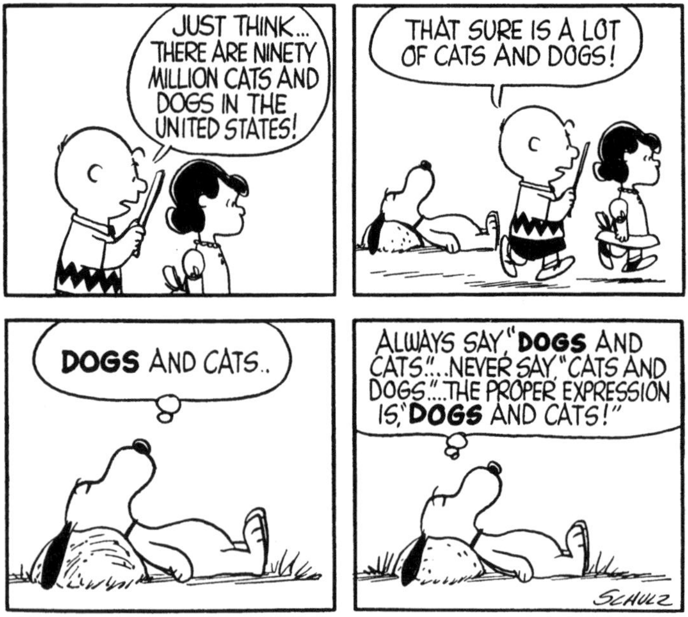
JUST THINK... THERE ARE NINETY MILLION CATS AND DOGS IN THE UNITED STATES!
THAT SURE IS A LOT OF CATS AND DOGS!
DOGS AND CATS..
ALWAYS SAY, "DOGS AND CATS"...NEVER SAY, "CATS AND DOGS"...THE PROPER EXPRESSION IS, "DOGS AND CATS!"
SCHULZ

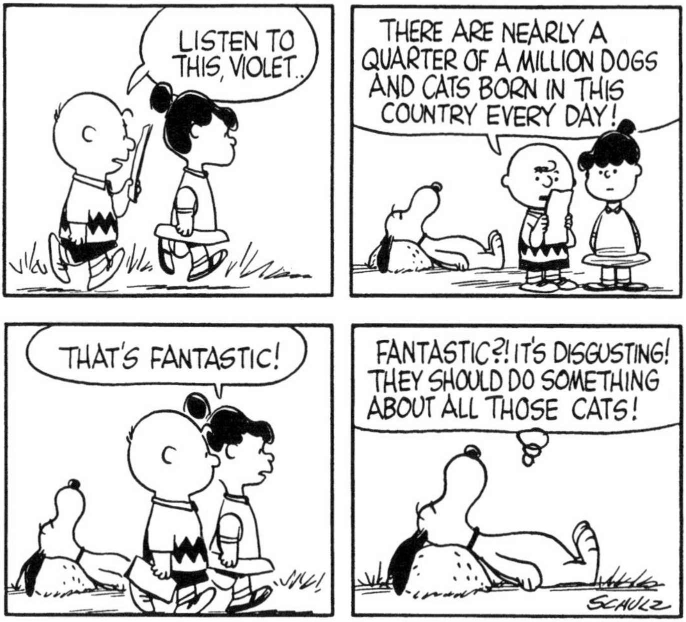
LISTEN TO THIS, VIOLET..
THERE ARE NEARLY A QUARTER OF A MILLION DOGS AND CATS BORN IN THIS COUNTRY EVERY DAY!
THAT'S FANTASTIC!
FANTASTIC?! IT'S DISGUSTING! THEY SHOULD DO SOMETHING ABOUT ALL THOSE CATS!
SCHULZ

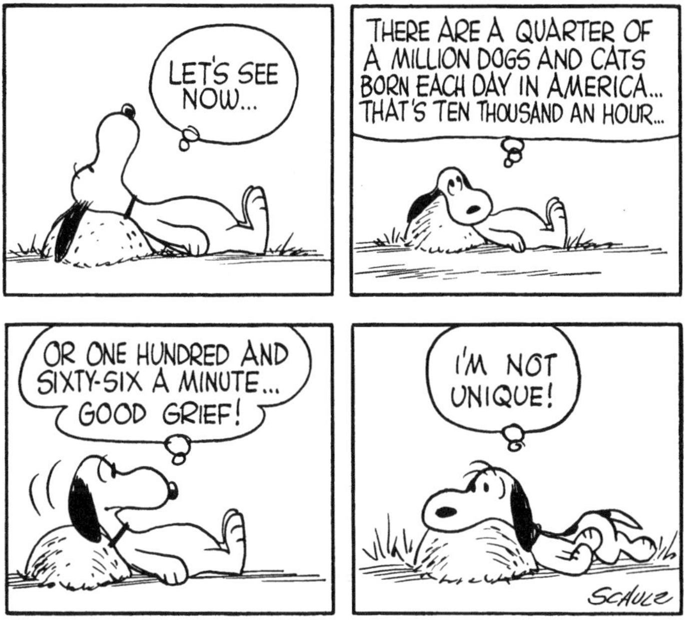
LET'S SEE NOW...
THERE ARE A QUARTER OF A MILLION DOGS AND CATS BORN EACH DAY IN AMERICA... THAT'S TEN THOUSAND AN HOUR...
OR ONE HUNDRED AND SIXTY-SIX A MINUTE... GOOD GRIEF!
I'M NOT UNIQUE!
SCHULZ

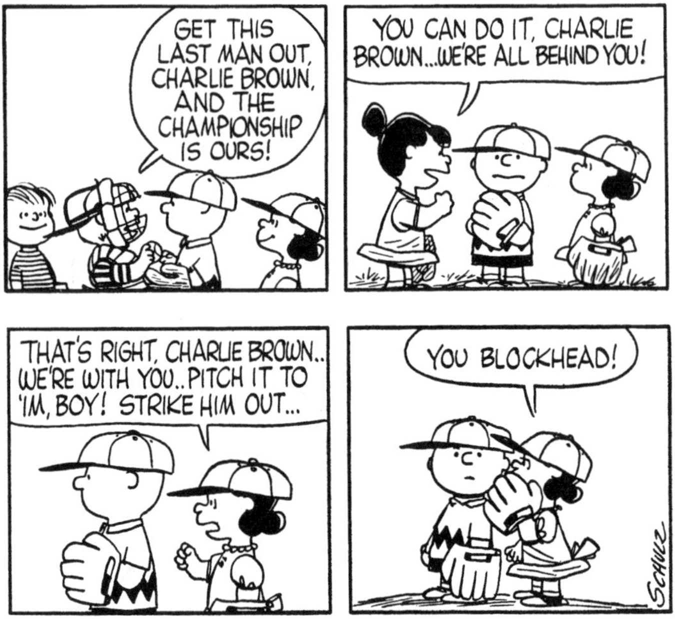
GET THIS LAST MAN OUT, CHARLIE BROWN, AND THE CHAMPIONSHIP IS OURS!
YOU CAN DO IT, CHARLIE BROWN...WE'RE ALL BEHIND YOU!
THAT'S RIGHT, CHARLIE BROWN.. WE'RE WITH YOU..PITCH IT TO 'IM, BOY! STRIKE HIM OUT...
YOU BLOCKHEAD!
SCHULZ

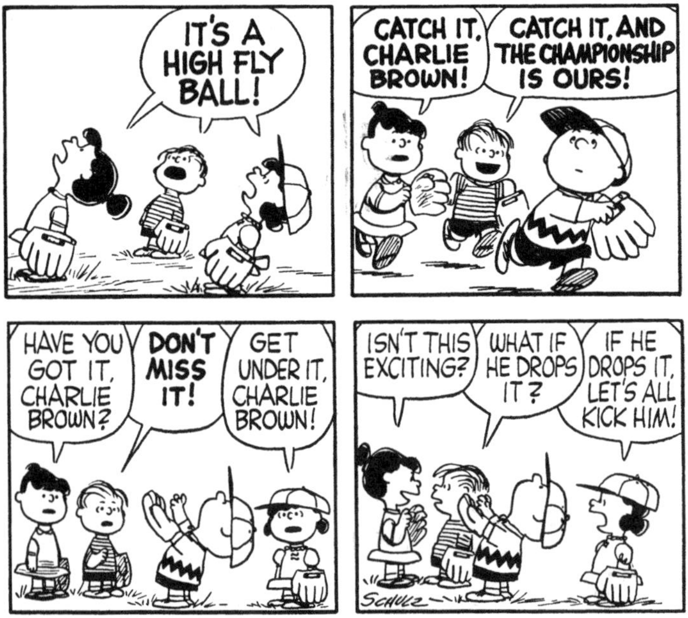
IT'S A HIGH FLY BALL!
CATCH IT, CHARLIE BROWN!
CATCH IT, AND THE CHAMPIONSHIP IS OURS!
HAVE YOU GOT IT, CHARLIE BROWN?
DON'T MISS IT!
GET UNDER IT, CHARLIE BROWN!
ISN'T THIS EXCITING?
WHAT IF HE DROPS IT?
IF HE DROPS IT, LET'S ALL KICK HIM!
SCHULZ

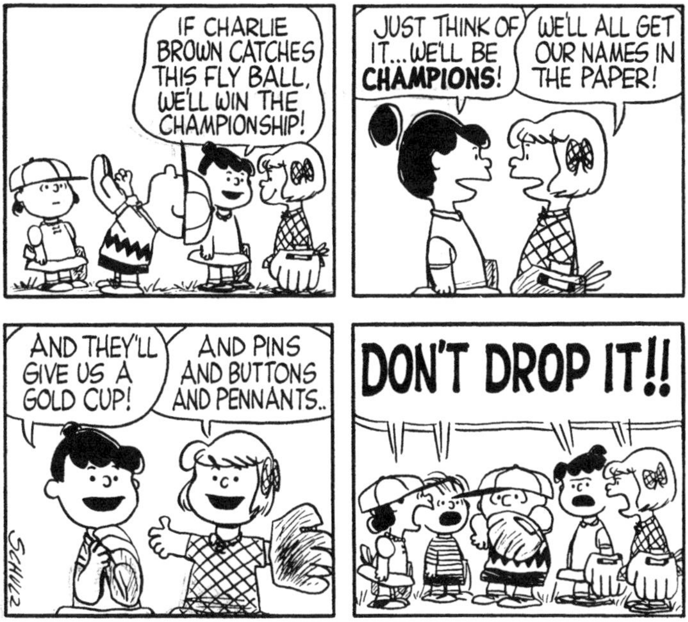
IF CHARLIE BROWN CATCHES THIS FLY BALL, WE'LL WIN THE CHAMPIONSHIP!
JUST THINK OF IT...WE'LL BE **CHAMPIONS**!
WE'LL ALL GET OUR NAMES IN THE PAPER!
AND THEY'LL GIVE US A GOLD CUP!
AND PINS AND BUTTONS AND PENNANTS..
SCHULZ
DON'T DROP IT!!

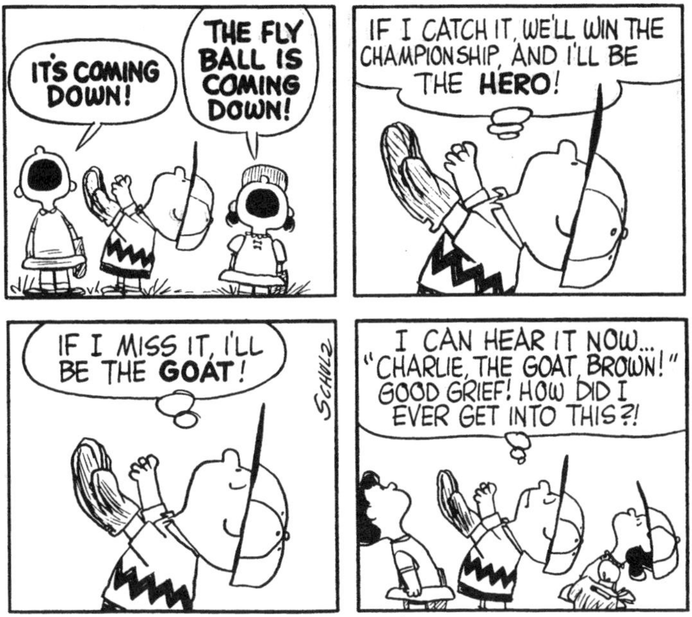
IT'S COMING DOWN!
THE FLY BALL IS COMING DOWN!
IF I CATCH IT, WE'LL WIN THE CHAMPIONSHIP, AND I'LL BE THE **HERO**!
IF I MISS IT, I'LL BE THE **GOAT**!
SCHULZ
I CAN HEAR IT NOW... "CHARLIE, THE GOAT, BROWN!" GOOD GRIEF! HOW DID I EVER GET INTO THIS?!

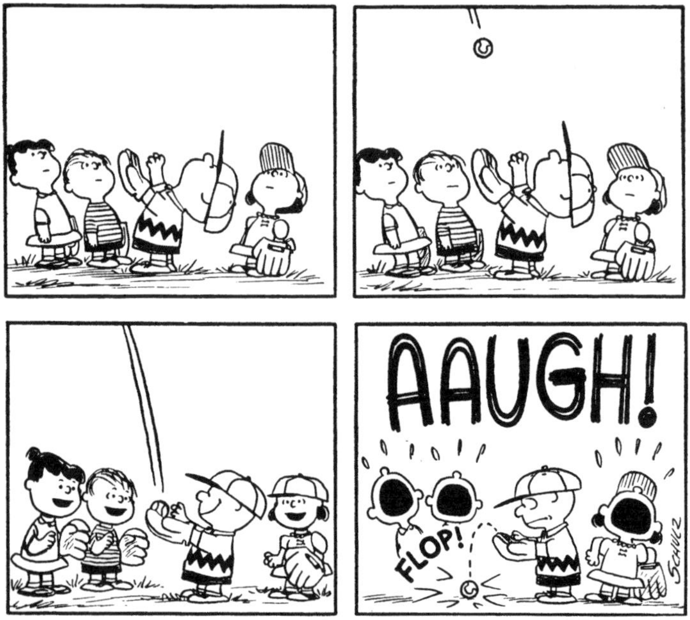
AAUGH!
FLOP!
SCHULZ

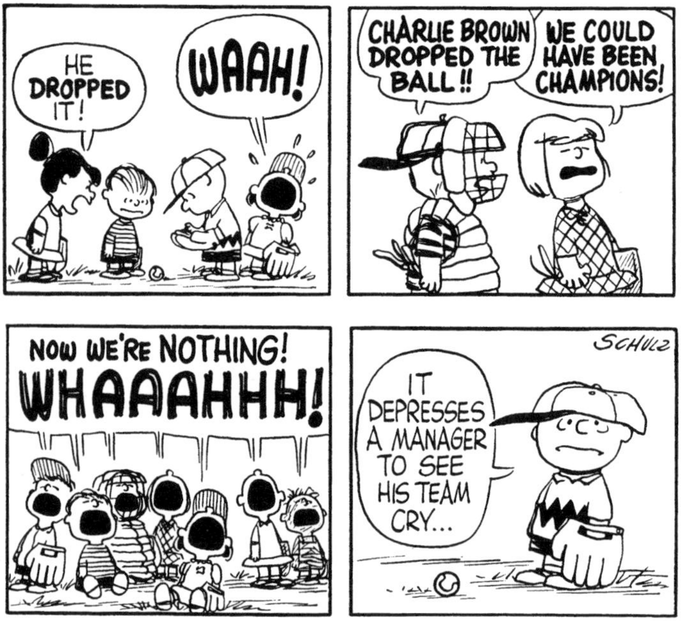
HE DROPPED IT!
WAAH!
CHARLIE BROWN DROPPED THE BALL!!
WE COULD HAVE BEEN CHAMPIONS!
NOW WE'RE NOTHING! WHAAAHHH!
SCHULZ
IT DEPRESSES A MANAGER TO SEE HIS TEAM CRY...

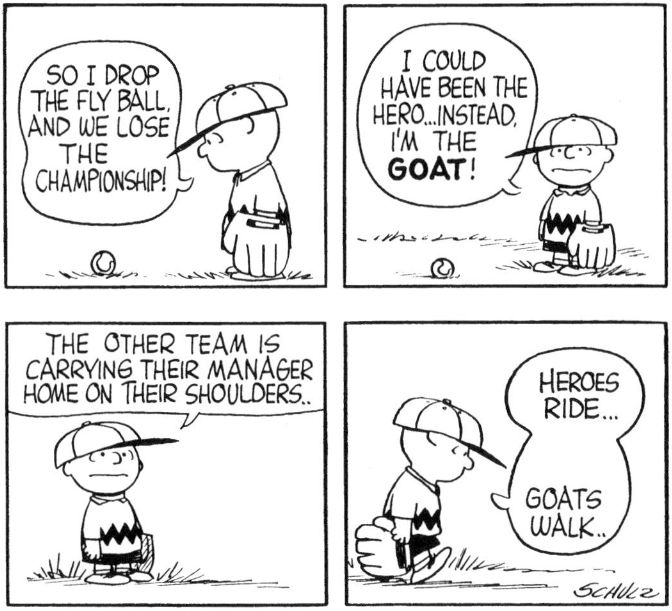
SO I DROP THE FLY BALL, AND WE LOSE THE CHAMPIONSHIP!
I COULD HAVE BEEN THE HERO...INSTEAD, I'M THE **GOAT**!
THE OTHER TEAM IS CARRYING THEIR MANAGER HOME ON THEIR SHOULDERS..
HEROES RIDE...
GOATS WALK..
SCHULZ

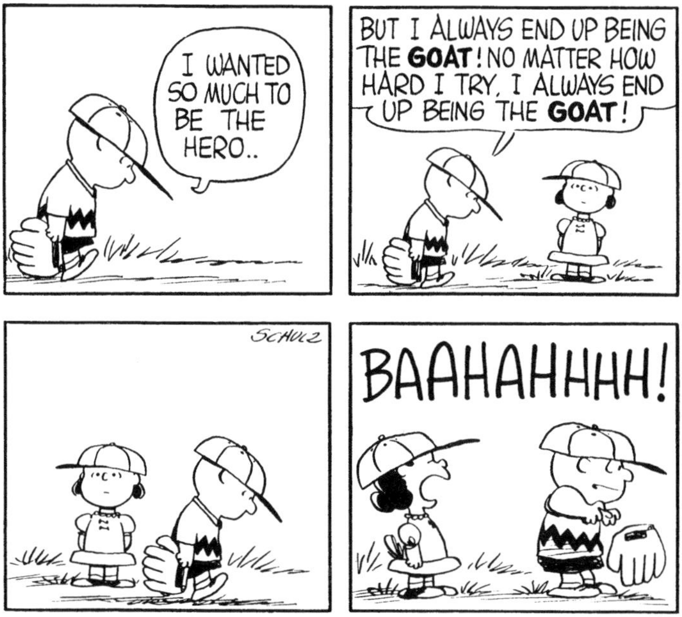
I WANTED SO MUCH TO BE THE HERO..
BUT I ALWAYS END UP BEING THE **GOAT**! NO MATTER HOW HARD I TRY, I ALWAYS END UP BEING THE **GOAT**!
SCHULZ
BAAHAHHHH!

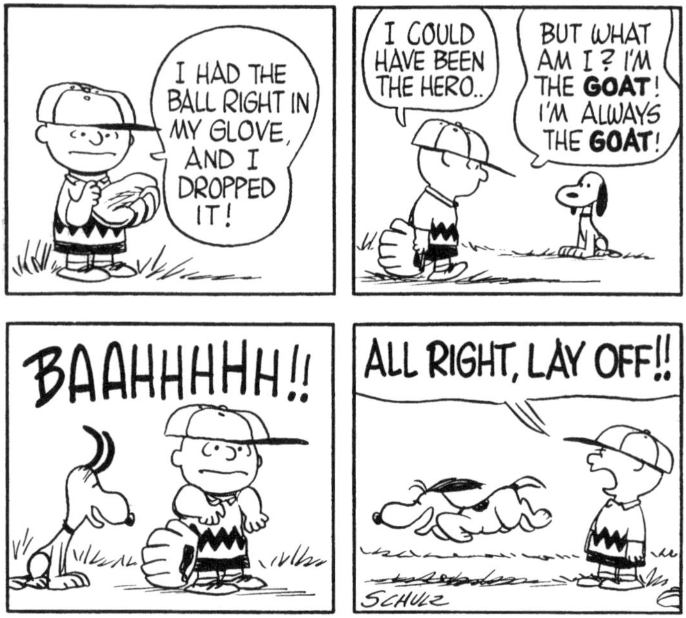
I HAD THE BALL RIGHT IN MY GLOVE, AND I DROPPED IT!
I COULD HAVE BEEN THE HERO..
BUT WHAT AM I? I'M THE **GOAT**! I'M ALWAYS THE **GOAT**!
BAAHHHHH!!
ALL RIGHT, LAY OFF!!
SCHULZ

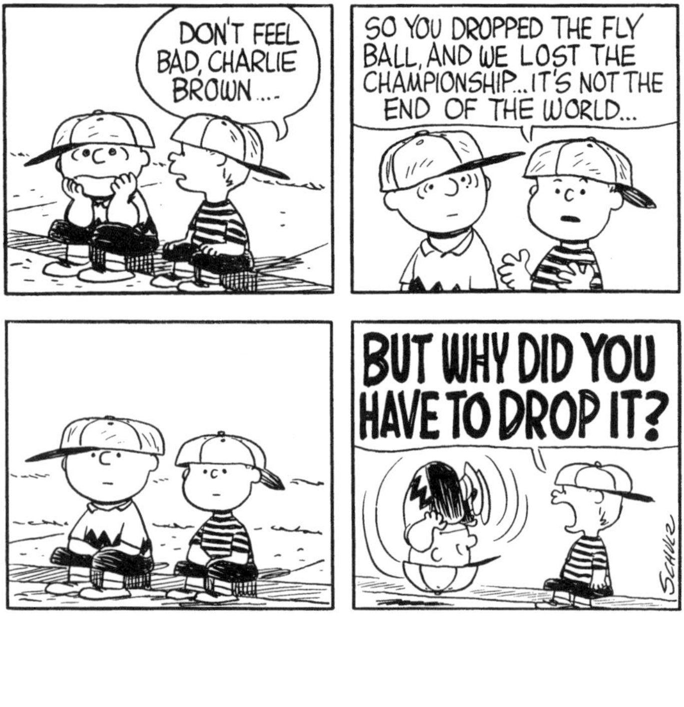
DON'T FEEL BAD, CHARLIE BROWN....
SO YOU DROPPED THE FLY BALL, AND WE LOST THE CHAMPIONSHIP...IT'S NOT THE END OF THE WORLD...
BUT WHY DID YOU HAVE TO DROP IT?
SCHULZ

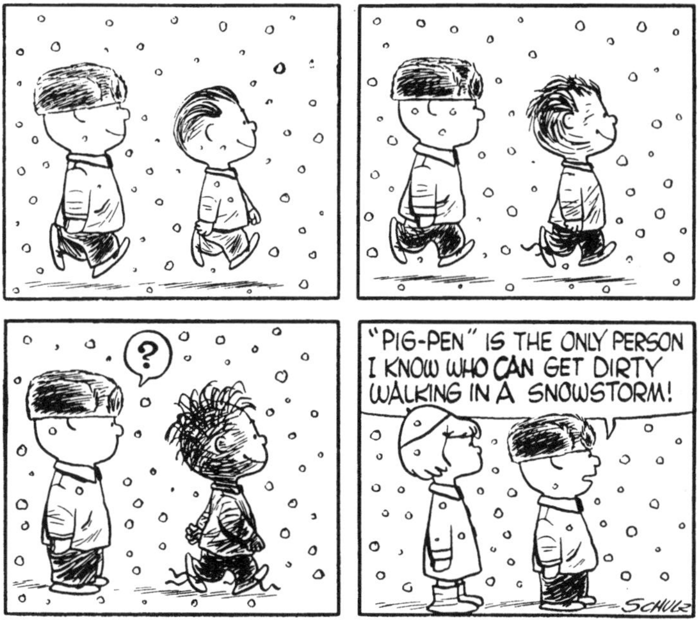
?
"PIG-PEN" IS THE ONLY PERSON I KNOW WHO CAN GET DIRTY WALKING IN A SNOWSTORM!
SCHULZ

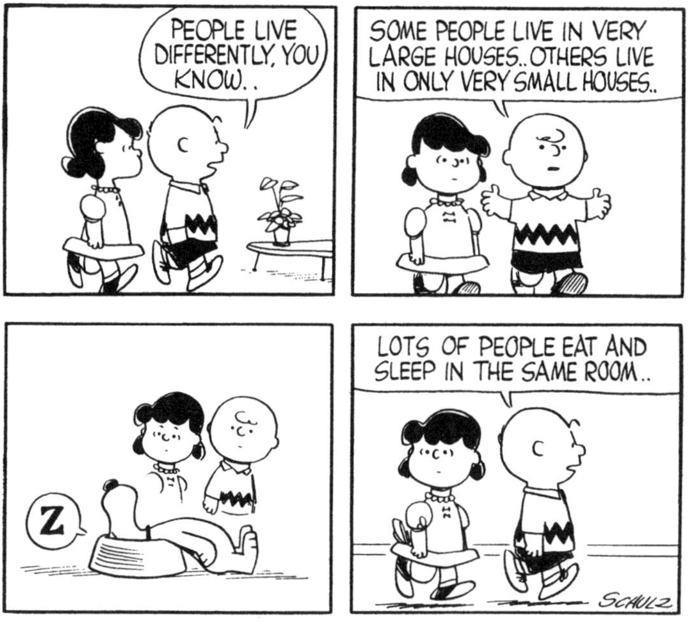
PEOPLE LIVE DIFFERENTLY, YOU KNOW..
SOME PEOPLE LIVE IN VERY LARGE HOUSES..OTHERS LIVE IN ONLY VERY SMALL HOUSES..
Z
LOTS OF PEOPLE EAT AND SLEEP IN THE SAME ROOM..
SCHULZ

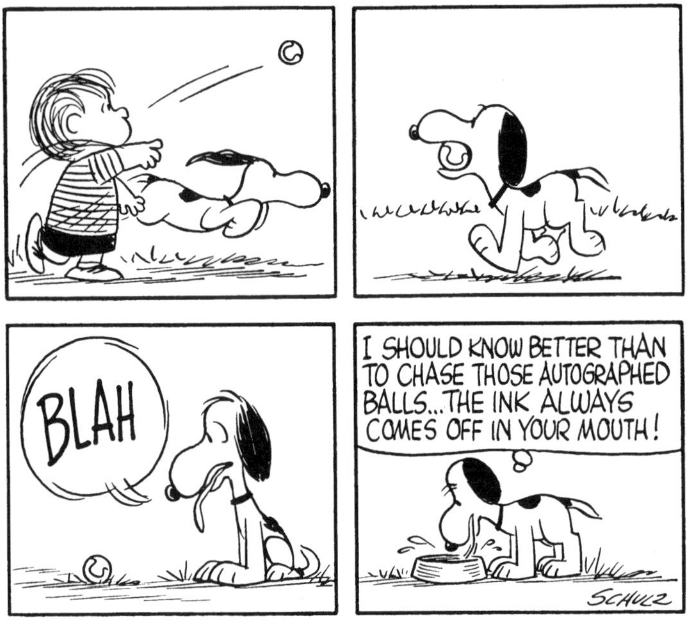
BLAH
I SHOULD KNOW BETTER THAN TO CHASE THOSE AUTOGRAPHED BALLS...THE INK ALWAYS COMES OFF IN YOUR MOUTH!

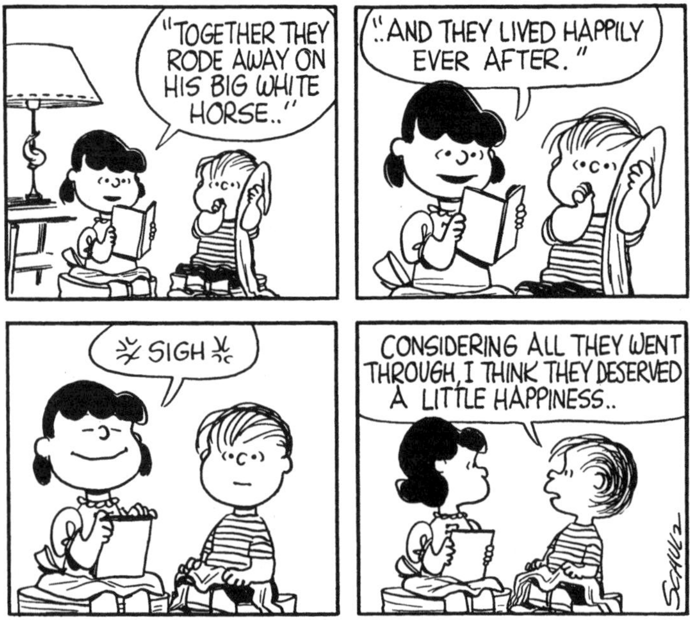
"TOGETHER THEY RODE AWAY ON HIS BIG WHITE HORSE.."
"..AND THEY LIVED HAPPILY EVER AFTER."
SIGH
CONSIDERING ALL THEY WENT THROUGH, I THINK THEY DESERVED A LITTLE HAPPINESS..

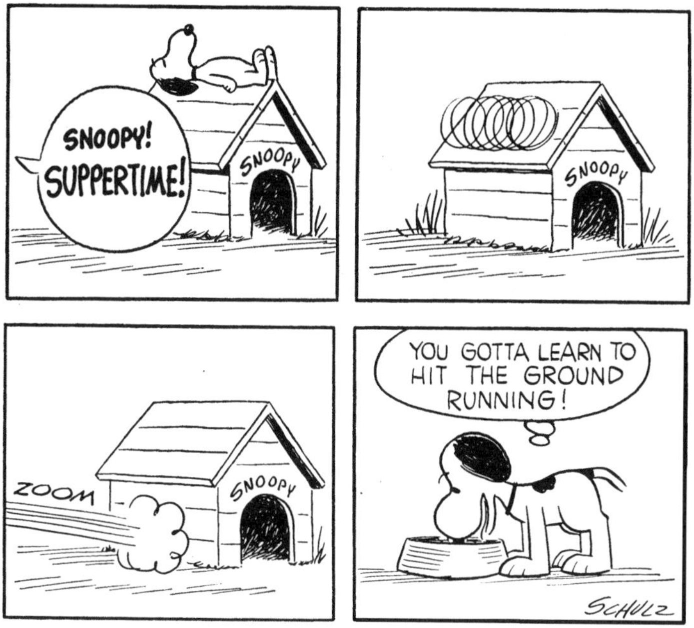
SNOOPY! SUPPERTIME!
SNOOPY
SNOOPY
ZOOM
SNOOPY
YOU GOTTA LEARN TO HIT THE GROUND RUNNING!
SCHULZ

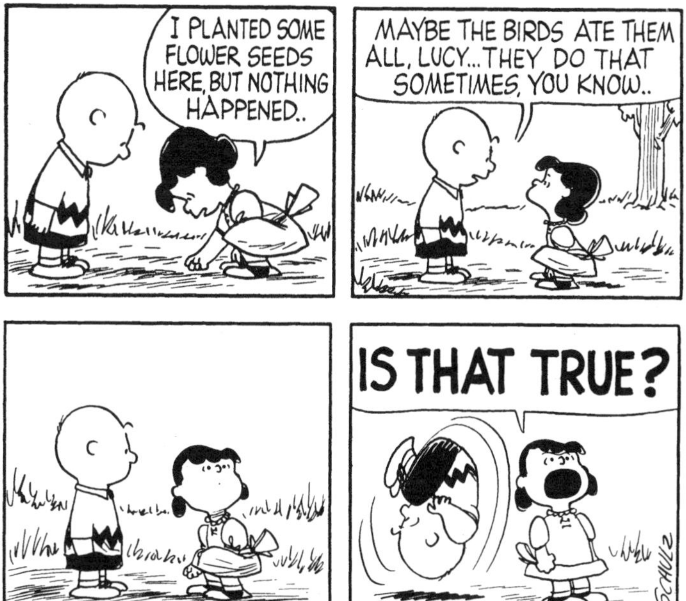
I PLANTED SOME FLOWER SEEDS HERE, BUT NOTHING HAPPENED..
MAYBE THE BIRDS ATE THEM ALL, LUCY...THEY DO THAT SOMETIMES, YOU KNOW..
IS THAT TRUE?
SCHULZ

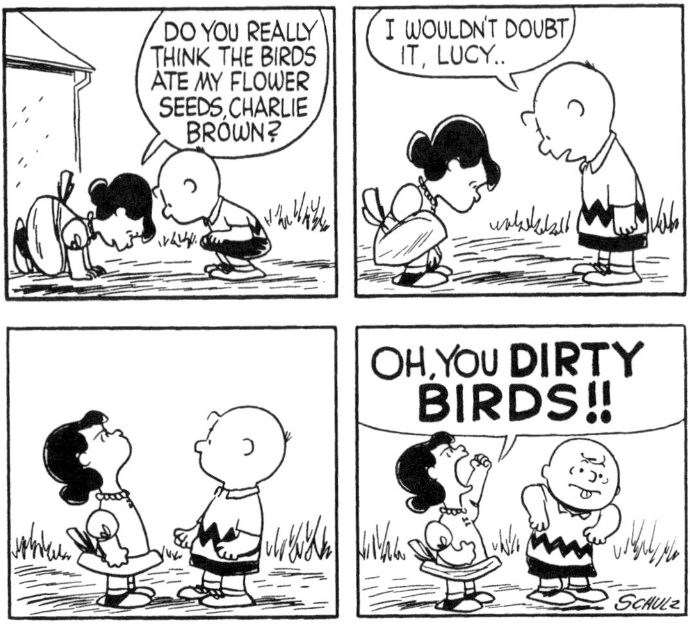
DO YOU REALLY THINK THE BIRDS ATE MY FLOWER SEEDS, CHARLIE BROWN?
I WOULDN'T DOUBT IT, LUCY..
OH, YOU DIRTY BIRDS!!
SCHULZ

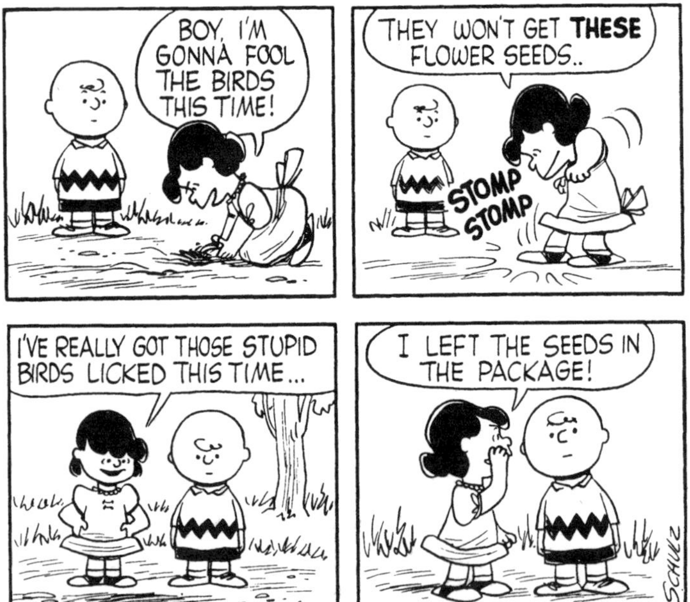
BOY, I'M GONNA FOOL THE BIRDS THIS TIME!
THEY WON'T GET THESE FLOWER SEEDS..
STOMP
STOMP
I'VE REALLY GOT THOSE STUPID BIRDS LICKED THIS TIME...
I LEFT THE SEEDS IN THE PACKAGE!
SCHULZ

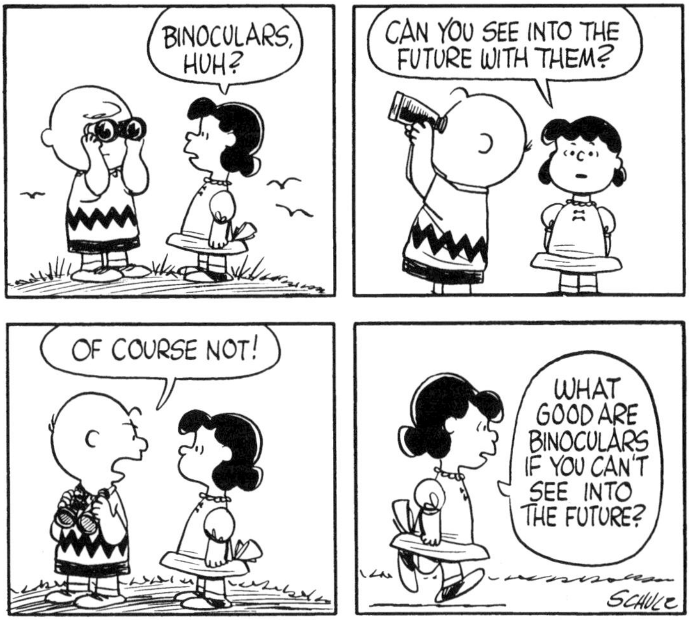
BINOCULARS, HUH?
CAN YOU SEE INTO THE FUTURE WITH THEM?
OF COURSE NOT!
WHAT GOOD ARE BINOCULARS IF YOU CAN'T SEE INTO THE FUTURE?
SCHULZ

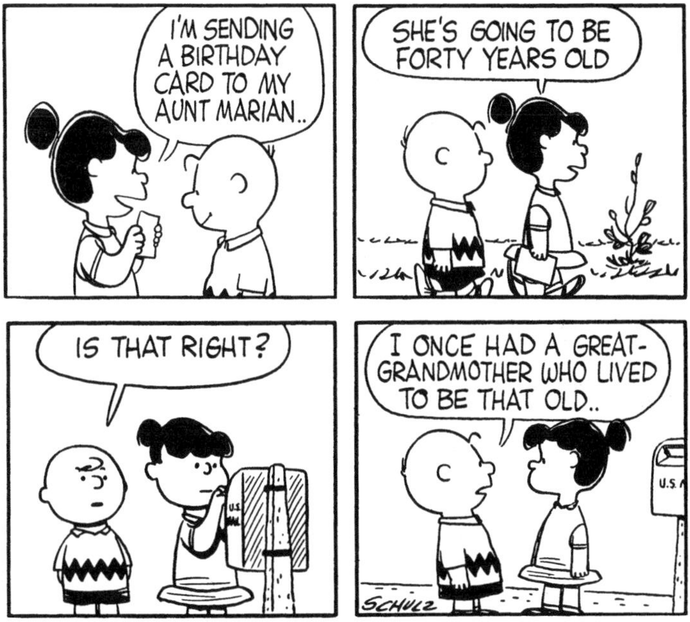
I'M SENDING A BIRTHDAY CARD TO MY AUNT MARIAN..
SHE'S GOING TO BE FORTY YEARS OLD
IS THAT RIGHT?
I ONCE HAD A GREAT-GRANDMOTHER WHO LIVED TO BE THAT OLD..
SCHULZ

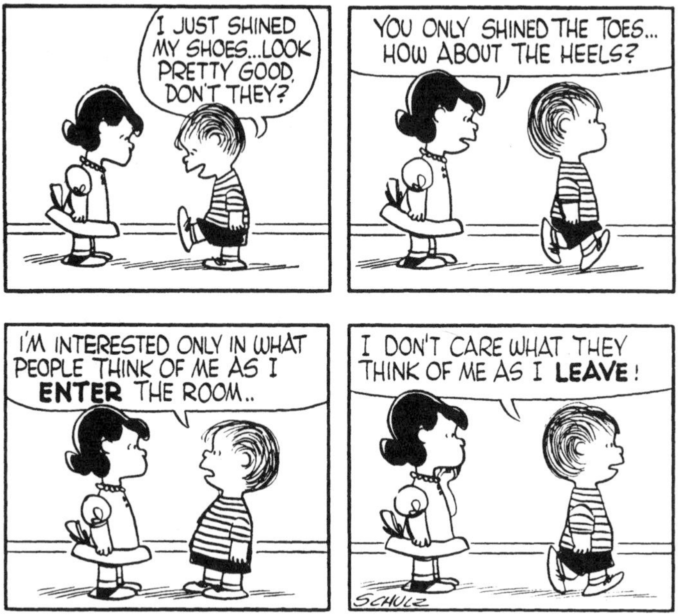
I JUST SHINED MY SHOES...LOOK PRETTY GOOD, DON'T THEY?
YOU ONLY SHINED THE TOES... HOW ABOUT THE HEELS?
I'M INTERESTED ONLY IN WHAT PEOPLE THINK OF ME AS I ENTER THE ROOM..
I DON'T CARE WHAT THEY THINK OF ME AS I LEAVE!
SCHULZ

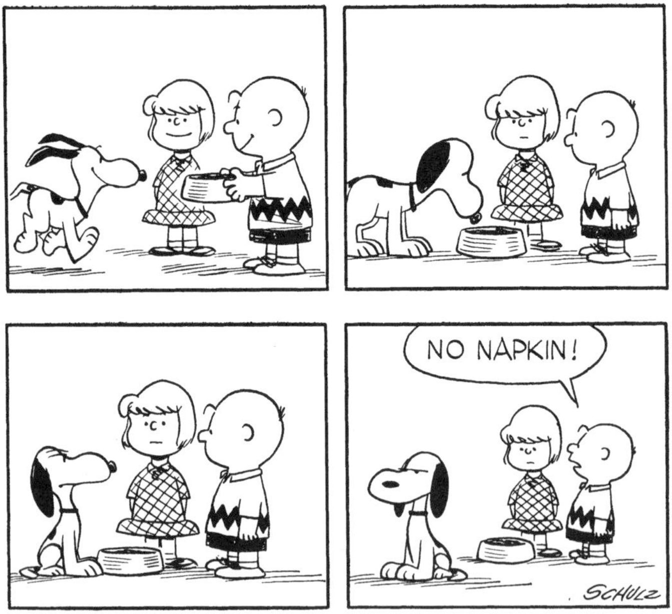
NO NAPKIN!
SCHULZ

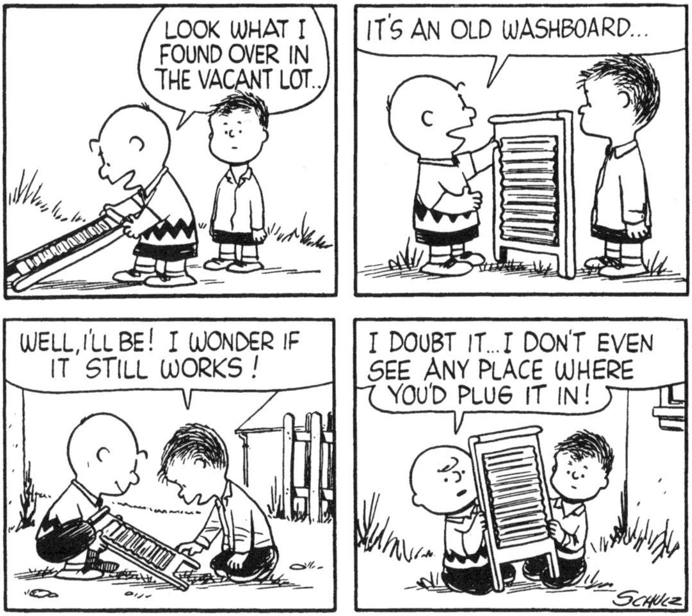
LOOK WHAT I FOUND OVER IN THE VACANT LOT..
IT'S AN OLD WASHBOARD...
WELL, I'LL BE! I WONDER IF IT STILL WORKS!
I DOUBT IT...I DON'T EVEN SEE ANY PLACE WHERE YOU'D PLUG IT IN!
SCHULZ

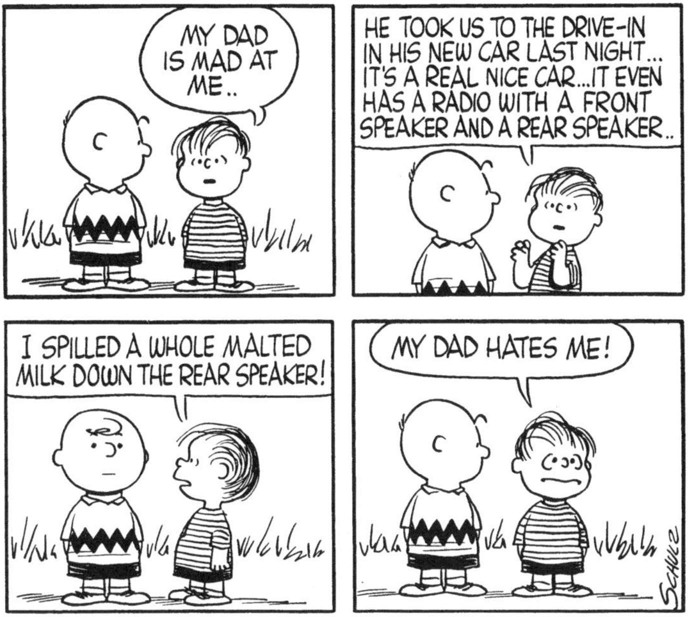
MY DAD IS MAD AT ME..
HE TOOK US TO THE DRIVE-IN IN HIS NEW CAR LAST NIGHT... IT'S A REAL NICE CAR...IT EVEN HAS A RADIO WITH A FRONT SPEAKER AND A REAR SPEAKER..
I SPILLED A WHOLE MALTED MILK DOWN THE REAR SPEAKER!
MY DAD HATES ME!
SCHULZ

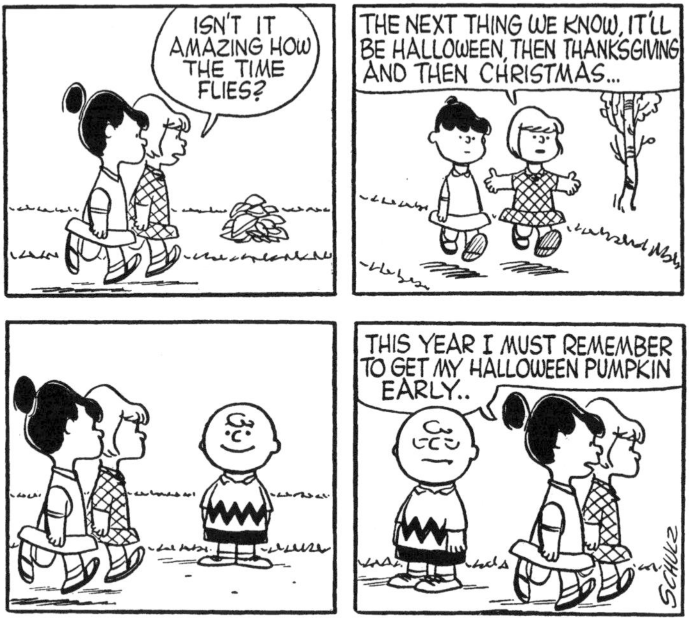
ISN'T IT AMAZING HOW THE TIME FLIES?
THE NEXT THING WE KNOW, IT'LL BE HALLOWEEN, THEN THANKSGIVING AND THEN CHRISTMAS...
THIS YEAR I MUST REMEMBER TO GET MY HALLOWEEN PUMPKIN EARLY..
SCHULZ

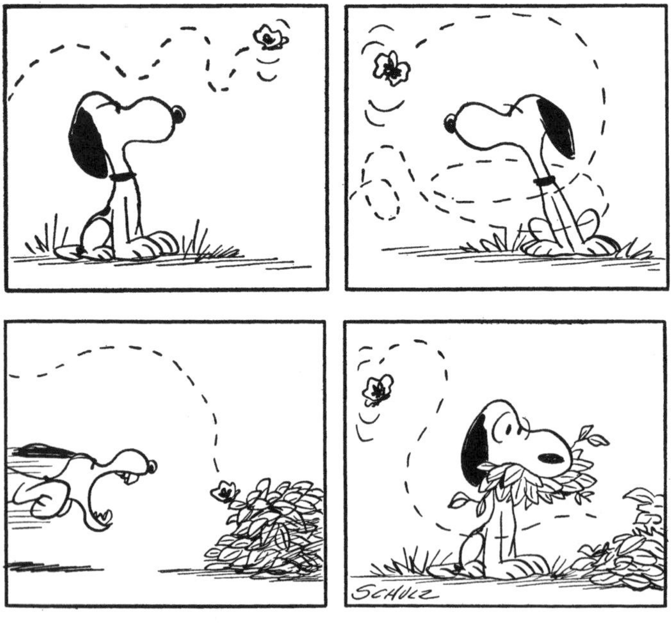
SCHULZ

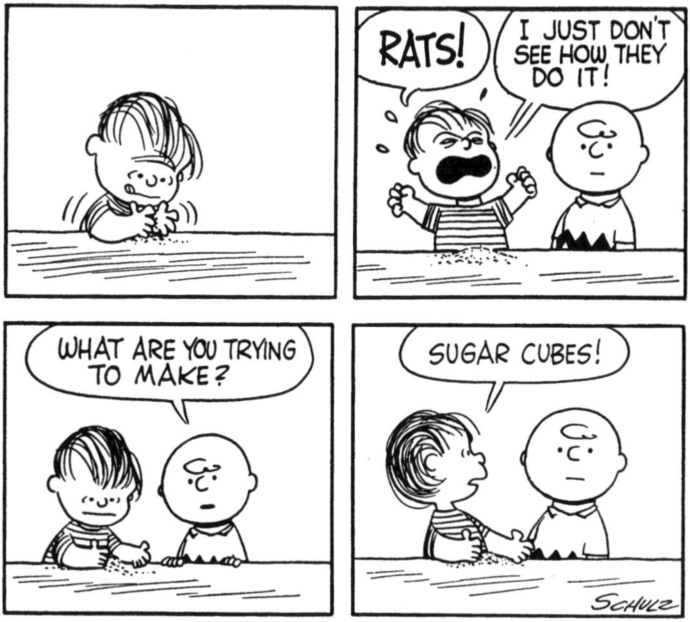
RATS!
I JUST DON'T SEE HOW THEY DO IT!
WHAT ARE YOU TRYING TO MAKE?
SUGAR CUBES!
SCHULZ

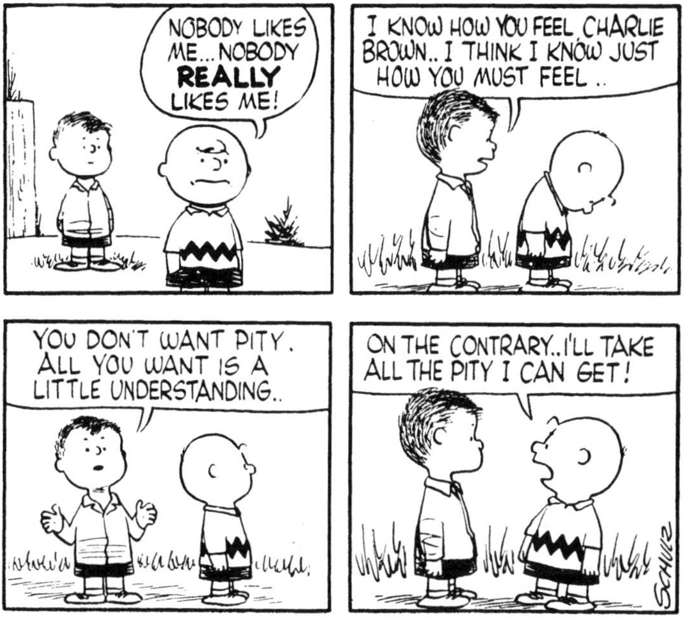
NOBODY LIKES ME... NOBODY **REALLY** LIKES ME!
I KNOW HOW YOU FEEL CHARLIE BROWN.. I THINK I KNOW JUST HOW YOU MUST FEEL..
YOU DON'T WANT PITY. ALL YOU WANT IS A LITTLE UNDERSTANDING..
ON THE CONTRARY.. I'LL TAKE ALL THE PITY I CAN GET!
SCHULZ

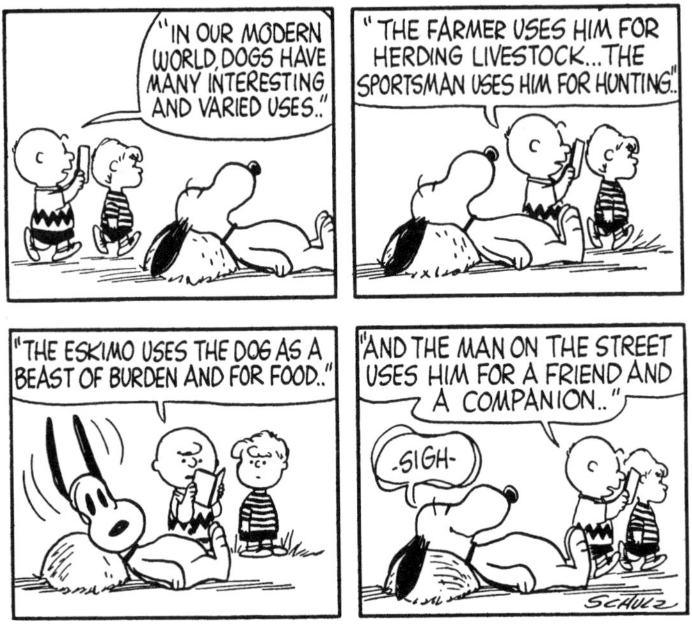
"IN OUR MODERN WORLD, DOGS HAVE MANY INTERESTING AND VARIED USES.."
"THE FARMER USES HIM FOR HERDING LIVESTOCK...THE SPORTSMAN USES HIM FOR HUNTING"..
"THE ESKIMO USES THE DOG AS A BEAST OF BURDEN AND FOR FOOD.."
"AND THE MAN ON THE STREET USES HIM FOR A FRIEND AND A COMPANION.."
-SIGH-
SCHULZ

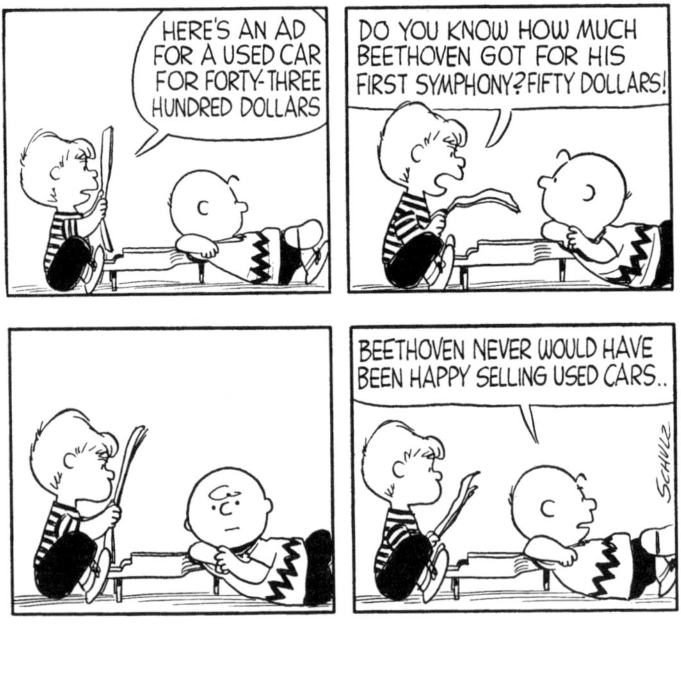
HERE'S AN AD FOR A USED CAR FOR FORTY-THREE HUNDRED DOLLARS
DO YOU KNOW HOW MUCH BEETHOVEN GOT FOR HIS FIRST SYMPHONY? FIFTY DOLLARS!
BEETHOVEN NEVER WOULD HAVE BEEN HAPPY SELLING USED CARS..
SCHULZ

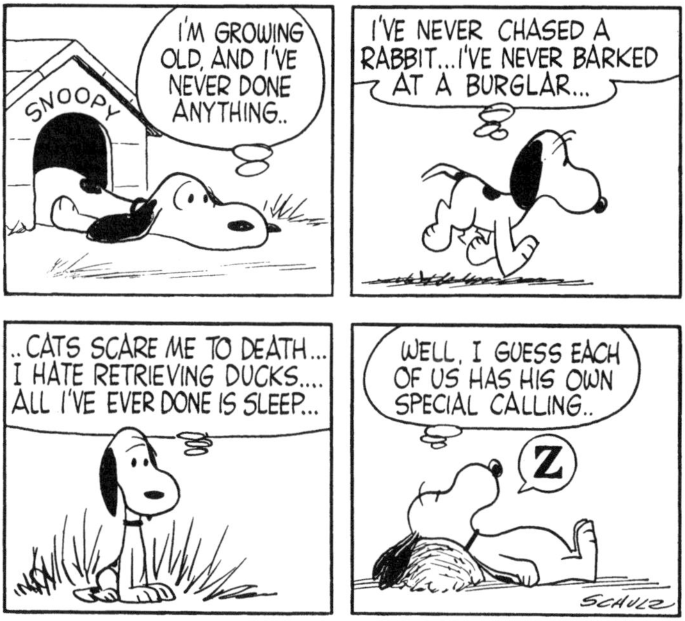
I'M GROWING OLD, AND I'VE NEVER DONE ANYTHING..
SNOOPY
I'VE NEVER CHASED A RABBIT...I'VE NEVER BARKED AT A BURGLAR...
..CATS SCARE ME TO DEATH...
I HATE RETRIEVING DUCKS....
ALL I'VE EVER DONE IS SLEEP...
WELL, I GUESS EACH OF US HAS HIS OWN SPECIAL CALLING..
Z
SCHULZ

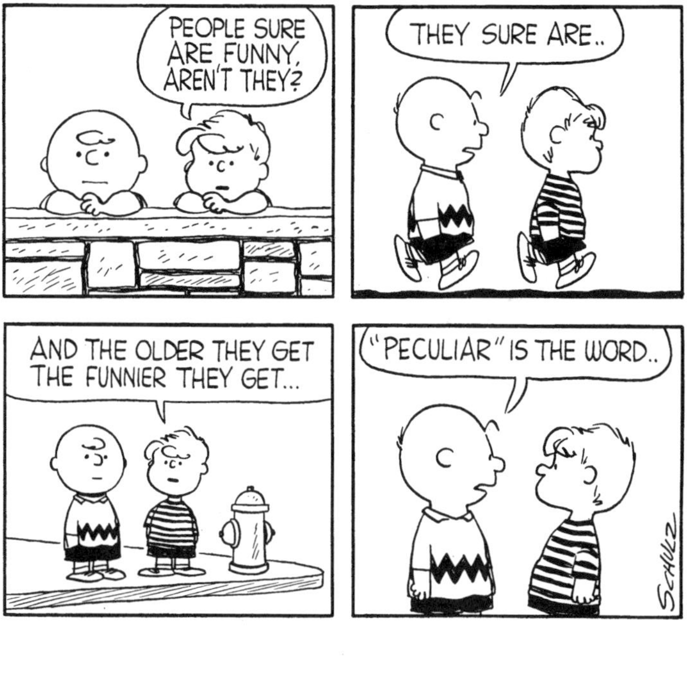
PEOPLE SURE ARE FUNNY, AREN'T THEY?
THEY SURE ARE..
AND THE OLDER THEY GET THE FUNNIER THEY GET...
"PECULIAR" IS THE WORD..
SCHULZ

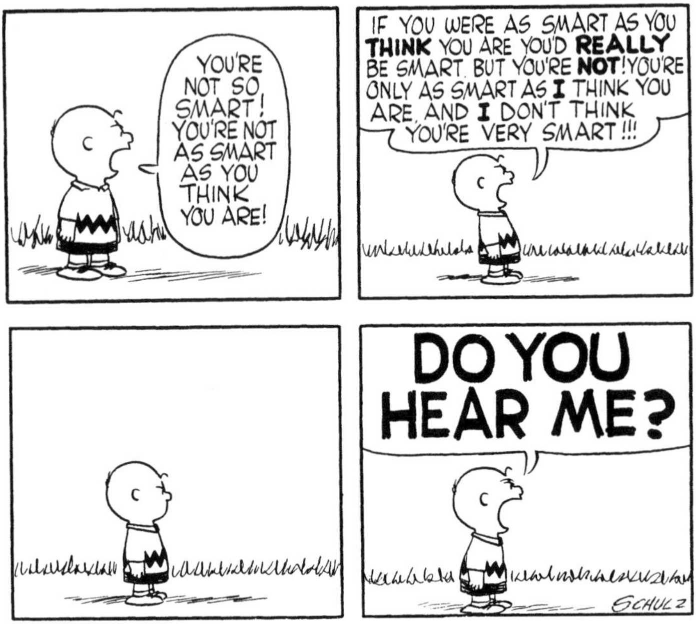
YOU'RE NOT SO SMART! YOU'RE NOT AS SMART AS YOU THINK YOU ARE!
IF YOU WERE AS SMART AS YOU **THINK** YOU ARE YOU'D **REALLY** BE SMART. BUT YOU'RE **NOT**! YOU'RE ONLY AS SMART AS **I** THINK YOU ARE, AND **I** DON'T THINK YOU'RE VERY SMART!!!
DO YOU HEAR ME?
SCHULZ

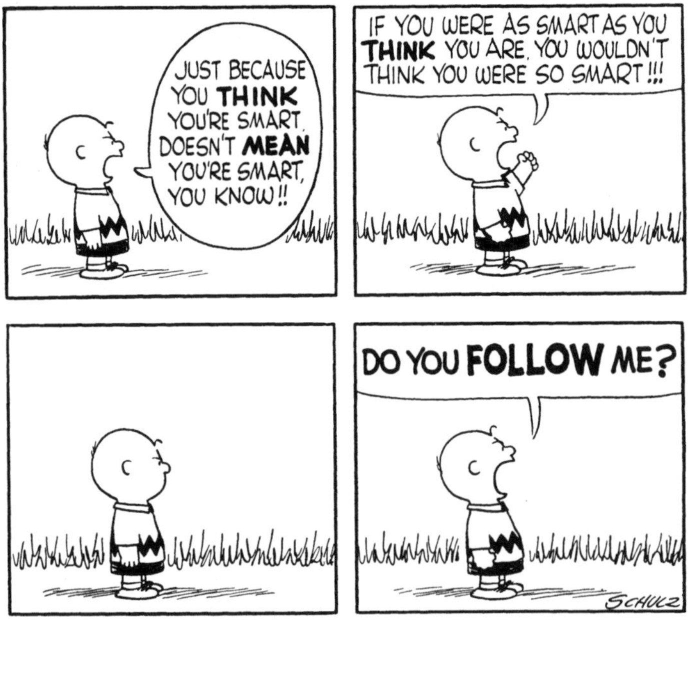
JUST BECAUSE YOU **THINK** YOU'RE SMART DOESN'T **MEAN** YOU'RE SMART, YOU KNOW!!
IF YOU WERE AS SMART AS YOU **THINK** YOU ARE, YOU WOULDN'T THINK YOU WERE SO SMART!!!
DO YOU **FOLLOW** ME?
SCHULZ

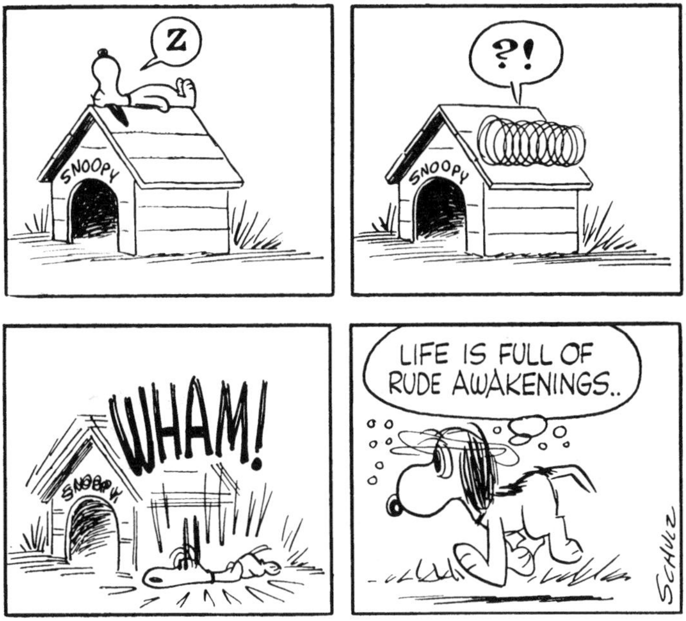
Z
SNOOPY
?!
SNOOPY
WHAM!
LIFE IS FULL OF RUDE AWAKENINGS..
SCHULZ

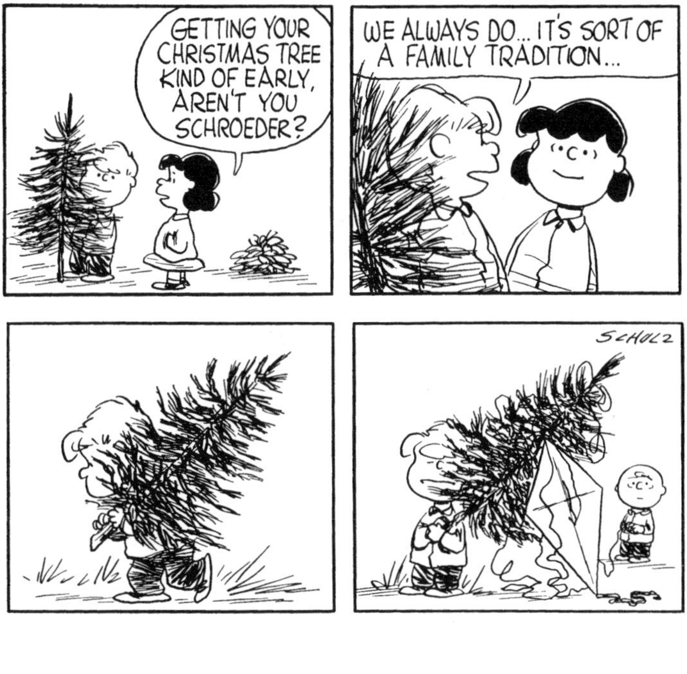
GETTING YOUR CHRISTMAS TREE KIND OF EARLY, AREN'T YOU SCHROEDER?
WE ALWAYS DO... IT'S SORT OF A FAMILY TRADITION...
SCHULZ

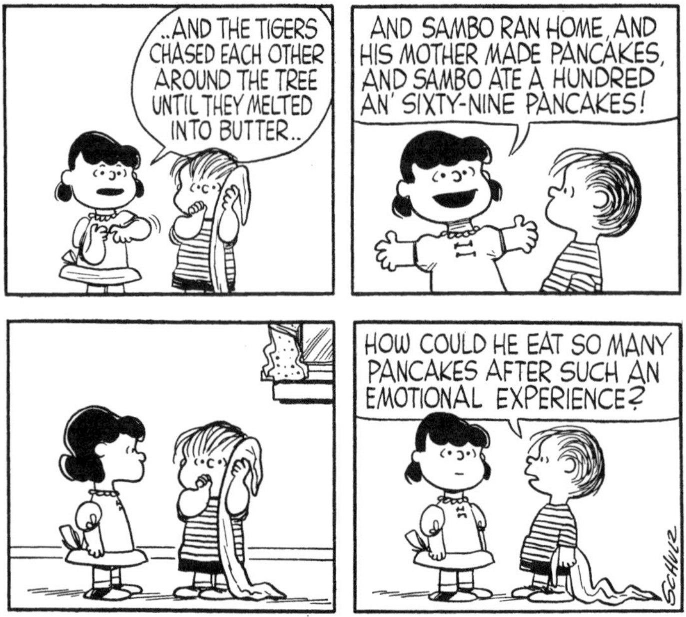
..AND THE TIGERS CHASED EACH OTHER AROUND THE TREE UNTIL THEY MELTED INTO BUTTER..
AND SAMBO RAN HOME, AND HIS MOTHER MADE PANCAKES, AND SAMBO ATE A HUNDRED AN' SIXTY-NINE PANCAKES!
HOW COULD HE EAT SO MANY PANCAKES AFTER SUCH AN EMOTIONAL EXPERIENCE?
SCHULZ

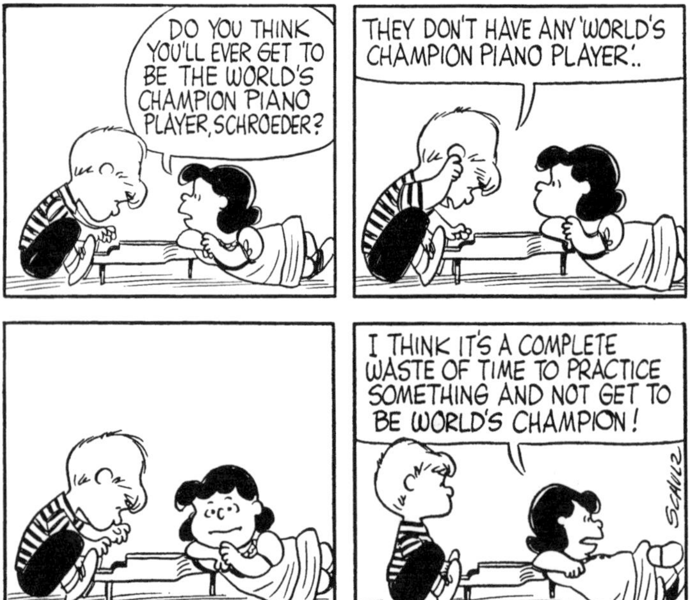
DO YOU THINK YOU'LL EVER GET TO BE THE WORLD'S CHAMPION PIANO PLAYER, SCHROEDER?
THEY DON'T HAVE ANY 'WORLD'S CHAMPION PIANO PLAYER'..
I THINK IT'S A COMPLETE WASTE OF TIME TO PRACTICE SOMETHING AND NOT GET TO BE WORLD'S CHAMPION!
SCHULZ

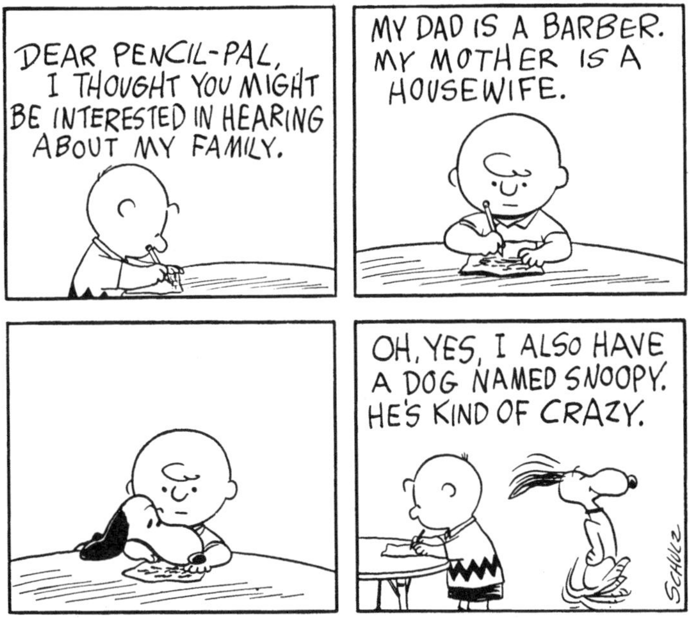
DEAR PENCIL-PAL,
I THOUGHT YOU MIGHT BE INTERESTED IN HEARING ABOUT MY FAMILY.
MY DAD IS A BARBER. MY MOTHER IS A HOUSEWIFE.
OH, YES, I ALSO HAVE A DOG NAMED SNOOPY. HE'S KIND OF CRAZY.
SCHULZ

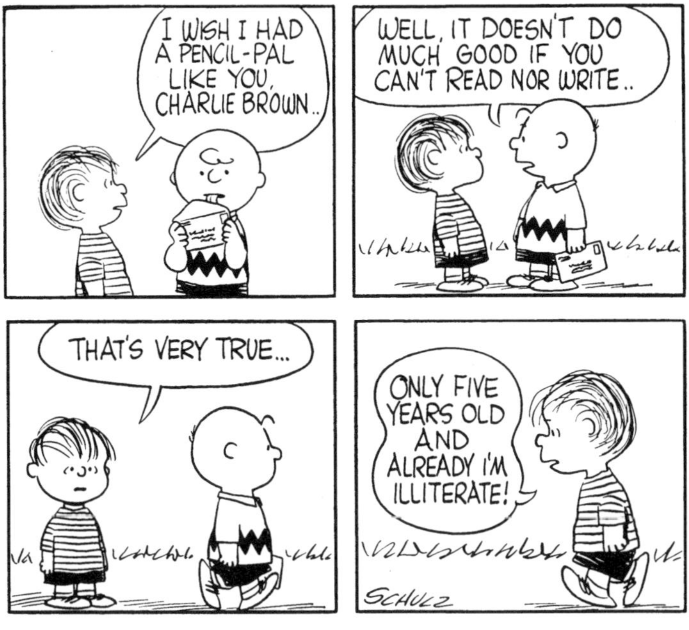
I WISH I HAD A PENCIL-PAL LIKE YOU, CHARLIE BROWN..
WELL, IT DOESN'T DO MUCH GOOD IF YOU CAN'T READ NOR WRITE..
THAT'S VERY TRUE...
ONLY FIVE YEARS OLD AND ALREADY I'M ILLITERATE!
SCHULZ

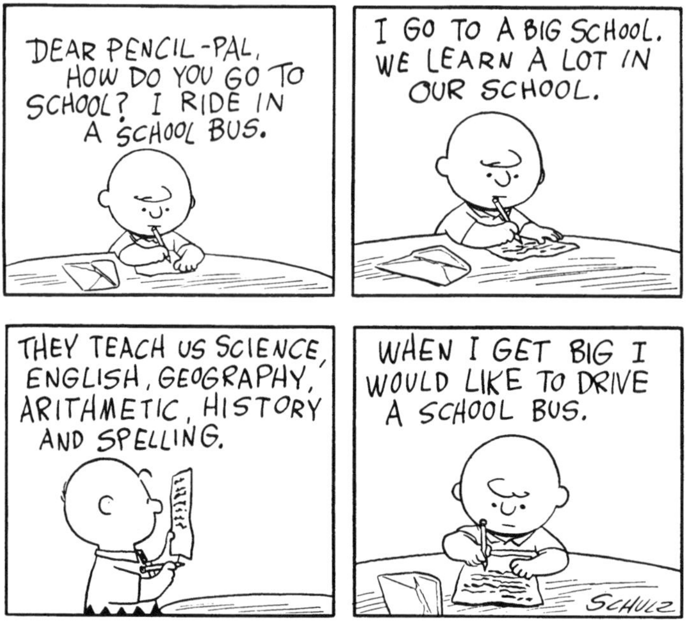
DEAR PENCIL-PAL, HOW DO YOU GO TO SCHOOL? I RIDE IN A SCHOOL BUS.
I GO TO A BIG SCHOOL. WE LEARN A LOT IN OUR SCHOOL.
THEY TEACH US SCIENCE, ENGLISH, GEOGRAPHY, ARITHMETIC, HISTORY AND SPELLING.
WHEN I GET BIG I WOULD LIKE TO DRIVE A SCHOOL BUS.
SCHULZ

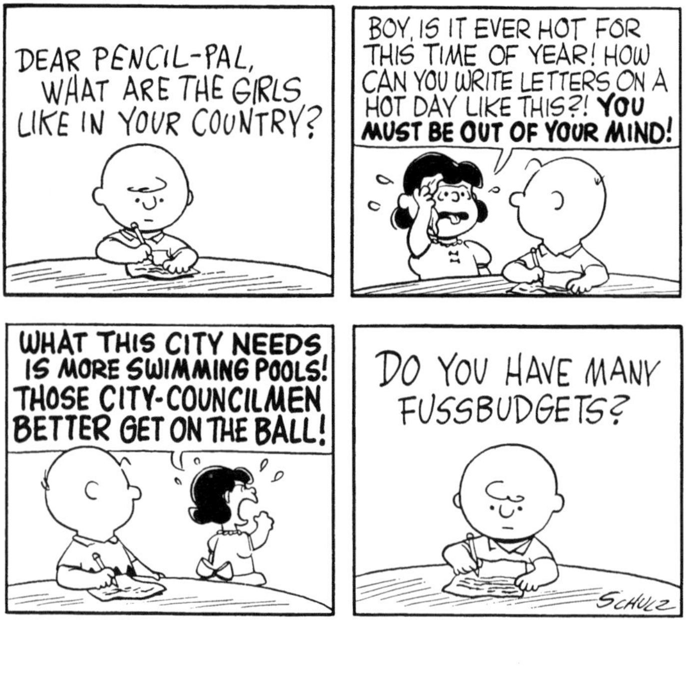
DEAR PENCIL-PAL, WHAT ARE THE GIRLS LIKE IN YOUR COUNTRY?
BOY, IS IT EVER HOT FOR THIS TIME OF YEAR! HOW CAN YOU WRITE LETTERS ON A HOT DAY LIKE THIS?! YOU MUST BE OUT OF YOUR MIND!
WHAT THIS CITY NEEDS IS MORE SWIMMING POOLS! THOSE CITY-COUNCILMEN BETTER GET ON THE BALL!
DO YOU HAVE MANY FUSSBUDGETS?
SCHULZ

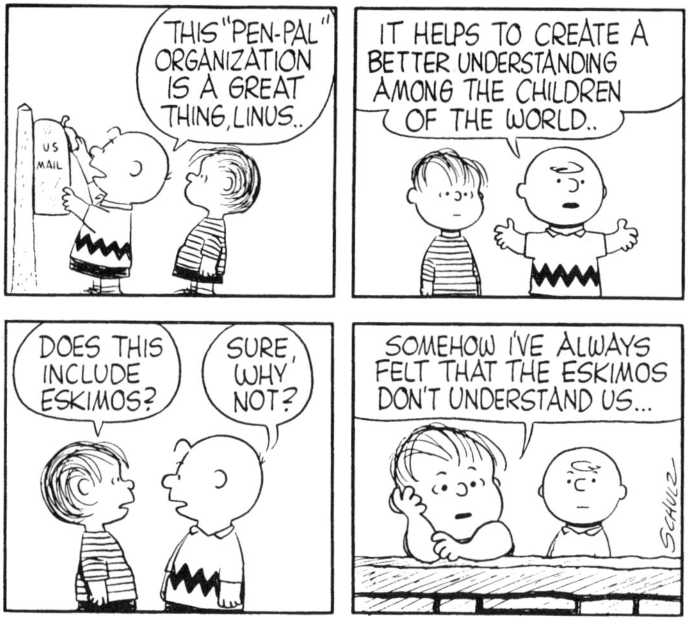
THIS "PEN-PAL" ORGANIZATION IS A GREAT THING, LINUS..
US MAIL
IT HELPS TO CREATE A BETTER UNDERSTANDING AMONG THE CHILDREN OF THE WORLD..
DOES THIS INCLUDE ESKIMOS?
SURE, WHY NOT?
SOMEHOW I'VE ALWAYS FELT THAT THE ESKIMOS DON'T UNDERSTAND US...
SCHULZ

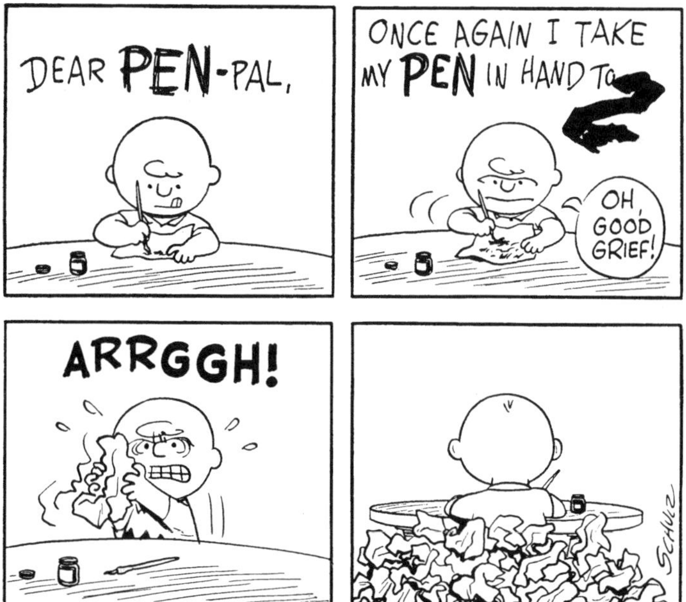
DEAR PEN-PAL,
ONCE AGAIN I TAKE MY PEN IN HAND TO
OH, GOOD GRIEF!
ARRGGH!
SCHULZ

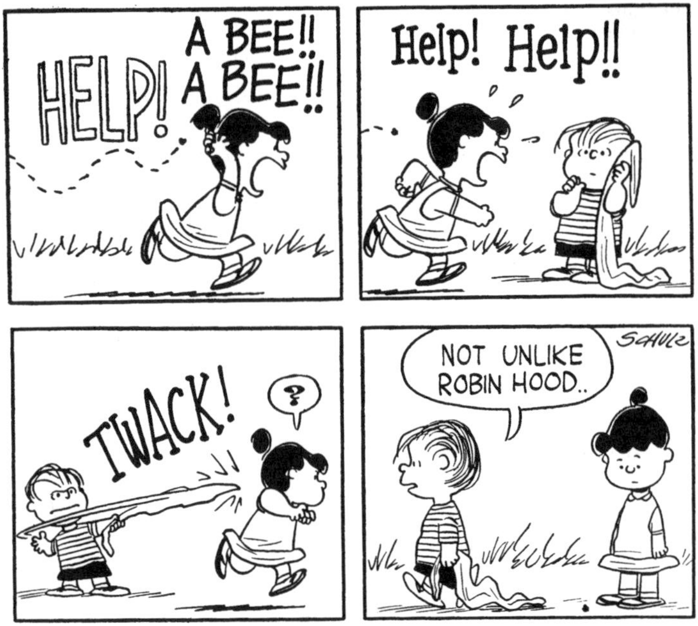
HELP!
A BEE!! A BEE!!
Help! Help!!
TWACK!
?
NOT UNLIKE ROBIN HOOD..
SCHULZ

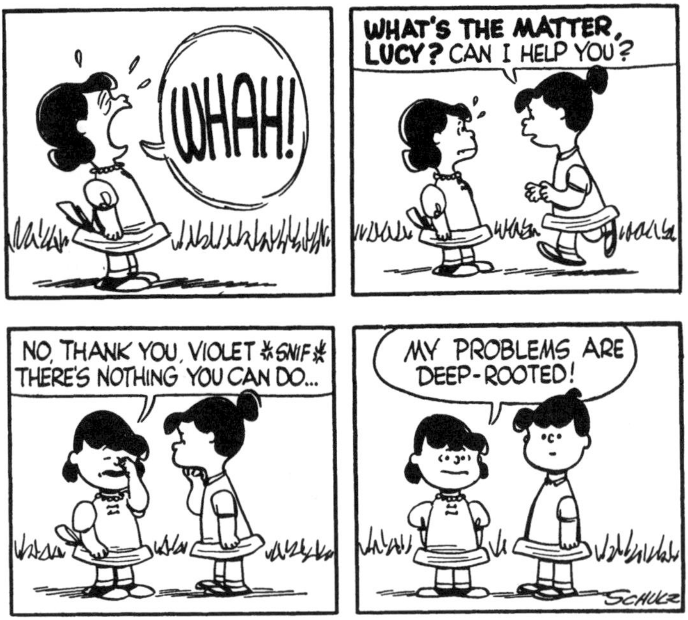
WHAH!
WHAT'S THE MATTER, LUCY? CAN I HELP YOU?
NO, THANK YOU, VIOLET *SNIF* THERE'S NOTHING YOU CAN DO...
MY PROBLEMS ARE DEEP-ROOTED!
SCHULZ

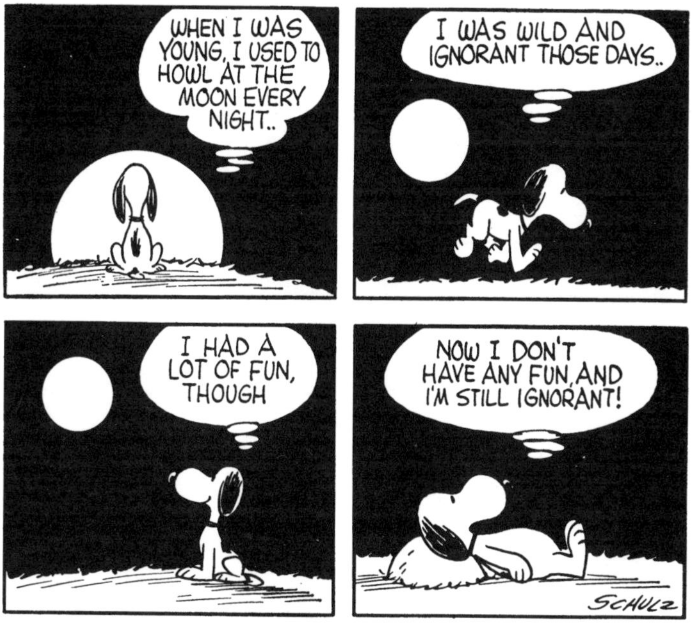
WHEN I WAS YOUNG, I USED TO HOWL AT THE MOON EVERY NIGHT..
I WAS WILD AND IGNORANT THOSE DAYS..
I HAD A LOT OF FUN, THOUGH
NOW I DON'T HAVE ANY FUN, AND I'M STILL IGNORANT!
SCHULZ

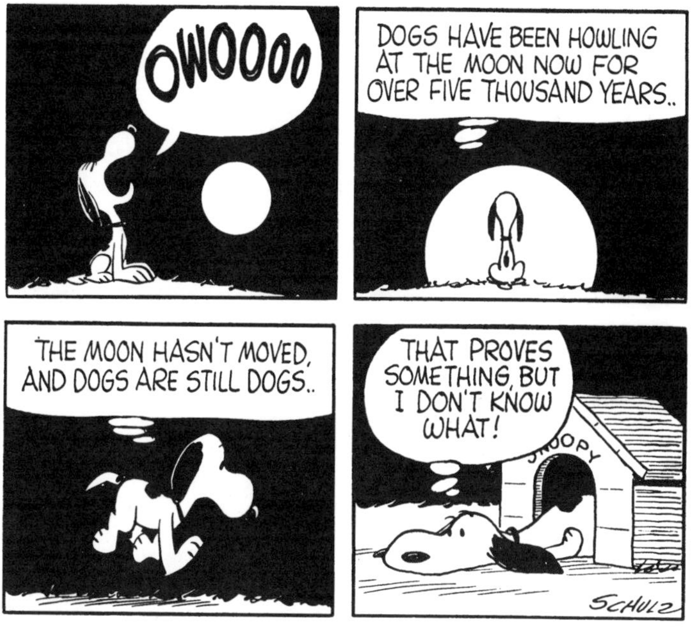
OWOOOO
DOGS HAVE BEEN HOWLING AT THE MOON NOW FOR OVER FIVE THOUSAND YEARS..
THE MOON HASN'T MOVED, AND DOGS ARE STILL DOGS..
THAT PROVES SOMETHING, BUT I DON'T KNOW WHAT!
SNOOPY
SCHULZ

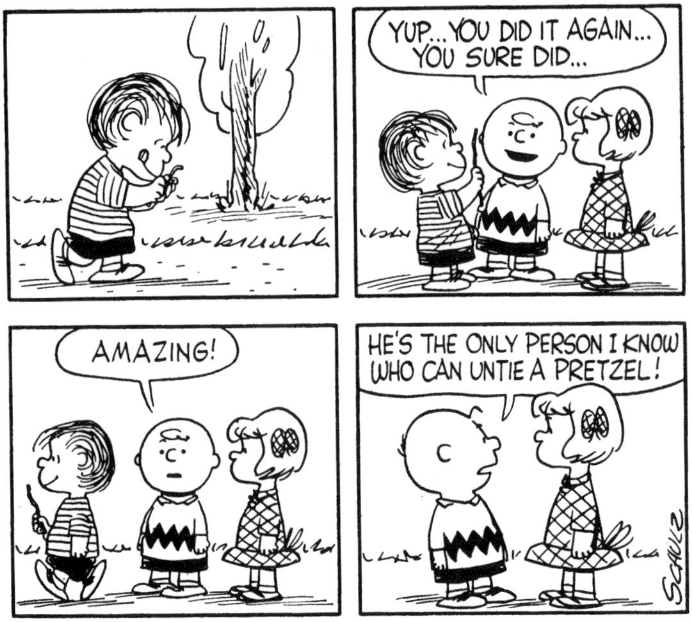
YUP... YOU DID IT AGAIN... YOU SURE DID...
AMAZING!
HE'S THE ONLY PERSON I KNOW WHO CAN UNTIE A PRETZEL!
SCHULZ

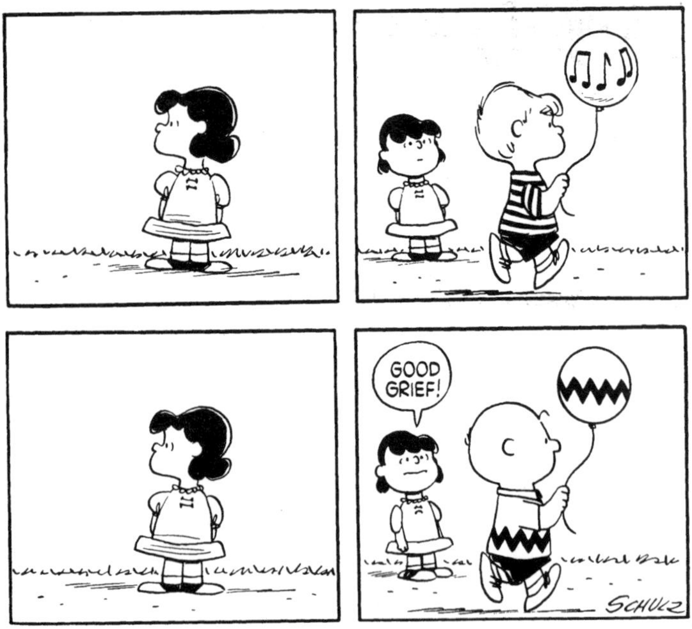
GOOD GRIEF!
SCHULZ